MILITARY INTERVENTION IN THE 1990s

Past intervention studies have gone so far as to examine the justification for military intervention. Richard Connaughton takes the opportunity presented by the new international order to take an important step further. He argues how and why it is possible for multilateral military intervention, as part of a collective security regime in the 1990s, to *succeed*. In this book he builds a plausible matrix of theories and principles which he tests by detailed reference to the Gulf Crisis. The book is the first comprehensive professional study of future interventions in terms of a complex of political and military issues at the operational level.

While the military and logistical considerations captured the headlines at the time, in the period since the Gulf War the economic and political issues have increasingly assumed a greater weight. With the fragmentation of the former Soviet Union, and the return of nationalism as a central issue in international affairs, the likelihood of new interventions under international control has increased dramatically. Humanitarian considerations are now beginning to claim equal weight with the absolute sovereignty of nation states. Yet, as in the case of Croatia and Yugoslavia, both the mechanics and the international law of intervention have been exposed to be uncertain.

Richard Connaughton's book, by considering the operational factors involved in all types of intervention, and by examining some of the historical precedents for these operations, provides a uniquely timely interpretation of a key issue of international affairs in the 1990s.

Richard Connaughton is the British Army's retiring Head of Defence Studies. Formerly a professional soldier, he has written and lectured widely on strategic, historic and international relations subjects. His two recent books, published by Routledge, are *The War of the Rising Sun and Tumbling Bear* (1989) and *The Republic of the Ushakovka* (1990).

THE OPERATIONAL LEVEL OF WAR
Edited by Michael Krause, Deputy Chief of the US Army
Center for Military History, and Andrew Wheatcroft

The Operational Level of War series provides for a theory of armed conflicts
in the present and the immediate future. Unlike many theories, it is not
rooted in abstractions but in the practice of war, both in history and the
immediate past.
The books in the series all contribute to the clearer understanding of the
potentials and the dangers of war in the 1990s.
The key contribution of the operational theory of war is to provide a link
between strategy and tactics, a connection which is of unique importance
in modern warfare.

Titles already published in the series include:

THE FRAMEWORK OF OPERATIONAL WARFARE
Clayton R. Newell

UNHOLY GRAIL
Larry Cable

Forthcoming titles include:

THE ROLE AND CONTROL OF WEAPONS IN THE 1990s
Frank Barnaby

THE SCIENCE OF WAR
Back to first principles
Brian Holden Reid

MILITARY INTERVENTION IN THE 1990s

A new logic of war

RICHARD CONNAUGHTON

Foreword by Sir Harry Hinsley

London and New York

First published 1992
by Routledge
11 New Fetter Lane, London EC4P 4EE

Simultaneously published in the USA and Canada
by Routledge
a division of Routledge, Chapman and Hall, Inc.
29 West 35th Street, New York, NY 10001

Typeset in 10/12 pt Palatino by DSC Corporation Ltd,
Cornwall, England

Printed in Great Britain by T.J.Press (Padstow) Ltd,
Padstow, Cornwall

British Library Cataloguing in Publication Data
Connaughton, R. M.
Military Intervention in the 1990s:
A New Logic of War
I. Title
355.02

Library of Congress Cataloging in Publication Data
Connaughton, R. M. (Richard Michael)
Military intervention in the 1990s: a new logic of war
Richard Connaughton.
p. cm.
Includes bibliographical references and index.
1. World politics—1945- 2. Intervention (International law)
3. United Nations—Armed Forces. I. Title.
D842.C64 1992
341.5′84—dc20 92-7938

ISBN 0-415-06524-0

0-415-07991-8 (pbk)

CONTENTS

Part II Postscript

SERIES EDITOR'S PREFACE

The concept which lies behind the operational level of war is immensely powerful. It grew directly out of a German philosophical tradition which underpinned the writings of von Moltke and the operation of the German General Staff. It provided the basis for Soviet defensive and offensive operations, when vast bodies of men and materiel were manoeuvred in unison over great distances, and it has produced a framework within which both the air-land battle and, at a different scale, low intensity warfare can be conceived, planned and, ultimately, executed.

How then will it adapt to the new conditions anticipated in the 1990s and beyond, as all the old verities of confrontation unravel? Part of the answer is given in this book. The author has used the events of the Gulf War to place the concept of 'intervention' within an historical context (he has already written on an earlier 'real life' intervention in the Russian Civil War). But he also looks to the future, at the theories and principles which underlie all interventions. The central question, he suggests, is: can interventions succeed, and if so, how can a positive outcome be secured?

This pragmatic approach has two aspects. First, political, by placing intervention within a changing framework of international relations and, second, technical, to assess what military organizations are expected to do under the conditions of an intervention.

The military would not, perhaps, in an ideal situation, be chosen to undertake the central role in interventions. Their current structure and training is being rapidly modified to accommodate the particular needs of working within an international force framework, and under conditions of constraint which frequently prove irksome. On the other hand, the military have a unique experience, through working with the United Nations, in the special circumstances of intervention, and no other group seems eager to take on this task. So it is fair to assume that this may well be a key role for some armies in the foreseeable future.

How does this fit within the framework of the operational level of war? I would suggest that the operational concept provides a most effective means of integrating the complex of logistic, political, social and economic

ix

factors which occur in all situations of intervention. Connaughton's book should provide an invaluable primer to the theory and practice of intervention, for which the Gulf War has already become a classic 'case study'.

FOREWORD

by Professor Sir Harry Hinsley

Colonel Connaughton turned his attention to the subject of this book long before events made it topical. When he started writing it the Gulf War was not in sight; it had not yet illustrated that states must be geared to carry out multilateral military intervention in some circumstances if they wish to maintain international order. It remained far from certain, moreover, that the momentous but still negative advance that we call the end of the Cold War would be consolidated by the rise of what he calls a new collegiality among the leading states – by their acceptance of the need for the positive collaboration between themselves without which the resort to multilateral military intervention in the Gulf would have been impracticable. He is to be congratulated on his foresight in anticipating these developments.

There are other reasons why his book is not only topical, but also of more than passing importance. The Gulf War has raised as many problems as it has solved. The collegiality which permitted it to be fought under the aegis of the Security Council may not be sustained, threats to international order are unlikely to decline; and it will become increasingly necessary to distinguish between those situations in which international action is proper and those in which it is not. Colonel Connaughton's discussion of these and associated issues will repay the closest attention; and it is particularly to be hoped that his emphasis on the need for revision within the United Nations is not ignored.

States in earlier international systems were beguiled by the maxim that if you want peace you must be prepared for war. The sentiment was sound enough, but in earlier international systems the absence of international machinery rendered the maxim self-defeating. Restated to meet the possibilities and the needs of our time, it acquires great force: if you want peace you must make sure that the Security Council is ready to act whenever international action is appropriate.

PREFACE

I could not have written this book without the advice and assistance of people too numerous to mention. They have freely given me the benefit of their time and their thoughts in the development of a subject I believed had been long neglected. I am most grateful.

Given its high political and international relations profile, the arena of this subject is not one that would seem naturally obvious for a former soldier to enter. However, in the absence of others coming forward to initiate the discussion of this important, though largely neglected, subject of military intervention, I thought it worthwhile to start the ball rolling. Those who subsequently agree or take issue with what I have written will, in time, finesse the area of study and improve our understanding.

The world of international relations is constantly moving. In a book such as this the line has to be drawn emphatically somewhere. In the time between this book going to the publisher and its publication, the German Foreign Minister, Hans-Dietrich Genscher, had left the Kohl government, NATO had reconsidered its out-of-area options, the Japanese government considered whether to deploy Japanese forces on peacekeeping operations, and change in the respective membership of the UN and CSCE appeared to be a weekly event. Against such a fluid background it is impossible to maintain constancy in detail. It is, however, a subordinate consideration to that of the underlying theory and principles.

This book is focused upon the Middle East. Indeed, when it was written it seemed unimaginable that there would be discussion of the possibility of sending expeditionary forces into Yugoslavia. However, international events tend to move in circles. It is certain that, in due course, the focus will return once again to the Middle East, involving different circumstances, different actors and a more subtle crisis.

I am, of course, alone responsible for the contents of this book and for any errors of fact or judgement.

Richard Connaughton
Camberley
June 1992

TABLES

LIST OF ABBREVIATIONS

ACC	Arab Co-operation Council
ACERRC	Allied Command Europe Rapid Reaction Corps
ANZUS Pact	Australia, New Zealand and United States Pact
ATPs	Allied Tactical Procedures
BARB	British Audience Research Bureau
CENTO	Central Treaty Organization
CFE	Conventional Armed Forces in Europe Treaty
CIA	Central Intelligence Agency
CIS	Commonwealth of Independent States
CND	Campaign for Nuclear Disarmament
COCOM(ME)	Co-ordinating Committee Controlling Middle-East Trade (a hypothetical organization)
CSCE	Conference on Security and Co-operation in Europe
DIA	Defence Intelligence Agency
EC	European Community
FAR	[French] Force d'Action Rapide
FOB	Forward Operating Base
FOO	Forward Observation Officer
GATT	General Agreement on Tariffs and Trade
GCC	Gulf Co-operation Council
GDP	Gross Domestic Product
GNP	Gross National Product
GOC	General Officer Commanding
IAEA	International Atomic Energy Authority
ICAO	International Civil Aviation Organization
ICJ	International Court of Justice
IEA	International Energy Agency
IEPG	Independent European Programme Group
IFF	Identification Friend-or-Foe
IGF	International Guarantor Force
IPC	[Iraq] Industrial Products Company

IRBM	Intermediate Range Ballistic Missile
JEWEL	Joint Endeavour for the Welfare, Education and Liberation
KIO	Kuwait Investment Office
LSC	London Suppliers Club
MIC	[Iraq] Military Industry Commission
MNF	[Lebanon] Multi-National Force
MPG	Military Planning Group
MPS	Maritime Prepositioning Ships
MSC	Military Staff Committee
MTCR	Missile Technology Control Regime
NACC	North Atlantic Co-operation Council
NATO	North Atlantic Treaty Organization
n.b.c.	Nuclear, Biological and Chemical
NIEO	New International Economic Order
NPT	Nuclear Non-Proliferation Treaty
OAS	Organization of American States
OAU	Organization of African Unity
OECS	Organization of East Caribbean States
OIC	Organization of the Islamic Conference
ONUC	Opération des Nations Unies au Congo
OOA	Out of Area
OPEC	Organization of Petroleum Exporting Countries
PLO	Palestine Liberation Organization
RMC	Revolutionary Military Council
ROE	Rules of Engagement
SALT	Strategic Arms Limitation Talks
SEATO	South East Asia Treaty Organization
SOF	[US] Special Operation Forces
SOPs	Standard Operating Procedures
SOTI	[Iraq] State Organization for Technical Industries
START	Strategic Arms Reduction Treaty
TAOR	Tactical Area of Responsibility
Templar	Tactical Expert Mission Planner
UAE	United Arab Emirates
UNEF	United Nations Emergency Force
UNESCO	United Nations Educational Scientific and Cultural Organization
UNFICYP	United Nations Forces in Cyprus
UNIFIL	United Nations Forces in Lebanon
UNIKOM	United Nations Iraq-Kuwait Mission
USAF	United States Air Force
USCENTCOM	United States Central Command
WEU	Western European Union

Part I

INTRODUCTION

The first problem to consider in any 'intervention' study lies in the defini-tion of the word. Within the literature there are expressions of caution that: 'A definition of "intervention" wide enough to take in all the meanings attached to the word will be masked by imprecision'.[1] The conclusion to be drawn from this truism is of the desirability of concentrating upon one aspect within the broad spectrum of coercive intervention. Within that spectrum, which includes many diverse forms, be they diplomatic, politi-cal, financial, economic or military, this work represents a study of the last of these: military intervention.

But then, military intervention can be initiated for quite varied social (such as anti-drugs crusades), environmental, humanitarian and politico-military reasons. In addition, the form which military intervention may take is subject to further subdivision. One of the more obvious and arguably simpler forms of military intervention is that involving naval forces, as was apparent in the Gulf towards the end of the Iran/Iraq War. A blockade can be imposed either as an independent measure or as a part of wider mea-sures. A clinical or surgical strike intervention is of the type which occurred against the Osiraq nuclear reactor in 1981 and which was launched unsuc-cessfully against Libya in 1986. These are described in outline as follows:

On 7 June 1981 two Israeli fighter-bombers carried out what was the world's first preventive strike against a nuclear facility. France had supplied Iraq with four charges of 93 per cent enriched uranium fuel, sufficient to manufacture four nuclear devices. It is believed that Israeli intelligence, monitoring the development of what Iraq alleged was an energy-producing reactor, discov-ered that towards the end of the 1970s, Saddam Hussein's scientists were on the way to manufacturing a nuclear weapon. Operation Sphinx was the codename given to the Israeli efforts to neutralize the Osiraq nuclear complex at Tuwaitha near to the town of Suwayah, twelve miles south of Baghdad. The Israeli fighters approached the facility under the 'shadow' of a Boeing 707, their 2,000 lb iron bombs destroying the Osiris-type nuclear reactor. An Israeli government statement of 9 June 1981 warned: 'Under no circumstances would we allow the enemy to develop weapons of mass destruction against our

1

nation; we will defend Israel's citizens with all the means at our disposal.'

The controversial US clinical strike air attack on Libya was conducted during the nights of 14 and 15 April 1986 by Sixth Fleet carrier-borne aircraft and F-111 fighter-bombers based in the United Kingdom. The attack was launched in response to a growing number of terrorist-inspired attacks in the West, allegedly at the behest of Libya's president, Colonel Gadaffi. The final straw appears to have been a bomb attack on 5 April 1986 against a Berlin discotheque frequented by United States servicemen. One of the two fatalities was a United States sergeant.

The aircraft struck at targets in Tripoli, the capital of Libya, Benghazi and the military airfield at Benina. Collateral damage was inevitable, given that a number of the targets were in built-up areas. But it had not been the best of demonstrations of precision bombing. The F-111s were ordered to attack at low level and their Pave Tac guided bombs proved to be ineffective.[2] There was some speculation that the intended target had been Colonel Gadaffi, but that would have run contrary to an administration executive order forbidding the targeting of heads of state in particular and assassinations in general. It is believed that ninety-five people were killed. A discredited report claimed that among those killed was Gadaffi's daughter. Subsequent intelligence information indicated that it might have been more appropriate (but much more difficult) to have bombed Damascus rather than Tripoli as a reprisal for the Berlin attack. Nevertheless, the long-term effect had been to lessen Colonel Gadaffi's involvement in terrorism.

A clinical strike is, therefore, in essence, an attack by bombs or missiles against point targets. Future clinical strikes could conceivably utilize redundant nuclear missiles armed with a conventional warhead. Such systems would not be affected by any blanket arms reduction agreement.

Traditional land intervention is subject to what Richard Little has described as the push and pull theories.[3] Citing examples from Morgenthau and Thucydides, he explains that the push 'concentrates on the motivation of the intervening actor when explaining intervention' while the pull 'refers the intervention response back to actors operating in the target state'. The power expressed by either push or pull action can be further subdivided according to whether the response is in a unilateral or multilateral form.

In order to remain within manageable proportions, this work is an examination of multilateral military intervention. Unilateral activity is not unimportant and it will be discussed but it differs from multilateralism because it has become a difficult operation to conduct and is arguably obsolescent. In general terms, domestic unilateral intra-state intervention (i.e. within national borders) is a legal action whereas uninvited, extra-state interventions (i.e. into the territory of other states) have tended to contravene international law. This is not a black and white area and there has been significant erosion of this principle.

The traditional definition of intervention suggests that it is 'a dictatorial or coercive interference by an outside party or parties in the sphere of jurisdiction of a sovereign state, or more broadly of an independent political community'.[4] This definition is really too broad for this study because it relates to a total intervention spectrum. A further, narrower definition describes intervention as 'forcible interference, short of declaring war, by one or more powers in the affairs of another power'.[5] The principal objection here is to the qualification 'short of declaring war'. Although it remains legally possible to declare war, the state of war since 1945 has been incompatible with the UN Charter. However, even before 1945, declarations of war were not at all common. A Channel Tunnel feasibility study (of 1881) investigated the number of occasions when hostilities had commenced without the prior declaration of war. Of the 117 conflicts identified between 1700 and 1870, war had been declared on only ten occasions.[6] The notion that Pakistan was at war with India in 1965 was dismissed by a commercial arbitrator.[7] Similarly, President Noriega's ill-thought-out declaration of war on the US in 1989 was widely regarded as bluster and rhetoric. Since 1945, it is not possible to identify one single legitimate instance of a declaration of war.

What exists today in lieu of war is an activity described as 'armed conflict'. Within that term lies the topic of this study, multilateral military intervention, an occurrence for which a new definition is offered: 'when one or more states intervene militarily within the territory or possessions of one or more other states. The threat or intention of the use of significant force on both sides is implicit'. A very general term to have emerged since the 1990–1 Gulf crisis is *Coalition Warfare*. There is, however, a world of difference between the coalition warfare evident in Operation Overlord, the Allied operations in Normandy, 1944 and the various Allied operations which evolved in Saudi Arabia in 1990–1. The former enjoyed the benefit from the outset of a recognized enemy, of pre-planning and recognizable command, control, communications and intelligence structures. The ultimate purpose of this book is to persuade its readership of the pressing need to formulate and establish structures for the future which are closer to the Normandy than to the Saudi Arabia model. It is unlikely that the next crisis will be contested in an environment as favourable as that for the Gulf coalition or in circumstances which permit the taking of a five month work-up period.

Today, it would be entirely unrealistic to believe that force, or more appropriately, the threat of force, could be avoided in bringing about the peaceful settlement of an international dispute. Sir Harry Hinsley has written:

You may count on the fingers of one hand the occasions on which agreements have been made and changes of sovereignty or transfers of territory have occurred in the modern world without the assistance of the possibility of a resort to force, if not of force itself. It is the possibility that force will be used, when it is not actual force, that alone makes agreements and changes possible – and that alone can stop them.[8]

3

In an intervention scenario, however, the overriding aim must initially be to deter rather than be obliged to use force. There are usually two options available to be considered prior to collective military action. Firstly, diplomacy and persuasion have to be given a chance. If that fails, coercion short of armed conflict in the form of sanctions may well be imposed against the aggressor state.

Hedley Bull concluded 'that intervention in the sense of coercive interference by outside parties in the sphere of jurisdiction of a state is an endemic or built-in feature of our present international arrangements'.[9] This coercive interference was traditionally manifested in three stages down a slippery slope and recorded for analytical purposes by Professor Richard Ullman as follows:

> The first stage is characterized principally by the provision of material and financial assistance.... The second stage of intervention is characterized by the limited participation of the supporting Power in military operations.... But in order for the intervening Power to get effective control, it is necessary to proceed to the third stage. Then the intervening forces become the dominant element in the war effort of the supported side.[10]

Today, that formula remains valid but it is no longer exclusive. The Falklands and Panama interventions did not follow that pattern but proceeded directly to the third stage, thereby indicating that modern intervention can be both a dynamic and immediate activity. The fact of immediacy is relevant in the sphere of the legal argument of self-defence but more importantly, in relation to planning and preparation.

Since 1945 there have been over 150 limited wars of the type that spawns military intervention. Few of these limited wars could have been foreseen six months before they occurred. Casualties have numbered 20 million.[11] Eighty-five per cent of those wars have been intra- rather than inter-state wars. Of these, 95 per cent have been fought outside Europe.[12] An important distinction should be drawn between intra- and inter-state conflict because of the relevance to peacekeeping and enforcement action. Intra-state conflict is less to do with territorial disputation than with ethnic, religious and ideological struggle. Conversely, inter-state conflict is more likely to be concerned with territorial claims and boundaries. It is in this latter field that peacekeeping has enjoyed its greatest success once the peace has been created to be kept. Inter-state and intra-state armed conflicts are not manifested in the same form. As a general rule, inter-state wars are conducted in accordance with the classical concept of armed conflict, yet intra-state wars are emphatically political, thereby requiring the supporting military response to be tailored accordingly. Setting aside the special circumstances prevailing in Cyprus, those circumstances when peacekeeping has been attempted in intra-state environments, such as the Congo and the Lebanon, have not always been auspicious events.

In the case of the United States, when the occasions of threat of force are added to the occasions where force has been used, the total since 1945 exceeds 500, most of which have been in the Third World.[13] In the 1950s and early 1960s 'the United States used its military power or paramilitary power on an average of once every eighteen months either to prevent a government deemed undesirable from coming to power or to overthrow a revolutionary government considered inimical to America's interests'.[14]

From earliest times, philosophers attempted to persuade states to forgo their sovereign right to go to war. Such men, who included Kant, Bentham and Vattell, were not so idealistic as to believe that war, or the threat of war, would be entirely eradicated. They sought to establish among right-minded states a system for collective security. Collective security has been described as 'a design for preserving the integrity of the anonymous victim of attack by the anonymous aggressor; it is no respecter of states, but an instrument to be directed against any aggressor, on behalf of any violated state.[15]

This desire to introduce an international system of collective security received substantial new impetus as a result of the extent and excesses of the First World War. France, which had suffered most in that war, attempted to give teeth to Article 10 of the League of Nations which required states to guarantee the territorial integrity and independence of every other state. France sought to form an International General Staff and standing forces to ensure that Article 10 would be observed. The American President Woodrow Wilson successfully objected to any such step, which would appear to turn the Covenant of the League into an outmoded military alliance. Among the founders of the League of Nations were those who had not understood that if there is a keen moral intention to introduce restrictive rules circumscribing a state's previous sovereign right to go to war, then there has to be a compensating enforcement mechanism. This was not the only hole in the fabric of the League's structure (sanctions proved to be ineffective) but it was certainly the most serious.

Even before the peace of 1945, the Allied Powers in San Francisco were drafting a charter for a new organization which would be more effective than the League. Both organizations proved to be much the same but important provision had been made in the Charter to repair the holes that had existed in the League. If there was a fault it lay in the assumption that the sinking of ideological differences that had been so essential in defeating Hitler would be perpetuated in the peace. The reality is outlined by Sir Brian Urquhart:

> The 'United' in United Nations came from the Atlantic Charter of 1941 and referred to nations united in war, not in peace. The permanent members of the Security Council with the power of veto were the leaders of the victorious wartime alliance, and the Charter assumed, with a stunning lack of political realism, that they would stay united in supervising, and if necessary enforcing, world peace.[16]

5

It was in giving to themselves the power of the veto that the great powers had contrived to build among themselves their own Trojan horse. Whereas the League had been compromised and destroyed by recognized pitfalls, the Charter was endangered at its inception by the one great chasm represented by the veto. It proved a necessary evil. Frequent use of the veto, first by the Soviets and then by the Americans, served to frustrate the workings of the UN. The veto was, nonetheless, a realistic mechanism, for in the early days it was impossible to force upon the superpowers a course of action which ran contrary to their national interest.

The enforcement chapter in the Charter of the United Nations is Chapter VII, 'Action with respect to threats to peace, breaches of the peace and acts of aggression'. The Security Council, in accordance with Article 39, 'shall determine the existence of any threat to the peace, breach of the peace, or act of aggression, and shall make recommendations, or decide what measures shall be taken in accordance with Articles 41 and 42, to maintain or restore international peace and security'. The reference here to 'peace' is generally regarded to mean international peace. When the Security Council does take action it does not always declare under which article it is acting. For example, it is believed that the Korean intervention was enacted under Article 39. By their Resolution 82 of 1950, the Security Council determined that a breach of the peace existed in Korea and two days later made recommendations that troops should be made available.

Article 40 empowers the Security Council to 'call upon the parties concerned to comply with such provisional measures as it deems necessary or desirable'. In some respects this is a misleading article for it attracts greater authority than at first appears the case. It has the authority to assemble the wherewithal to ensure that provisional measures are heeded and to report back on the effectiveness of the measures implemented. 'The Security Council shall take account of failure to comply with such provisional measures.' In the chronology of action, it can even precede Article 39, being either a recommendation or a mandatory measure when linked to Article 25. ('The Members of the United Nations agree to accept and carry out the decisions of the Security Council in accordance with the present Charter.') It is Article 40 which is often the constitutional basis for the setting up of Security Council military operations. It was the basis under which observer groups were first established in Indonesia in 1947 and Palestine in 1948.

Article 41 embraces all sanctions other than the use of armed force. It is, however, Article 42 which is the ultimate military sanction available to be initiated once Article 41 is found to be inadequate. The Security Council

> may take such action by air, sea or land forces as may be necessary to maintain or restore international peace and security. Such action may include demonstrations, blockade, and other operations by air, sea or land forces of Members of the United Nations.

6

This is the significant point of departure from the weaknesses found in the Covenant of the League of Nations. Moreover, under Article 43(1) of the Charter, all members

> in order to contribute to the maintenance of international peace and security, undertake to make available to the Security Council, on its call and in accordance with a special agreement or agreements, armed forces, assistance and facilities, including rights of passage, necessary for the purpose of maintaining international peace and security.

Article 43(2) specifies further that: 'such agreement or agreements shall govern the numbers and types of forces, their degree of readiness and general location, and nature of facilities and assistance to be provided'. (This article has never been tested. Therefore, the more obvious questions of who pays and whether a state has the reserved right to decline to support interventions which, for that state, are politically difficult or impossible, have not been addressed.) There is even provision under Article 47 for a Military Staff Committee (MSC) consisting of the chiefs of staff of the permanent members of the Security Council, or their representatives, to advise and assist the Security Council in the 'maintenance of international peace and security, the employment and command of forces placed at its disposal, the regulation of armaments and possible disarmament'.

Thus far, for practical and political reasons, these ultimate military sanctions enshrined in Articles 42 and 43 have never been initiated. Even on 29 November 1990 when the UN Security Council adopted Resolution 678, which authorized the United States, Britain and other Allies in the Gulf to use all necessary measures against Iraq to liberate Kuwait and 'restore international peace and security in the area', Article 42 was not invoked. Nevertheless, not since the Korean War had the UN approved of armed conflict to defeat an aggressor.

Efforts were made in 1947 to put together an impressive though inflexible standing military force, principally from the resources available among the permanent members of the Security Council in accordance with Article 43 although the Charter does not limit the provision of forces exclusively to them (see also Article 45). On 16 May 1947 the MSC established a sub-committee to examine Item I on its programme of work. This involved gathering

> the preliminary estimates of the overall strength and composition of armed forces to be made available to the Security Council by Member Nations of the United Nations, including the determination of the overall strength and composition of the three principal Services of armed forces – land, sea and air.[17]

Further objectives were to consider force structures made available from the five permanent members and force structures from other members. On

25 June 1947 the Security Council requested the MSC to submit an estimate of the overall strength of the armed forces which should be made available to the Security Council. They were required to indicate the strength and composition of the separate components and the proportion of that overall strength that should be provided on the basis of equality by the five permanent members.

Table 1 shows the estimates submitted in the report. The figures proposed by the five permanent members represented the overall strength of the armed forces which should be made available to the Security Council by all UN members in accordance with Article 43 of the Charter. Nationalist China supported the British estimate and chose to give it full support in

Table 1 Proposed force structure to be made available to the Security Council

	France	UK	US	USSR
AIR FORCES				
Bombers	775	600	1,250 (includes only	600
Strategic	(225)		strategic and	
Medium	(150)		tactical	
Light	(400)		bombers)	
Fighters	300	400	2,250 (includes fighter bombers)	300
Reconnaissance	200	—	—	—
Miscellaneous	—	200	300	300
TOTAL:	1,275	1,200	3,800 (does not include air transport requirements)	1,200
GROUND FORCES				
Divisions	16	8–12	20	12
Armoured	(3)			
Airborne	(3)			
Motorized or mountain	(10)			
NAVAL FORCES				
Battleships	3	2	3	—
Carriers	6	4	6	—
Cruisers	9	6	15	5–6
Destroyers	18–24	24	84	24
Escort vessels	30	48	—	24
Minesweepers	30	24	—	24
Submarines	12	12	90	12
Assault shipping and craft for number of divisions shown	1	$\frac{2}{3}$*	6	—

*(2 regimental combat teams or brigade groups)

Source: Yearbook of the United Nations 1947–1948, 495.

order to facilitate the draft report and to minimize divergent views.

A second request from the Council, that the MSC should indicate what proportion of the overall strength shown in Table 1 should be provided on the basis of equality by the permanent five, was never resolved. Although France and the USSR considered that the major portion of the armed forces should be supplied by the Five, both Nationalist China and the USA stated that no overall fraction of the overall strength could be supplied on the basis of equality by the Five. Britain was unwilling to give an answer until the first question, relating to the overall strength, had been resolved. General R.L. McCreery, the British Chairman of the MSC, wrote to the Chairman of the Security Council:[18]

Inasmuch as unanimity could not be achieved on the question of the overall strength and composition of the United Nations Armed Forces [Item I of the Programme of Work], it was, *a priori*, impossible to consider Items II and III of the Programme of Work, dealing with the contributions by Member Nations.

Such grandiose ideas had presupposed the continuation of harmony and unanimity among the victorious Allies as well as the willingness to fund in peacetime substantial standing armed forces. The principal objections and original source of obstruction arose from the USSR. Table 1 reveals that the United States was consistently out of step with the other permanent members of the Security Council regarding force structures. The United States' expectations were far greater than the others, a fact which caused immediate suspicion within the Soviet camp. They took the view that there was no possible rationale for such large standing forces unless they were intended for deployment against a major power. To that end, they sought to clarify the circumstances under which the force would be employed. Other problem areas that were cited were those concerned with command and parity. Essentially, the Soviets did not want to see a USA-dominated United Nations wield such considerable military power. It was, in the main, their deliberate obstruction at that time which killed off any prospect of the UN sponsoring collective security measures.

As a result of this frigidity, which heralded the Cold War, collective security devolved down through the regions to collective defence systems such as NATO, the Warsaw Pact, the Baghdad Pact redesignated as CENTO (Central Treaty Organization), SEATO (South East Asia Treaty Organization) and ANZUS (Australia, New Zealand and United States Pact). This inability to initiate enforcement measures led to a fortuitous compromise with the emergence within the UN of a peacekeeping function, something not provided for by the Charter.

The original 1947 peacekeepers were military observers overseeing ceasefire agreements and truces. It was not until the 1956 Suez crisis that forces were deployed on peacekeeping activities and it was not until the

1973 UNEF (United Nations Emergency Force) II, when peacekeepers were dispatched to Egypt and Sinai following the Middle East War, that peacekeeping procedures were standardized into a format that is recognizable today. Whereas multilateral military intervention would fall within Chapter VII of the UN Charter, it is Chapter VI, 'Pacific settlement of disputes', which has evolved as the umbrella for the conduct of peacekeeping operations predicated upon the non-use of force except, in the last resort, in self-defence. Peacekeeping is therefore more a political activity than intervention, owing its strength to its obvious weakness. Multilateral military intervention under UN auspices would be conducted in circumstances where there is no peace to be kept, possibly as a precursor to peacekeeping or peacemaking activities.

In recent years it has become increasingly apparent that, while Chapter VI and Chapter VII are rigorously distinct, there is, in operational terms, a real problem in maintaining that distinction. This is a direct reflection of escalating levels of conflict, principally in the Third World. The problem first became apparent during the Congo crisis when the peacekeeping function and the use of force proved incompatible. The Katanga episode of 1961–3, however, is the only occasion when Chapter VI has been thoroughly compromised. Yet it is clear from subsequent peacekeeping operations, most notably in UNIFIL (UN Interim Force in Lebanon), that the obligatory abstention from the use of weapons other than in self-defence in an environment where the settlement of disputes by armed force is the norm, is becoming increasingly difficult to sustain. Recent debate has examined the upgrading of peacekeeping activities by giving the 'blue berets' more teeth. This high-profile peacekeeping is known euphemistically as 'Chapter VI $\frac{1}{2}$'. The term was first used by Dag Hammarskjöld to describe an option for UN peacekeeping lying midway between Chapters VI and VII. If, for example, Palestine were to be divided between two states, there seems little doubt that the peacekeepers deployed in support of a UN settlement would require a quite different status of forces agreement and rules of engagement from those which emerged in 1973.

The United Nations has become the largest of the international organizations. It has a substantial, sometimes overwhelming, infrastructure but it has the significant benefit of the force of international law to support Security Council resolutions. Whereas it seems the ideal choice to oversee the introduction of a collective security regime, it is nevertheless appropriate to examine the role, purpose and capabilities of the other main, sometimes contending, regional international organizations. There is ample justification for considering the relationship between the UN and regional organizations this early in the discussion because it is a key issue. Regional organizations have often had a chequered existence. Impartiality has been a problem in the past but, properly managed and supported by their constituent actors, they have the potential, either working independently or in association with the UN, to be important agencies for world stability.

Winston Churchill's concept of a new post-Second World War order was based on the hopeful re-emergence of the old Concert or Council of Europe cemented by a separate alliance between Britain and the United States.[19] Discouraging the United States from returning to its previous isolationism was central to his policy, and the way Churchill believed this could be achieved was through an effective international organization. Roosevelt was reluctant to support a concept of internationalism which Churchill intended to be regional in nature but which was essentially Eurocentric. In Churchill's plan there would be three regional councils – Asia, Europe and the Americas – reporting to a supreme council. He intended that the United States and the Soviet Union should also be represented in the main European regional council; it fitted his vision of the Great Power management of world affairs. He envisaged the United States remaining within the mainstream of European politics to balance the growing power of the Soviet Union, whose inclusion as a power-sharer in the grand design for Europe was a reflection of the Soviets' strength.

Churchill's idea, circulated in 1943, of regional organizations revolving around a central European pillar did not survive into 1944. The Dominions proved to be hostile but it was the strong American and Soviet opposition expressed both at Quebec and at the Moscow Conference which ensured the idea died an early death. How ironic, therefore, in 1990 that Gorbachev should have been beating on the door of the 'common European home' asking to be admitted. Stranger still, and something Churchill would have found extraordinary, was the USA playing host in New York to the foreign ministers of the Helsinki process, the Conference on Security and Co-operation in Europe (CSCE). The ministers' discussions there centred on the evolution of a structure to manage the affairs of a pan-European Alliance. America's role was not altruistic but pragmatic, aimed at preserving its influence in Europe.

CSCE emerged as a contender to wear the mantle of European security once the earlier East–West divisions in Europe evaporated. The hope of the supporters of the CSCE process is to merge the previous separate NATO and Warsaw Pact collective security systems into a single collective security regime. It is a pan-European organization in so far as it includes the states of Western and Eastern Europe and indulges in some Atlantic pond-jumping to include America and Canada, both NATO members. The Soviet hope that CSCE will eventually supersede NATO and the defunct Warsaw Pact is matched by an American intention to maintain NATO's primacy for European security. The reality of the weakening of America's voice in Europe and the new emphasis placed on NATO's political rather than military function could mean that NATO will compete for collective security pre-eminence with a host of other disparately represented European organizations. It is this proliferation of competing European regional security options which may well perpetuate division, indecision and overwhelming weakness.

The question does need to be asked, and it applies equally to all regional organizations: how effective can CSCE be? Is it realistic or does it incline too far towards idealism in attempting to maintain an anti-bloc character? Critics could say, with some justification, that an organization which spans almost totally the land mass of the northern hemisphere from Vancouver to Vladivostock is not a regional organization. Some would say that its size, fifty-two states, is too large to reach sensible conclusions by obligatory consensus rather than by simple vote. Others suggest that the decision-making process can be blurred by the insistence that working groups are chaired by neutrals who have undue and undeserved prominence. Certainly, the CSCE spawns bureaucracy not least through the existence of six official languages: English, Russian, German, Italian, Spanish and French. However, setting aside impulse, bias, intuition and partisanship, this analysis is concerned with the assessment of the efficacy of CSCE as a collective security system.

CSCE has already had its undoubted successes in the fields of human rights and in establishing East–West dialogue as a prelude to European assimilation. In the future it could have a part to play in confidence-building measures, conciliation and verification. If Germany has its way, the function of the CSCE could be further expanded so that 'the protection of minorities must form part of the common legal order',[20] and a European centre would be established 'for the early detection and settlement of conflicts'.[21] A Conflict Prevention Centre was established in Vienna as a measure arising from the 1990 Charter of Paris. Given its inherently weak decision-making structure, the CSCE would be best suited to the management of crisis avoidance rather than crisis management.

The first step towards any problem-solving is to examine the rules, and the CSCE rules are contained in the Helsinki Final Act signed in 1975 by the then thirty-five participating states. The Act is a dual-track agreement which combines western standards on human rights issues with the promise of ameliorating Soviet security worries. In some quarters, doubt has been expressed at ministerial level whether the Final Act is legally binding. However, what is immediately evident from the examination of the Helsinki Final Act is that, although it does go further in some areas, it is nevertheless written around the framework of the United Nations Charter. CSCE states have reaffirmed:

> in conformity with their membership in the United Nations and in accordance with the purposes and principles of the United Nations, their full and active support for the United Nations and for the enhancement of its role and effectiveness in strengthening interna-

12

tional peace, security and justice and in promoting the solution of international problems, as well as the development of friendly relations and co-operation among states.

The Helsinki Final Act does not and cannot give CSCE the unilateral legal authority to take action within its region in the interest of collective security. The CSCE has the authority to act in the interest of collective self-defence under Article 51 of the UN Charter but is still obliged to report back to the UN. The United Nations is the organization more suitably geared to crisis management than anything likely to emerge in Europe. That much was evident during the Yugoslav crisis 1991–2. The Charter does permit the United Nations to delegate its authority down to regional organizations. Europe's principal problem is in deciding the form of conflict to which it needs to address its endeavours. It seems unlikely today that any credible regional organization would act in a manner contrary to the wishes of the United Nations. What is rather more likely is that CSCE, and similar regional organizations, will behave as the coagulant for common national interests in support of a broader response to their own regional problems.

CSCE is the largest but not the only European political organization vying for a collective security dimension. The failure of the so-called truly European pillar to rise to a position of prominence was due in the main to the large number of organizations involved with European security, with their different membership, interests and priorities. The risk to NATO in moving its weight quite significantly from the military to a political rationale is that it could become just another competitor in an overpopulated European collective security field. In reality, what has happened in NATO is not so much an obvious increase in its political activity as the rather obvious decrease in its military responsibilities. The presence of the United States in a future European-polarized NATO could be less important than the absence of France. Much depends upon France's future position, but it is significant that since 1945 the United States has contributed more to European security than France.

France is not a member of the Eurogroup, founded in 1968 and part of NATO. Eurogroup's principal interest is in the field of defence equipment collaboration yet it has no charter and is therefore not a strong contender. France is a member of the thirteen-nation Independent European Programme Group (IEPG) which is designed to promote equipment collaboration. However, this group, formed in 1976, and institutionalized in 1989 with the formation of a secretariat, remains an informal group. None of its decisions are binding on its members. A weightier organization is the Western European Union (WEU).

The WEU is the senior European security organization. It has its origins in the 1948 Brussels Treaty and therefore predates NATO. It has proven at times to be a resilient organization, as was evident in 1954 when the reinvigorated WEU allowed Europe to shrug off the problems associated with the ill-fated European Defence Community. It was the organization which arranged the integration of West Germany into NATO, from which point it fell under NATO's shadow, becoming dormant for thirty years.

The WEU today comprises nine European countries – Belgium, France, Germany, Italy, Luxembourg, the Netherlands, Portugal, Spain and the United Kingdom. It does not therefore include all twelve members of the European Community (EC). Since its preoccupation is with matters of defence and foreign policy, it cannot be all-embracing. It would be difficult, for example, for Ireland to be a member. The WEU is, nevertheless, an organization which has had success. In 1987 it co-ordinated the European naval response in the Gulf. What limits its potential for wider success is the political tension that exists within the body.

The future of the WEU has not always been secure and it remains the source of high-level international debate. There have been proposals that NATO could cultivate the WEU and in some way compensate for the latter organization's lack of permanent military support. In the past, some influential Europeans have made a case for the WEU to be subsumed by the EC. That prospect had been receding but is now back on the agenda. Whereas the original Treaty of Rome precluded the EC from adopting a defence role – not least because of the presence of neutrals – it is a fact that the EC does have security and commercial interests which combine to provide an inescapable defence dimension. There is a difference, however, between maintaining an interest in economic and political security and going so far as to define a defence role. Equally, the EC does not have any transatlantic linkage, which is a disadvantage if the USA retains a strongish military presence in Europe. The proliferation of European security agencies, the emergence of the trans-European possibilities within CSCE and the existence of wider political and economic problems within the EC reinforce the conventional wisdom of the EC keeping faith with its civil origins.

This is not to say that in the future the EC will not mould the European security agenda to some degree. Over a period of time and during the potentially difficult transition from collective defence to collective security, recurring crises might cause one, or more, of the European political organizations to emerge in a pre-eminent position. That lead organization will have adapted to the circumstances and retailored its charter and infrastructure to fall into line with the conceptual changes now so self-evident. Those European political organizations which find themselves in a secondary position will nevertheless still find a complementary role to play in a collective security cat's cradle.

NATO is currently the most plausible and cohesive collective security option for Europe to work under the umbrella of a UN crisis-management mechanism. It does not, however, have such a role. It not only has the crisis management structure to deal with threats arising both within and outside the region but also the integrated military assets with which to respond to a whole range of multi-intensity conflicts. An organization which is openly admired by its former opponents must have some attraction. If, as appears likely, CSCE is unable to provide Eastern Europe and the former Soviet Union with the security dimension they at first envisaged, there seems to be a compelling argument for an expanded NATO. The formation of the North Atlantic Co-operation Council (NACC), which includes ten of the independent states of the former Soviet Union, including Russia, is a cautious step in this direction. A future Europe promises to provide that organization with new and very different scenarios. It remains true that the European theatre will continue to be NATO's only concern. In a shrinking world, however, NATO will need to look beyond Europe into other regions whose activities impinge upon European and transatlantic interests. In order to move with comfort into a new, future phase in NATO's life, it is essential that linkages and bridges are built with the United Nations Organization.

Outside Europe there are of course other notable regional organizations: the Organization of American States (OAS), the Organization of African Unity (OAU), the Arab League and the Gulf Co-operation Council (GCC), to name a few. Analysis reveals that they are often seriously divided, disorganized and ineffective. There is the prospect, however, of the organizations being a greater force for regional security when supporting the United Nations initiatives.

The OAS supported the USA's stand against Cuba in 1962 and the intervention went ahead. The OAS did not support the USA's invasion of Panama in 1989, yet it went ahead. For reasons which are explained later, it is evident that the United States' scope and capacity for unilateral action, even in Central America, has diminished and will continue to diminish.

But then, it must be recognized that regional organizations have a charter which requires them to do rather more than maintain peace and security within the region. The OAU's chairman Mengistu Haile Mariam said of that organization in 1983 that it was 'The only forum in which we can express one common voice'. 1983 had proved to be a make-or-break year for an organization which suffered a major crisis associated with the nineteenth summit scheduled in 1983 for Libya but reconvened in Addis Ababa. A contemporary description illustrates the OAU's broader *raison d'être* and explains that the impact of an OAU collapse

> would have catastrophic consequences for the continent, as well as for international peace and security. It would eliminate any restraint on interference in internal affairs and violation of the inherited frontier, thus opening Africa to endless armed conflict of various types. It would destroy the cohesion of the African Group at the United

Nations with regard to major issues of common concern. It would weaken the national liberation movements in southern Africa to the point of dangerous dependence on ideologically-motivated funds and support from inside and outside Africa. It would revive bloc politics in Africa and bring back the era of the Casablanca Group versus the Monrovia Group.[22] It would weaken non-alignment in Africa, if not end it, hence paving the way for superpower rivalries for the purpose of carving out spheres of influence. It would eliminate any hope that subregional organizations might work together with an all-Africa purpose in mind, a development that would pit them against one another. It would weaken all programming for the advancement of African economic integration. It would destroy nation-building in Africa on the premise of Africa being one sphere of common concern to its peoples. It would shatter Africa's image and respect of itself on the world stage.[23]

The desire to express 'one common voice' can be applied quite literally to the Arabs and the Arab League and can also be extended to include the existence of a common religion. Yet it is insufficient to prevent the League from being divided into the distinct format of sub-regional groups which had so worried the OAU. Saddam Hussein's Arab Co-operation Council (ACC) consisting of Egypt, Jordan and the then North Yemen was established to confront Syria in the Lebanon and also to pursue collective interests in the Middle East, the Gulf and Africa. The onset of the 1990 Gulf crisis saw Egypt emphatically dissociate herself from Iraq and, despite the presence of strong nationalist sentiments, Jordan took an initial latitudinarian position. The crisis caused a confused response in the recently united Yemen.

It is not appropriate here to be drawn into discussion of the failure of the Gulf Co-operation Council (GCC) to react to Iraq's invasion of Kuwait by mobilizing its rapid reaction force, or Peninsula Shield. That comes later. Despite all the polite mouthings of phrases such as 'the brotherhood of all Arabs' and the need for 'an Arab solution', in the final analysis the Arab world failed to respond to the north's encouragement to take the initiative. The political and economic divisions among the Arabs came to the fore. Some Arab states feared Iraq, its power and its proven willingness to exercise that power. Others simply resented the GCC's exclusivity and wealth and were not to be disturbed unduly by the invasion of Kuwait. The crisis showed that, in the Middle East, members of regional organizations react according to the nature of the crisis. As has become evident elsewhere it is the very nature of the crisis which will form the alliance according to the national interest of each state. But these 'hot' alliances are essential because in the Middle East the activities of outside parties behaving unilaterally is a unique and almost certain recipe for polarizing previously-divided attitudes in Arabia, particularly when the action is aimed against one claiming to champion the Arab cause. The political and military tangle in Arabia is not unique: it is replicated throughout the world.

The purpose of this work is to determine whether the time may once again be right to attempt to adopt co-ordinated global collective security measures in the form of multilateral military intervention for the 1990s. In 1939, E.H Carr wrote in *The Twenty Years' Crisis*:

> The advocate of a scheme for an international police force or for collective security or some other project for an international order generally replied to the criticism not by an argument designed to show how and why he thought his plan will work but by a statement that it must be made to work because the consequences of its failure to work would be so disastrous.[24]

This unintended challenge is taken up by developing an argument to show how and why a new plan for collective security might work. It is logical to tackle the *why* (necessity and opportunity) before the *how*. It is also addressing the simpler question first. The argument can be previewed as follows:

Why?

Instability in large parts of the Third World;
the new collegiality among the permanent members of the UN Security Council;
the failure and difficulties in achieving military intervention.

How?

Establish the 'rules of the game', namely:
- select and maintain the aim;
- operate under the auspices and co-ordination of a valid and support-ive international organization;
- establish a simple and agreed unified command, control, communi-cations and intelligence organization;
- establish an effective *cordon sanitaire* around the target area;
- plan the force extraction concurrently with the planning of force insertion;
- maintain consensus;
- agree and adhere to national contributions;
- operate within the law;
- remember that military intervention is the last resort of a collective security machine.

Utilize the UN's legal mechanism;
Restructure the UN's military organization;
Design a strategy;
Allocate resources.

WHY?

INSTABILITY IN LARGE PARTS OF THE THIRD WORLD

The conventional stability which has developed between East and West explains the rationale for concentrating the greater part of this study in the Third World. This is not to say that the so-called 'north' is entirely stable, for the lifting of central Communist control over Central and Eastern Europe has uncovered, amongst others, the Balkan problem and also reminded us that ethnicity is neither a recent nor an un-European phenomenon. The inflammation of the Balkan ulcer has continued apace. However, there was no rush to intervene militarily by other concerned parties. There was an undoubted fear that intervention in Yugoslavia might create a precedent which would be applicable to other areas of turmoil within Europe. Was this, for example, a preview of what might happen in the former Soviet Union whose republics, to paraphrase something Charles de Gaulle said, each contained the seeds of another Algeria? Hopefully not, but the point is that these are not fertile areas for future successful military intervention.

At the beginning of a new decade, arms limitation discussions and SALT (Strategic Arms Limitation Talks) were seen to be generating overall military stability in the 'north' while the proliferation of weapons in the 'south' was giving rise there to increasing instability. This is true in Latin America and Asia but more particularly in the Middle East, where the sword of Damocles is permanently poised as the Arab–Israeli problem persistently defies solution. It is this growing, dangerous instability in large parts of the Third World which emphasizes the importance both of examining the avenues leading towards a new, world collective security regime and of beginning this investigation of the reason 'why'.

Instability in the Third World has obvious geopolitical and economic causes. Whereas it is true that weapons themselves do not equal instability, arms transfers are a cutting edge of the problem. The current holders of arms stockpiles are certainly a cause for concern, but what is of more concern is what is happening within the so-called 'threshold' states (India,

18

Pakistan, Brazil, Argentina, South Africa and Israel) and weapon developments elsewhere. Strangely, Iraq is not described as a threshold state.

At a time when the USA no longer has chemical weapons within the military structure of NATO and bilateral plans on stock reduction between the USA and the former USSR are progressing well, there is a widespread belief that twenty countries possess chemical weapons. Yet the USA, France and the former USSR together with Iraq are the only four states to have admitted to their possession. After proving its willingness to use chemical weapons by killing 5,000 Iraqi Kurds at Halabja and against Iranian troops, the Iraqis could hardly have done otherwise. In addition to the twenty countries thought to have chemical weapons, there are others which could develop the weapons in a short period. The 'right to reply' if attacked has been reserved by a significant number of states. Defensive research into the production of chemical agents continues in the Third World as well as elsewhere. Until now, the chemical weapon has been regarded by many as the Third World's nuclear alternative. It seems likely that during the course of this decade there will be a gradual change in that situation as some Third World states seek to gain a nuclear capability.

Despite the existence of the Missile Technology Control Regime (MTCR) there has been a proliferation of missile development. The *Economist* has assessed that at least twenty-two Third World countries are trying to buy or build ballistic missiles (see Table 2).[25] This assessment is confirmed by the Stockholm International Peace Research Institute. By the year 2000,

Table 2 Short and intermediate-range systems in
development, 1989

Country	Missile	Range (km)
Argentina	Condor-2	900
Brazil	MB/EE family	150–1,000
	SS - 300/1000	300–1,000
China	M family	600–1,000
Egypt	Condor-2	900
France	Hades	480
	S4	3,500
India	Prithvi	250
	Agni	2,500
Iran	Iran-130	130
Iraq	Al Abbas	900
	Condor-2	900
Israel	Jericho 2	1,500
Pakistan	Hatf 1	100
	Hatf 2	300
South Africa	Arniston	1,500
Taiwan	Sky Horse 1	950

Source: Jane's Defence Weekly, 23 December 1989, 1384.[27]

fifteen countries will have a nuclear launch capability.[26] Such missiles could of course be armed with either chemical or nuclear warheads. An examination of those nations leading the charge in this direction – the so-called threshold states and Iraq – cannot all justify these developments due simply to the absence of a collective security mechanism.

Not only does India, one-time apostle of non-violence, have 1.362 million men under arms, an airforce equipped with Mirage 2000s and MiG-29s, and substantial and growing maritime aspirations, she also has a space programme. In 1980 she was the sixth country to launch a satellite into orbit with indigenous equipment. On 22 May 1989 India test-fired an Intermediate Range Ballistic Missile (IRBM) at the Chandipur launch site. The Agni (meaning 'fire') came down in the sea 1,000 km to the south of the firing point, but its maximum range with a 2,200 lb warhead is said to be up to 2,500 km. With such a range, targets in the former USSR, Pakistan, China, Iran and Saudi Arabia are vulnerable.

President Gadaffi of Libya is becoming less equivocal regarding the development of IRBMs. If he were to deploy a similar system to Agni in the region of Tripoli, its northern radius of operation would include the Anglo-Scottish border and reach out beyond the north German coastline. Yet India maintains that Agni is not a missile but a 'test vehicle'. It is difficult not to reflect upon the irony of the poverty in which the majority of India's population exists and the selfsame poverty which precludes India from taking essential environmental initiatives. India's external debts are of the order of $64 billion but her defence budget from 1981 (US $2.75 billion) has more than tripled.[28] For the moment, however, South Asia is a less immediate problem than the Middle East.

Whereas it was the growth of Germany and the resultant imbalance of power which finally destroyed the Concert of Europe, the equilibrium of 'no war – no peace' in the Middle East has been sustained through a cultivated imbalance of power. This much was claimed by Richard Nixon in a presidential campaign, when he said that US policy should ensure that Israel would have sufficient military power as a deterrent to preclude an Arab attack. He believed that 'the balance must be tipped in Israel's favour. An exact balance of power ... would run the risk that potential aggressors might miscalculate and would offer them too much of a temptation'.[29] Due largely to the progress of Iraq, the Arabs were moving closer to an approximate balance of power, something that might have been achieved this decade. It was Winston Churchill who warned, in 1934, 'If you wish to bring about war, you bring about such a balance that both sides think they have a chance of winning.'[30]

Analysts' estimates of Israel's nuclear arsenal suggest that Israel has between 50 and 150 nuclear weapons. There was a belief that Israel would maintain regional stability through the exclusive possession of nuclear weapons into the middle of the next decade. The recent nuclear develop-

Table 3 Arms transfers to the Third World 1984–8
(US $ billions, at 1985 prices)

Leading exporters		Leading importers	
1 USSR	45.9	Iraq	16.0
2 USA	23.5	India	13.3
3 France	14.7	Saudi Arabia	9.3
4 China	7.7	Egypt	8.0
5 Great Britain	6.6	Syria	7.1
6 West Germany	3.6	North Korea	5.8
7 Italy	2.4	Angola	4.4
8 Brazil	1.4	Pakistan	3.4
9 Israel	1.2	Iran	3.3
10 Spain	1.1	Libya	3.1

Source: From Die Ziet/Globus, Stockholm International Peace
Research Institute.[31]

ments and progress with delivery means in Iraq had been regarded as bringing forward the possibility of a nuclear contest into this decade.

At first Iraq denied that she had aspirations to become a nuclear power, and from 29 October 1969 became a signatory to the Nuclear Non-Proliferation Treaty (NPT). However, few doubted President Saddam Hussein's determination to develop an atomic bomb. It was after the Israeli attack on the Baghdad reactor on 7 June 1981 that the Iraqi president appealed to all 'peace and security-loving nations of the world' to help the Arabs build an atomic bomb to counter Israel's nuclear arsenal. Hussein saw this desire as completely 'rational' and a remedy to the existing situation in Israel.

The Times of 24 June 1981, quoted Hussein: 'What would happen to the Arabs and humanity if Israel were to impose conditions and the Arabs refused them, and Israel would then use the atomic bomb against the Arabs because of this?'

In 1990 Iraq was generally thought to have been perhaps three years away from the production of nuclear warheads, emphasizing a shift away from the Cold War in Europe and the evolution of a potential 'hot war' in the Middle East.

It is third-party holdings such as these which take on greater importance as a bilateral START (Strategic Arms Reduction Treaty) progressively reduces superpower holdings of strategic weapons. Prior to START, Great Britain and France, who are currently excluded from the discussions, possessed only a fraction of US holdings. When START has run its course into the middle of the next decade, Anglo-French holdings, compared with the superpowers, will rise significantly. When these figures are extrapolated into what is possible in the Third World, particularly the Middle East, it serves to shake cosy self-congratulations based upon the accumulating East–West disarmament accords. The problem of nuclear war has not gone away, it has simply moved out of Europe, and unless controls are effective, it will reappear in the Middle East: 'The Arab–Israeli conflict today, and others tomorrow, are about to evolve into the hair-trigger balance of terror that kept Americans, Russians and Europeans in nuclear thrall for 30 years'.[32]

For the selfsame Americans, Soviets and Europeans as well as the Chinese this is a case of *déjà vu*. There is considerable irony in the fact that the top five arms exporters to the Third World are the five permanent members of the *Security* Council (see Table 3). 'Traditionally,' write Hare and Joynt, 'arms aid has been used by states to build up allies and substitute arms for the use of one's own forces, to influence the balance of power in an area of the world where important interests were involved, to maintain or overthrow the status quo inside other states and for reasons of profit.'[33] Arms transfers had become the proxies through which the superpowers exercised a unique form of intervention to gain influence and leverage. There are now so many new actors on the arms transfer stage – for China it represents her principal source of foreign exchange – that it is the client who calls the tune and little prospect remains for the exporter to derive influence and leverage through the sale of arms.

Sixty-one per cent of all weapons exported prior to the 1990–1 Gulf War went to the Middle East. Whereas NATO spends 3.8 per cent of Gross National Product (GNP) on defence, the Middle East spent 18 per cent. The Soviets had the largest share of this market, at 34 per cent, with the United States second, at 16 per cent. *Jane's Defence Weekly* quoted Soviet Foreign Minister Shevardnadze as saying that while the world is changing both politically and militarily, many people in the Middle East 'still think that you can accomplish anything with a gun'.[34] A former British Middle East diplomat estimated that, prior to the 1990–1 Gulf War, the region contained one tank for every 2,000 head of population.

There is evidence that the industrialized nations are now concerned by the implications of the proliferation of missile systems as well as by the development of nuclear and chemical warheads. France for example has sold nuclear know-how to both Israel and Iraq. There were also plans for France to supply Baghdad with the high technology necessary to develop an aerospace industry.[35] One specialist has said of France's arms sales policy that 'generally [France] has been considered to be the most permissive of the major suppliers, with the assumption often made that the French government is willing to sell arms to almost anybody'.[36] It seems that after the Gulf War France's attitude to arms transfers may be subject to review.

Efforts at gentle persuasion targeted at the more extreme developments in the Third World have been unsuccessful. For example, India was particularly resentful of US efforts to stop the testing of the Agni IRBM. However, now that the former Soviet Union – who, like China, has much to lose – has agreed to support the principles of the 1987 Missile Technology Control Regime (MTCR), there is the prospect of some order where none had previously existed. There are still important missile manufacturing countries who are not signatories, namely Argentina, Brazil and North Korea. In addition, there are companies within countries who have signed the agreement, such as Italy and West Germany, who have evaded MTCR agreements. The London Suppliers Club (LSC) is a group of nuclear exporting states who, in similar circumstances as those in the MTCR, act as a controlling mechanism on the export of nuclear information and material.

One aspect of Vienna's Conventional Forces in Europe (CFE) talks has important implications and that is the amount of equipment that is to be given up. Although ratification questions remain, it was originally assessed that if all the armour scheduled to be forfeited by the Soviets was to be placed nose to tail, it would stretch from Paris to Bonn. A further consideration is 'Cascading', which describes an activity whereby good, serviceable but surplus to requirement equipment is transferred to allies and friends, who release for disposal and destruction what may well be their own obsolete or obsolescent weapons. Even if controls are effective in ensuring that NATO and former Warsaw Pact weapons do not cascade into the Third World, intense pressure will fall on arms suppliers to market their wares in what may well be the only significant market open to buyers – the Third World.

How, therefore, if the need arose, might this steady build-up of weapons and forces be combated? There is no simple answer. Libya has almost as many fighter aircraft as West Germany and more tanks than Great Britain and France. In fact, Libya and Syria each have more tanks than the US Army had in its units in Europe prior to CFE reduction. A dozen or more Third World countries have over 1,000 main battle tanks.[37] 'Syria,' said a French government official to the author, 'has 350 fighters. What sort of force structure is required to combat that?' The purely numerical consideration does of course need to be tempered by a qualitative appraisal. By the end of July 1982, for example, when Israel launched her Operation Peace for Galilee, the Israeli airforce had shot down eighty-nine MiG 21/23 aircraft for no loss and destroyed twenty-nine surface to air missile sites for the loss of two aircraft to ground fire.[38]

Working from interior lines, Israel is in an advantageous position to restore her regional superiority and improve her security through the means of pre-emptive clinical strikes. This thought will not be developed further here because the legality of such action would need to be considered. In addition, it is not strictly relevant to this specific study, and begins to encroach into the area of 'how'. Nevertheless, it does make the point that external powers do not have the benefit, for example, of a state enjoying Israel's geographical position. It seems rather obvious now that military intervention in the Middle East could not be attempted by one single state, unilaterally. The ideal course of action must in some way involve the United Nations, the United States and the regional actors. The reason why there have never been better political prospects for the development of a new collective security regime is to do with the new collegiality that has developed among the permanent members of the UN Security Council.

THE NEW COLLEGIALITY AMONG THE PERMANENT MEMBERS OF THE UN SECURITY COUNCIL

The collapse in 1948 of the UN concept of collective security coincided with the end of the conceptual, or first distinct, phase in the evolution of the UN. The second phase, one of western domination, most particularly by the USA, extended into the mid-1950s. During the period 1945–54 the Soviets used the veto fifty-eight times to the USA's nil. The great numerical expansion in UN membership heralded a new third phase beginning in 1955 with the so-called 'package deal'. It began with the influx of new members from the Afro-Asian countries, their championship by the USSR and the eventual overturning of the West's automatic majority in the General Assembly. During the period 1970 to 1980 the Soviets used their veto only nine times whereas it was used by the USA on twenty-two occasions. The veto illustrations used here indicate a trend rather than bald fact, because raw statistics cannot reflect the behind-the-scenes manoeuvring that went on.

It is the belief that the UN has very recently entered an important fourth phase in its evolution which provides the rationale for feeling that collective security in general and legitimate multilateral intervention in particular, given the right conditions, can be distinct possibilities. International organizations are bound to be behind the developments in international relations, particularly when those developments have been so frenetic as during 1989–92. There are indications that the UN has moved out of the third phase and that these origins were discernible as early as the 1960s once the idea of limited nuclear war became discredited. The irony of what could develop into a highly significant change in the UN's fortunes is that the new wave was led by the nation primarily responsible for the organization's original impotence: the USSR.

The avoidance of war became central to the Soviet policy of *perestroika* and peaceful coexistence. The incongruity of Marxism-Leninism had never been starker in comparison with modern western economic developments. The unequivocal conclusions drawn by the leadership were that interstate relations not only had to be de-ideologized but also had to be subordinated to the primacy of domestic considerations. An almost total conceptual revolution in Soviet foreign policy had occurred. While internal affairs were subjected to urgent reassessment, external affairs were required to be conducted in a non-adversarial, non-confrontational status quo environment. The United Nations was tailor-made to suit the new Soviet circumstances. The timing was equally opportune, for the incidence of the use of force to secure national aims in international relations had declined appreciably, to be replaced by the broad

24

recognition of the value of interdependent action in a multilateral world.

There are four reasons for believing that the UN has entered the fourth phase in its development. First, the significant improvement in East–West relations heralded a greater preparedness on the part of the superpowers to work together in resolving regional problems. It was a truism that nothing of real importance could come about in international affairs without the support of one or both the superpowers. Their own particular failures in their interventions in Vietnam, Afghanistan and the Middle East prior to the 1990–1 Gulf conflict have been due to a greater or lesser degree to the active opposition of the other superpower. In the past there have been rare occasions when it has suited both the USA and the USSR to co-operate. For example, the post-Second World War withdrawal of the USSR from Austria was decided upon on the basis of the recognition by the USA of the neutrality of the alpine republic. It was the USA and USSR which stopped the 1956 Suez intervention and saved Jordan from her Arab neighbours. What has happened in the very recent past is that these longish intervals of co-operative activity have closed up.

The new-found cordiality transformed the work of the Security Council. Pressure was successfully brought to bear on Baghdad and Tehran to end the Gulf War in accordance with Security Council Resolution 598. The trend towards de-ideologizing regional conflicts, in so far as they become truly local matters rather than superpower issues afforded them greater prospect of early resolution. With the Soviet troop withdrawal from Afghanistan, peace in Namibia, progress in the Western Sahara, Cyprus and Cambodia, and lately, superpower agreement over Nicaragua, the UN is now taking a central place on the world's stage. The 1988 award of the Nobel Peace Prize for peacekeeping activities did much to raise the UN's flagging morale. The most recent evidence of collegiality is in the use of the UN's auspices to restore Kuwait to her own nationals.

Secondly, there has been a transformation in the Soviet Union's attitude towards the UN. For a long time the Soviet Union's regard for international organizations had been ambivalent. The UN appealed to Gorbachev as a platform for his own style of public relations and New Thinking. He felt that internationally the Soviet Union had become ostracized and he needed a political platform from which to discuss important issues as they emerged. In October 1987 he dropped the old Soviet reservations about UN peacekeeping activities and won a significant propaganda coup by beginning the repayment of the Soviet debts to the UN. This act contributed to the return of the USA to a more active role and encouraged her to begin repaying her own debts, which had by then grown to US $500 million. 'Behind differences in social structures, in ways of life, and in the preference for certain values, stand interests,' said Gorbachev.[39] Today it is in the former USSR's interest to be a supportive leader in the UN, building it into 'a comprehensive system of security'.

Moscow currently wants the UN to become the guarantor of international peace and security through a standing army and the revitalization of the UN's MSC. Further evidence that the USSR wanted to strengthen the power of the UN is reflected in the recommendation that foreign ministers of the permanent members of the Security Council should attend Council meetings.

The third and fourth reasons are interlinked. They are the changing attitudes of the USA and the Third World. The phase-three attitude of the USA towards the UN was one of sulking indifference, undisguised contempt and obstruction. She is the hostess to the UN and furnishes 25 per cent of the budget.[40] Her sense of inequity is further fuelled by observation that states smaller in all respects than the Isle of Wight enjoy the same voting rights as she, and in the General Assembly over 50 per cent of the 179 membership pay less than 1 per cent of the budget.[41] These facts, the ongoing problem with Israel and the concerted attacks upon the USA from the Third World in the early 1980s resulted in the US withholding her contribution to the UN budget. Other displays of displeasure included the ignoring of a judgment of the International Court of Justice over Nicaragua and her withdrawal with others, from UNESCO. These years of confrontation did enormous harm to what little was left of the UN's authority and effectiveness.

The wind of change blew strongest not from the direction of the USA but from the Third World. This display of realism and pragmatism was the involuntary recognition that the ground had shifted. It was an admission by the Third World that their rhetoric of the 1970s had been unproductive. They now accepted that the industrialized states could not be forced to embrace and adopt the New International Economic Order (NIEO). One observer described the aspiration to develop NIEO by Third World leaders as (among other things) 'an attempt to increase the price of their raw material exports, obtain more imported technology and thus to finance a new stage of development'.[42] But it did not work; it could not work. Many Third World leaders had to face the fact that they were facing bankruptcy. At the same time, they recognized that the political and economic changes prevailing in the USSR and China meant that their prospects for economic salvation and influx of capital lay in the West, not the East.

In the USA had dawned the realization (in contrast to the Nixon era) that the USA needed a sense of international legitimacy for its actions in the world. The change in US president proved equally opportune. Bush is more qualified to use the UN effectively than any other president. He was ambassador there from 1971 to 1973, and enjoyed a good reputation with the Third World, whom he did not attempt to browbeat. A career diplomat was appointed as US ambassador to the UN, so was therefore accountable to the White House as well as to the State Department. As a member of the cabinet, there was the prospect of greater harmony – or greater confusion! The US has also supported the eight new peacekeeping initiatives begun over the past four years.

Although the UN's entry into a distinct fourth phase in its evolution is undeniable, it is not a phase that has yet been consolidated. The capacity to behave boorishly still exists and is indeed exercised. In November 1989 the United States responded to a Palestine Liberation Organization (PLO) attempt to be recognized as a state by advising the organization that if such a resolution were accepted, it would result in the cessation of US contributions to the United Nations.

It is also true to say that there are two sound reasons why the new superpower cohesion will never truly reflect the oligarchy and centrality of power enjoyed by the Concert of Europe. First, because today's permanent members of the Security Council are not exclusively the five most powerful states. Castlereagh, Britain's Foreign Secretary in 1815 rebuffed King Bernadotte of Sweden's attempt to approach the high table at which the five powers mapped out the world's affairs. It was these five, according to Castlereagh, 'with whom the principal concerns must rest'. In 1816 the members of the Quintuple Alliance enjoyed a relative balance of power derived from their economic, military and political position. Today that is not the case with the five permanent members of the Security Council. Moreover, there are stronger actors who remain outside who have the capability of mobilizing their influence to undermine that elite club. These outsiders must be regarded as having the potential to disrupt world order for as long as they are excluded from permanent membership of the Security Council. There might be some advantage to be gained in expanding the permanent membership of the Security Council by embracing larger, significant world powers, but if it becomes too large it becomes unwieldy. It is a matter of balance. The real difficulties which would arise in assessing the diverse claims of the more obvious contenders would in reality indicate that the prospects for change this decade are probably zero.

Additionally, the passage of a Security Council Resolution requires nine votes. Given unanimity among the permanent members, there is still a requirement for the concurrence of at least four of the ten non-permanent members. It should not be assumed that this support is automatic, since invariably seven of the non-permanent members will come from the Non-Aligned Movement. It is possible, therefore, that they can block a resolution with what is known as the sixth veto.

Secondly, because today's smaller states enjoy greater collective power they will not be so easily fobbed off as King Bernadotte of Sweden. The Third World countries account for more than 70 per cent of the world's population and over 58 per cent of its land area. Their differing conditions and circumstances are reflected in the regional organizations from which they derive their collective strength.

It would be quite illusory to believe that a collective security regime could function effectively without drawing on the influence, knowledge and persuasive capabilities of these regional powers. However, the inbred fear of the small state of multilateral domination by the great powers needs to be recognized. It is a sensibility that has to be acknowledged and developed rather than being ridden rough-shod over.

Observers are coming to recognize that now that the Security Council is beginning to function as a collegial body there is greater potential for the adoption of enforcement measures. This is possible in power management terms due to the emergence of a hybrid system balancing, on the one hand, 'balance of power' and, on the other hand, a collective security enforcement system. 'Enforcement actions to deter, disrupt or punish perpetrators of morally obnoxious forms of violence probably represent a clear text-book case for Security Council co-operation'.[43] Hopes such as these place the onus for positive action upon the members of the Security Council. They will need to make positive efforts at positive internationalism rather than pursue their own narrow national goals, at times of international danger. The real significance of reaching this new threshold in international relations is that it represents a return to the old comity of nations, re-emphasizing a moral obligation of the so-called civilized states to maintain mutual respect for separate interests.

Some important countries have found it extraordinarily difficult to act as positive internationalists while others choose not to. In the case of the United States, she has often exercised what can only be described as an involuntary form of foreign policy due to what Richard Neustadt has described as 'separated institutions sharing power'.[44] The reason British officials were not best informed with regard to the American intervention in the former British colony of Grenada was because the British Embassy was monitoring activity in the State Department when the decision-making was taking place in the White House. The same error was not evident at the time of the Falklands episode. Sir Nicholas Henderson, the egregious former ambassador in Washington, explained the situation to a House of Commons Select Committee desirous to know what the Administration's view of the Falklands had been. 'When you say the US Administration, I am sorry to be pedantic but there is the Pentagon view, the State Department view and the White House view'.[45] To which he later added '... they do not necessarily communicate with one another'.[46]

The existence of pressure groups, lobbies and domestic considerations can influence US foreign policy to the extent of verging on the irrational. It is reported that Bush's warning to Gorbachev not to intervene in the Baltic states following on from the US invasion of Panama had left the Soviet president 'flabbergasted'. Such inconsistency can only be emphasized by Bush's suggestion to Gorbachev that a 1989 Soviet intervention in Romania would be welcome. At a time when it was in the United States' and international interests to preserve the Gorbachev regime, the Soviet president was denied the benefits of 'Most Favoured Nation' trading privileges, which were offered by the administration to Deng Xiao Peng and coincided with the first anniversary of the Tienanmen Square massacre. A strong Jewish lobby, keen to encourage immigration among Russian Jews, had taken a political initiative which effectively served to tie President Bush's hands.

France's claim to be a good internationalist has been seen to be flawed in relation to arms transfers, but what is of most concern to France's friends is her apparent willingness in the past to negotiate with terrorists. The evidence is more circumstantial than actual but the return to Libya in 1989, for example, of three impounded Mirage fighter-bombers, in contravention of the 1986 European arms ban, was yet one more episode prejudicial to those who would wish to take an international counter-terrorist line. France insisted that the release of the jets was unconnected with the release of Gadaffi's hostages, Jacqueline Valente and her family. Besides, argued Paris, since Libya had only 200 trained pilots to man 500 combat aircraft, the French action had not been significant.

It is this French independent line and concept of autonomy that needs to change if practical internationalism is to become a reality. 'It is still an open question whether major powers are prepared, in practice, to forgo, in all circumstances, unilateral options and to put the weight of their authority and power behind a genuinely international system of common security.'[47] So, although there are still some grounds for continuing pessimism, the scope for real internationalism in terms of the UN's life has never been better. At a time of danger, when national interests converge, the Security Council could exercise its legal constitution of taking action in the interest of world peace and security.

THE FAILURE AND DIFFICULTIES IN ACHIEVING MILITARY INTERVENTION

It is the political change in international relations as well as a change in superpower fortunes which indicate that the days of successful unilateral intervention are past and that multilateral military intervention might only succeed in exceptional circumstances. Even before the changes in these relationships had occurred, both the old USSR and the USA discovered in the most dramatic way the true impotence of their power in the intra-state conflicts of Afghanistan and Vietnam respectively. Not least, the cost of unilaterally inspired intervention was horrendous. The total bill for Vietnam was $190 billion while the Soviets spent $3–4 billion for each of the years their forces were fulfilling no useful purpose in Afghanistan.[48]

The fact is that most military interventions undertaken this century should never have been embarked upon, for they were doomed to failure. The reason for this has tended to be due to misplaced faith in national capabilities as well as a misappreciation of the size of the problem. By way of illustration it is appropriate first to relate international theory to the concept of military intervention, followed by a current overview essentially of the two states most traditionally involved in military intervention, the former USSR and the USA.

The Charter and Realist paradigms have been regarded as distinct, mutually exclusive and incompatible entities. The Charter paradigm's origins can be found in the idealist and utopian traditions and it is modelled today on international organizations such as the United Nations. Its principles are formulated on sovereignty and non-interference. Non-intervention is the key principle of international organizations, with member states retaining domestic jurisdiction and abiding by the principles of international law and the rules of the international organization to which they belong. The Realists take a different view. They see international organizations as being founded upon great power management. A key mechanism within their international system was the sphere of influence where intervention occurred more or less to order, whether politically, economically or militarily. Stability was maintained through the balance of power providing equilibrium within the international organization.

The recent changes in international relations, most notably the ending of the Cold War, have served to make it possible for these paradigms, thus far regarded as being quite separate, to merge. This is a fundamental premiss of this work, namely that the post-Cold War international system contains enough incendiary material for the future conflagrations to make collective security a vital necessity. That is so in the Third World and who knows what the developments there might uncover? What is central to this argument is the possibility of embracing Charter concepts, yet pursuing at the same time goals which are steadfastly Realist. Examine Robert Rothstein's description of realism:

> It is always a doctrine which takes for granted the primacy of foreign policy and the dominance of the security issue defined in terms of simple notions of power. It is, *in sum*, not only the classic version of a state-centric doctrine but also an affirmation of the rightful dominance of the Great Powers and the autonomy of their foreign policies.[49]

Present circumstances, which oblige the great powers to recognize the impact of interdependence upon their foreign policy and also the desirability of operating within the norms of international law, undermine the earlier adversarial view of what were competing paradigms. The examination of the normative and prescriptive elements in the context of a volatile post-Cold War international system in which a form of collective security has rarely been more essential, indicates conclusively the comfortable coexistence of the idealist and Realist paradigms. The United Nations' challenge is to formalize this convergence.

The question which needs to be addressed is: why has past state practice in relation to intervention more often than not ignored the norms of international law? The answer is because intervention 'is the single issue around which the Realist and Charter conceptions of order most flagrantly diverge, the former accepting it as a contribution to order and the latter as the most palpable evidence of violation of international norms'.[50] The evidence indicates that where a national interest exists, that interest will not always be tempered by considerations of international law. Such is apparent from the examination of five cases: Suez 1956, Cuba 1962, Afghanistan 1979, Grenada 1983 and Panama 1989.

Suez

On 26 July 1956 President Nasser of Egypt, the then-rising star of Arabia, made an announcement in Cairo that, as he spoke, the Suez Canal was being taken over and nationalized. The jointly owned Anglo-French canal and its equipment were due to be handed over gratis to Egypt in 1968 on the expiry of the original hundred-year-old concession. The Suez Canal Company's administrative offices were in Paris but it had been established under Egyptian law with its head office in Egypt. The Egyptian president had therefore nationalized an Egyptian company. Nasser stated that compensation would be paid based on the canal's value on the stock market but such payment would only be made on surrender of all the company's assets.

Anthony Eden's view that Nasser was becoming a dangerous, destabilizing force in the Middle East was a view shared by the Americans, who had earlier withdrawn financial support for the prestigious Aswan Dam project. The Baghdad Pact, founded in 1954, included Britain, Pakistan, Iran, Iraq and Turkey. The United States was only an associate member, yet was represented on the economic and defence sub-committees. Ostensibly, the Baghdad Pact was anti-Soviet, aimed at preventing expansionism and at protecting the Middle East's oil wealth. From the British position, however, the Pact was very much an anti-Nasser instrument. Certainly as far as Eden was concerned, Nasser was yet another Hitler or Mussolini threatening British interests. It was Nasser who went on to wreck the Baghdad Pact and whose influence on the King of Jordan had led to the dismissal of Glubb Pasha (Sir John Bagot), the British commander of the Arab Legion. During the currency of the previous Labour government's term in office, Mohammed Mossadeq nationalized British oil interests in Iran. Now Nasser was imitating that affront to Britain's prestige and position in the Middle East.

It is clear that the British cabinet had decided at a very early stage to regain the nationalized Suez Canal from Egypt. Although France was preoccupied with events in Algeria, she was of like mind. Anthony Nutting wrote:

My suggestion that at least the Foreign Office legal adviser, Sir Gerald Fitzmaurice should be brought in on a matter which involved taking the law into our own hands met with the flattest of negatives. 'Fitz is the last person I want consulted,' Eden retorted. 'The lawyers are always against us doing anything. For God's sake keep them out of it. This is a political affair.'[51]

A secret meeting at Sèvres on 22 and 24 October 1956 was attended by representatives of the British, French and Israeli governments. Those attending the meeting contrived to 'set Egypt up' so as to lend legality to the proposed intervention. It was agreed by the three parties to give Egypt (and Israel) what proved to be for the former an impossible ultimatum – to cease hostilities and withdraw ten miles from the canal. Nasser's predictable refusal provided Britain and France with what they argued was their justification for intervening: 'Our action would be defensible in international law; for we should be intervening to prevent interference with the free flow of traffic through the canal, which was an international necessity.'[52] Fitzmaurice warned those who might have influence on the cabinet that armed intervention would be contrary to international law. The future international judgement that the Suez intervention had been an illegal act was made without awareness of the secret connivance at Sèvres.

A high price was subsequently paid for that ill-advised intervention. Britain suffered her greatest humiliation since the war in the Far East. A run on the pound occurred, which the USA proposed to allow to continue until the interventionists (including France and Israel) agreed to withdraw. Throughout the Middle East, Britain's influence and authority were undermined, not least in Iraq, where the pro-British government was overthrown. The United States, in a providentially opportunist and systematic move, filled the vacuum created by the demise of Anglo-French fortunes in the Middle East. Concurrently, in Europe, the Soviet Union had the benefit of the diversion of the Suez affair when putting down the Hungarian uprising.

Cuba

In October 1962 US reconnaissance flights produced incontrovertible evidence that Soviet intermediate ballistic missiles were being installed on the island of Cuba. Photographs revealed that some were already *in situ* while others were *en route* aboard Soviet ships. This act was clearly something that US strategy could not permit. The legal arguments did not rise to much prominence because final decisions were based on an almost exclusively political rationale. From a technical point of view, Cuba's action in putting missiles on her own sovereign territory did not contravene international law. It could be said that US missiles in Turkey represented a similar threat to the USSR. There is no law which prevents Cuba from entering into an alliance with the USSR or which places limitations on the types of weapons Cuba might utilize. What the USSR had done was politically unacceptable to the USA, for it threatened to destabilize the balance of power in a particularly sensitive sphere of US interest.

At the time of the Cuban crisis in 1962, Dean Acheson remarked:

> the propriety of the Cuban Quarantine is not a legal issue. The power, position and prestige of the United States had been challenged by another state, and law simply does not deal with such questions of ultimate power – power that comes close to the sources of sovereignty.[53]

Professor Henkin, the eminent US international lawyer, responded to Acheson's statement that 'such a view would indeed be a negation of law that no legal system could tolerate'.[54] In fact the selection of the less confrontational of the plausible options – to invade, launch an air strike or blockade – had much to do with a legalistic rationale. Similarly, legal arguments were adduced to justify the action to NATO and the OAS. 'It demonstrates,' wrote Schachter, 'that states require a basis of legitimacy to justify their action to their citizens and, even more, to other states whose co-operation or acquiescence is desired.'[55]

As a comment on the 1962 Cuban missile crisis, Professor Henkin wrote: 'But by 1962, in Latin America surely, the day of unilateral intervention by the United States seemed over, replaced by collective judgement if not by truly collective action.'[56] But that was not to be. Despite the availability of the most sophisticated of decision-making machinery, the USA finally intervened unilaterally in the Dominican Republic in 1965 on the whim of President Johnson, because someone had shot at the US ambassador. The underlying reason had been the typical US fear of leftish regimes. There was no real attempt to legitimize the intervention, because Johnson perceived the happenings in the Dominican Republic not to be of concern to any other important state. Only after sending in the troops did the president address the problem of how the troops were to be withdrawn.

Afghanistan

It had long been a Russian aspiration to dominate an Afghanistan strategically placed between what was then India and Persia and is now Pakistan and Iran. Politically, Afghanistan in the 1970s had some empathy with the Soviets for, when the monarchy was abolished in 1973, it was replaced by the Afghan Communist Party, which did enjoy an admittedly localized mandate. Relations between the two countries were cemented in 1978 with the signing of the Afghanistan–USSR Treaty of Friendship. The relationship was tenuous to say the least, due to the factions and infighting within the

Afghan Communist Party. The overthrow and death of one party leader, Nur Mohammed Taraki, and his replacement by a new leader by the name of Hafizullah Amin, did nothing to bring peace either to the turbulent party or to the troubled land. After the assassination of a senior Soviet general and the evidence of the hopeless state of the Afghan Army had been accepted in Moscow, a number of Soviet divisions entered Afghanistan in a military intervention. The military build-up was so slow and ponderous that it failed to be seen as a convincing exercise in the protection of Afghanistan against counter-revolution.

The reasons advanced for the intervention followed a dual-track justification. The first reason was that the Afghan government had invited the USSR to intervene. The rationale of the second was based on the theory of limited sovereignty embodied in the Brezhnev Doctrine.

The Soviets had used the invitation card before when they intervened in Hungary. There are striking similarities between the Hungarian and Afghanistan interventions. Moscow acted when, on 2 November 1956, Imré Nagy publicly disowned the Warsaw Pact and appeared ready to declare Hungary's neutrality. Nagy was overthrown and executed that year and replaced by a puppet ruler, Janos Kadar. It was allegedly in response to Kadar's invitation that the Soviets intervened but, as was to happen in Grenada, it was a retrospective invitation. The cautious Czechoslovak intervention did not follow the pattern of intervention by invitation, if only because the Soviets could not identify anyone prepared to invite them in.

During the course of the Afghanistan intervention Amin was executed and speedily replaced by a new leader, Babrak Kamal, who was flown into Kabul from Czechoslovakia in a Soviet aircraft. This critical change of leadership arising when it did facilitated the Soviet claim that they were responding to an invitation. Whether that invitation came from Amin or Kamal was never elucidated. Nevertheless, there was a serious attempt to justify the intervention under the aegis of international law. Central to the Soviet thesis was Article 4 of the Treaty of Friendship but, in the absence of a genuine invitation from the constitutional or *de facto* government, there can be no right of unilateral intervention.

In the Nicaragua judgment, the International Court of Justice ruled that the provision of advisers and financial and logistic support did not justify the response of an armed attack. The Soviets had been foremost among those who had applauded that judgment. Logically therefore, they had debarred themselves from utilizing the claim of necessity of self-defence under Article 51. Additionally, it would have been impossible to prove that Afghanistan had been threatened by external forces.

The other thread which had been developed as the rationale for the Afghanistan intervention was the Brezhnev Doctrine, a charter for the maintenance of Soviet imperialism. At the Fifth Polish Party Congress on

12 November 1968, Brezhnev declared that when 'a threat to the cause of socialism' arose in a given country, it 'becomes not only a problem of the people of the country concerned, but also a common problem and the concern of all socialist countries'.

The whole theory of 'limited sovereignty' ran contrary to international law and there were valid questions as to the applicability of the Brezhnev Doctrine to Afghanistan. Article 5 of the Friendship Treaty recognized Afghanistan as a non-aligned state, so it was never in the same category as either Hungary or Czechoslovakia. But then, the definition of the Brezhnev Doctrine is very subjective and international law, as it applies to the doctrine, is of questionable validity to a Marxist-Leninist.

The intervention was finally drawn to a conclusion by the 1988 Geneva Conference. Inevitably, the blame for the ill-advised adventure was laid squarely at the feet of Brezhnev, who had died in 1982. The experience and impact of Afghanistan upon the Soviet government and people will exert a strong dampening influence when debates are held on future external involvement of states within the old USSR.

Grenada

The 1983 Grenada intervention, Operation Urgent Fury, was a ploy to remove the unwanted extremist successors (not that they were legitimate successors) to the left-wing Bishop government. It is a valuable case study, which shows how regional organizations can be manipulated to provide a justification for military intervention. A particularly revealing case, it deserves wider examination than the foregoing studies.

Grenada is a small island situated in the south-east Caribbean Sea 1,600 miles from the United States. Its territory covers a mere 133 square miles and in 1983 it had a population of 110,000. The country had been a British colony for many years prior to independence in 1974. Grenada retained a constitutional monarchy with the Queen as head of state and represented on the island by a governor-general, Sir Paul Scoon. The Queen, as Queen of Grenada, was obliged to act on the advice of the Grenadian government, not the British government. In fact, the British government had no say in Grenada nor any right to interfere or give advice.

Until March 1979, Grenada functioned under a parliamentary government led by Prime Minister Sir Eric Gairy. Gairy was no democrat and his hard-line government was overthrown and replaced by Maurice Bishop's New Joint Endeavour for the Welfare, Education and Liberation (JEWEL) Movement. In June 1981 the smaller Caribbean nations of Grenada, Dominica, St Kitts and Nevis, St Vincent and the Grenadines, St Lucia, Antigua and Barbuda, and Montserrat formed the Organization of East Caribbean States (OECS). The larger regional states did not join. The majority of the leaders of the states who formed the OECS, with the exception of Grenada,

35

were politically more like old-fashioned British socialists, which made their support for the US-led intervention all the more significant. Relatively speaking, therefore, they were a good deal less left-wing than the Bishop government, which gradually became more extreme and isolated.

The 1967 constitution was suspended in March 1979 by the Bishop government. In its stead, a series of People's Laws were proclaimed which vested all 'executive and legislative power' in the People's Revolutionary Government. Sir Paul Scoon retained only limited minor powers of appointment and removal, but was permitted to continue as the Queen's representative. Bishop did not make Grenada a republic, as Dominica had become. Bishop went on to develop left-wing ties and friendship with the USSR, Eastern Europe and, more particularly, Cuba.

On 12 October 1983 a military coup toppled Bishop's pro-Marxist regime. On 18 October the United States made a formal enquiry regarding the safety of American nationals in Grenada and the US joint chiefs of staff laid down contingency plans to intervene. On 19 October, the day Barbados pressed for intervention, Bishop, together with seven ministers and close associates, was murdered at Fort Rupert by 'revolutionary armed forces' on the orders of his deputy, Bernard Coard. On that same day a sixteen-member Revolutionary Military Council was formed with the army commander, General Hudson Austin, designated its 'nominal head'. On Friday, 21 October the OECS met, but no Grenadian was present. A secret decision was taken to use force. Barbados and Jamaica were invited to intervene and later the US was included, essentially because the West Indians had no amphibious capability. Britain was also invited to take part in the intervention, a request considered at the next normal working day of the cabinet on Monday, 24 October. After the cabinet had considered the invitation from the OECS, Sir Geoffrey Howe announced to the Commons that he had seen no evidence of an imminent intervention.

On 22 October two US diplomats and a UK diplomat, the Deputy High Commissioner, David Montgomery, visited Grenada. The British diplomat's function was to ascertain whether British nationals were in immediate danger. Subsequent Foreign Office reaction would tend to indicate the conclusion that British nationals were not thought to have been in imminent danger. On 23 October the Revolutionary Military Council announced that the 1,000 US medical students and retired citizens would not be harmed. At the same time, the Grenadian military authorities warned against military intervention. At dawn on Tuesday, 25 October 1983 1,900 US Marines and Rangers supported by 300 West Indian troops invaded Grenada and were met by force from Cubans and Grenadians. Although the military operation was code-named Urgent Fury it was to be an exercise in muddle and confusion.

Mrs Thatcher heard on the evening of 24 October of President Reagan's decision to intervene in the Commonwealth's only Marxist state. In his autobiography, President Reagan admitted that his withholding of information from Mrs Thatcher over America's decision to invade Grenada 'troubled me because of our close relationship'. Margaret Thatcher put a call through to the president as soon as she heard of the USA's intentions. The call coincided with the president's operational briefing.

> She said she had just learned about the impending operation [probably from British officials on Grenada] and asked me in the strongest language to call off the operation. Grenada, she reminded me, was part of the British Commonwealth, and the United States had no business interfering in its affairs .... She was very adamant and continued to insist that we cancel our landings on Grenada. I couldn't tell her that it had already begun.[57]

There is more to observe from the above than the fact that the Commonwealth is not 'British', a mistake that Mrs Thatcher is unlikely to have made. The British High Commission for the region is based in Barbados. There was only a vice-consul in Grenada at the time of the intervention. The emergency communications were in John Kelly's, the vice-consul's, office yet he would have been confined to his house for much of the day by the curfew imposed after Bishop's murder. Due to the time difference of five hours, the British High Commission in Barbados did not learn of the Thatcher/Reagan conversation until after the intervention had begun. The British diplomats in Barbados were given a few hours' notice of the intended intervention by the Barbadians and this was passed to the Foreign Office at their opening time on Tuesday, 25 October. It appears that this was the first news the Foreign Office had heard of the intervention.

The strength of Mrs Thatcher's fury took the president aback following on so soon after the Falklands conflict. The United States had hoped for reciprocal moral support that was not forthcoming. Realists have seen through the transparency of the US being presented with an opportunity to act dramatically in the Caribbean to inflict military defeat on a Communist dictatorship, establish a democratic government and hopefully to get away with it virtually unscathed. However, a threefold justification was advanced. First, the USA took part in an OECS regional operation; secondly, she intervened at the request of the Governor-General to restore law and order and, finally, it had been necessary to intervene to protect the lives of US nationals. A great deal of the literature cites other legal justifications but these are the ones with which the State Department persevered.

Regional action was the centre of the argument. It is an argument that is seriously flawed because the OECS had no right to issue an invitation to intervene, nor was there an entitlement as a matter of general international law to intervene. The regional Charter does not address intervention although Article 8 does provide for the protection of a member from threats originating outside the OECS. Any decision to take action had to be unanimous. When the OECS met to consider the matter, Grenada was not present and Montserrat was unable to participate. Montserrat, a Dependent Territory, was represented by its Chief Minister, who sympathized with the OECS decision but was unable to take action because at that time, as now, responsibility for defence affairs remains with Her Majesty's Government. The Chief Minister referred the matter to London and Montserrat took no further part in the intervention. The decision was therefore legally invalid. The validity of the argument cannot even be stretched to cover the external Cuban influence. There were Cuban troops and civilian advisers in Grenada but there was no indication that Cuba was behind Bishop's overthrow. They had nothing to gain from the death of Bishop.

It is an important point to make that the Revolutionary Military Council (RMC) in Grenada never had time to legitimize itself, even at home (where the Governor-General was kept under house arrest), still less abroad. One of the reasons the OECS and USA moved so expeditiously was to pre-empt the recognition of the newly formed RMC by Cuba and hence forestall further Cuban military reinforcement. So was the OECS action regional peacekeeping? The answer is negative, because it is a breach of the norms of peacekeeping to send troops into a territory to deal with internal unrest contrary to what was an admittedly embryonic government's wishes. The UN peacekeeping initiative in the Congo was established with the consent of the host state. Under Article 53 of the UN Charter, a regional organization can only engage in enforcement action with the approval of the Security Council.

There were also some selective general arguments. Some, rather than argue the case of collective self-defence, argued the regional issue, although it was left to the OECS to attempt to justify collective self-defence. Professor Richard Gardner, a former ambassador under the Carter regime, suggested that the building of the airfield was a prelude to a Cuban invasion, therefore the OECS states could intervene and invite the USA to assist. The argument was legally sound but was not borne out by the facts. There did not appear to be a likelihood of imminent attack.

If it is true that the Governor-General invited the OECS to intervene it would have made a substantial difference. The letter of consent, however, for the intervention to proceed originated in the State Department, which drafted it and sent it to Barbados for onward transmission for Scoon's signature. It was also backdated. While it carries the date 24 October, it has been alleged that it was not signed until 26 October when most of the fighting had ended.[58] If the letter had been written on 24 October, there was no way Sir Paul Scoon could have got the letter to the Americans, since his last contact with them was on the 22nd. Even if the request had preceded the intervention, it is doubtful whether the Governor-General had the necessary authority in international law. Had there been absolutely no functioning government in Grenada, the Governor-General would have been the only remnant of legal authority and as such could invite help; but the request must precede the intervention.

If the US nationals had been in danger, the most severe response that would have been justified in terms of proportionality would have been an Entebbe-style operation. The Americans were not under imminent threat, there was moment for deliberation and there was a choice of means. As an argument, the protection of civilians cannot stand alone and needs to work with others such as humanitarian intervention to protect Grenadians from extremists. This argument cannot be given real credence, nor in state practice is there much evidence to support humanitarian intervention. There is a view that the Americans did originally plan a limited, Entebbe-style operation. The mission was to rescue their civilians, and hold the airport and south-west corner of the island long enough for the evacuation of the civilians. It is believed that, in the course of planning, the Americans realized that with the addition of only 1–2,000 more troops, they could take the whole island, which is what the OECS wanted them to do.

The question of the Governor's status is rendered academic by the allegation that the key letter was not signed by him until the day after the intervenors arrived in Grenada. The *American Journal of International Law* summarized the intervention as follows:

On balance the Grenadan episode does not augur well for either international law or regional security. It appears to have been a case of unilateral intervention by the United States, expressly approved in advance by neighboring Island States and undertaken without due regard for the territorial sovereignty or political independence of Grenada. That the ends attained were good and just is laudable; the means used to fulfil that ambition, however, emerge as legally regrettable.[59]

Panama

The invasion of Panama, Operation Just Cause, advanced what is the worst legal justification for military action since 1936 [with the possible exception of Iraq's invasion of Kuwait]. This lingering legacy of the Monroe Doctrine, or the belief that the USA can intervene unilaterally at will in the Central American region, leads a body of opinion to suggest that unilateral intervention could well continue. The more the USSR becomes introspective, the more likely is the USA to take the view that she has greater freedom to embark upon an intervention in that region. If that is the view, then the wrong lessons have been learned from what was a politically and militarily fortunate invasion of Panama.

Panama has had a special relationship in the United States' security considerations since 1903 when the Canal Treaty established the Canal

Zone as US territory. It is a loose relationship shared with the Philippines and South Korea. In or within all three countries there is a strong American garrison, and hence an inescapable and entangling commitment. The 1989 intervention in the Philippines at the request of the democratically elected government was legal, uncomplicated and now largely forgotten. Having troops *in situ*, as in Panama and the Philippines, overcomes many of the problems in launching a military intervention. Troops, equipment, intelligence and logistics will be available in beneficial quantity. This is, in French parlance, the 'glass of water strategy', which aims to use garrison troops to douse the flickering fire *ab initio* before it grows out of control and requires the attention of a larger fire brigade. The Panamanian intervention became a significant morale booster for a massive standing force keen to demonstrate to the world what it could do, exorcizing the spectre of Vietnam, the Iran hostage affair and Grenada.

In 1904, at the time of the Panama canal's early beginnings, President Theodore Roosevelt's conscience was troubled at having taken the zone from Colombia and he sought to legalize what the United States had done. It is alleged that his attorney-general cautioned: 'Oh Mr President, do not let so great an achievement suffer from any taint of legality.'[60] Panama is decidedly within the United States' sphere of influence and in 1989 there was no superpower conflict of interest to prevent another in a series of regional interventions. 'The US has a long history of intervention in Central American affairs,' confirms Marko Milivojevic. 'Rarely, if ever, does this benefit the host countries, rather it tends to cripple economies and fuel anti-American nationalism. It seems unlikely that such policies will solve the problems of the region.'[61]

If the Central American region is indeed the last bastion where unilateral action can be conducted, is it really in America's best long-term foreign policy interests to pursue such a policy? The available evidence suggests that it is decidedly not. It is true that interventions often attract collateral benefits, which become apparent at the cessation of hostilities. By that token it is true that the Panama invasion did isolate Cuba and weaken Castro. It also gave democracy the opportunity to succeed in Panama, but it came perilously close to causing long-term harm to the anti-drugs war.

The domestic problems that have occurred in the former Soviet Union have enabled the USA to switch from an anti-Communist crusade to an anti-drugs and environmental campaign. For a nation with an estimated 14.5 million drug users spending US $100 billion annually on drugs,[62] the priority would seem to be fostering regional co-operation. It does not matter greatly what the private face of the OAS offered by way of support to the US invasion of Panama. Only El Salvador, Canada and the United Kingdom approved of the invasion. Otherwise, the vote of condemnation in the General Assembly underlined the hardening attitude against such conduct in world affairs:

If Washington decides that the end of the international cold war authorises the commencement of a hot inter-American war, no-one is safe – not even Mexico. Any reason to intervene will do: the war on drugs, electoral fraud, political instability, immigration or the protection of some tourist suffering sunstroke in Puerto Vallarta. In those circumstances who is safe from being saved by a providential White House?[63]

What the foregoing suggests, therefore, is that the prospects for the projection of unilateral, Realist goals are perhaps relics of past behaviour in international relations. International law will continue to be broken *in extremis* but civilized relations are built around the ability to avoid extreme cases. The compromise today's neo-Realist will need to make is to recognize the option of exercising his national policy through an international organization, thus serving to underline the convergence of the Realist and Charter paradigms. The Kuwait intervention of 1991 is an obvious case in point. Before the argument for the selection of multilateral rather than unilateral paths can be substantiated it will be necessary to identify the changed circumstances which now exist among the two principal actors.

Military intervention is a most hazardous, expensive and difficult activity to execute satisfactorily. It is no accident that almost all military interventions which have required anything more ambitious than the crossing of contiguous borders, such as Iraq's 1990 invasion of Kuwait, have been conducted by the super or medium powers. The truth is that military intervention takes with it the seeds of its own destruction. In today's volatile national and ethnic climate, there is a grave risk that military intervention which does not enjoy the authority of the United Nations and therefore attract legitimacy will be self-defeating. This is not to say that it may not be self-defeating even with a cloak of legality. Interventions have a tendency to harden and polarize resistance within the target country.

The historic preoccupation of both superpowers in developing their military power has found them badly off balance at the beginning of a new decade which promises to be dominated by economic rather than military power. Neither of the superpowers is in a sufficiently strong position to be able to switch its power projection capabilities away from military channels into economic ones. The greatest irony of this wealth of disposable military power has been its past inability to guarantee success against inferior opposition. There have been many more failures than successes.

The USA dropped a greater number of bombs on Vietnam, her peasants and the North Vietnamese Army than in the European theatre during the Second World War. The 200,000 casualties the USA suffered in Vietnam[64] was more than during the course of the war in the Pacific. The effect the legacy of Vietnam has upon domestic public attitudes would preclude even the sending of US peacekeepers into Cambodia. The US component in the

Lebanon Multi-National Force (MNF) 1982–4 suffered 10 per cent casualties, which served to highlight the difficulties the USA might experience in the Middle East. Yet the Pentagon is continually working on contingency plans for intervention in the Lebanon, the Philippines and Central America. The new approach is to use the Unified Commands co-operating with local actors to take multilateral paths towards problem-solving. Unless the legality of the proposed actions is properly squared away, the original problem is unlikely to be satisfactorily solved. Unlike the Soviet Union, the United States' behaviour in international affairs does not always reflect the relative decline in her power. What she has done on the home front, however, is to limit the president's power to draw the nation into precipitate armed conflict by the 1973 War Powers Act. The Act followed the aftermath of the Vietnam War but no president has thus far recognized its constitutional power of giving to Congress a vote if US forces are still confronted by hostilities after sixty days have elapsed.

The Soviet Union's attitude to military intervention beyond her borders was a better reflection of that nation's declining power. It is also true that Afghanistan has had a very wide impact upon the new Commonwealth of Independent States' (CIS) public opinion. Afghanistan was a small operation in comparison with Vietnam, yet the Soviets admitted that among the 100,000 killed there were 13,310 Soviet troops.[65] Vietnam's impact on US public opinion represents more a regional taboo, which would not translate into short, sharp action in other areas such as the Gulf, Central America, the Philippines or even South Korea. In 1989 a social scientist in Moscow pointed to the high incidence of intervention failures.[66] He thought that the general public and the leadership were reluctant to become further involved in foreign adventures. He emphasized the considerable impact Afghanistan had had upon public opinion, so much so that he could not envisage Soviet troops embarking again upon interventionist operations. He believed that Moscow's support of other interventionist troops might be acceptable but he reminded the author that traditionally UN forces have not included superpower components. He said ruefully that even the Soviet airlift support for Cuban troops in Angola had been roundly condemned.

There is a view that the former Soviet Union has finally succumbed as the latest of the weary Titans. Her preoccupation with domestic problems should not, however, mask the fact that she still retains awesome military power, containing within her borders the most powerful force in Europe. She has, after all, been a one-dimensional military superpower since the 1960s, from which point the military justified, until recently, the USSR's status and superpower ranking. Yet it has been the necessity of the *perestroika* programme which has emphasized her economic weakness. Gorbachev admitted at the 1986 twenty-seventh Communist Party Congress that the visible decline in economic growth began in the 1970s, or rather during the Brezhnev era of 'the years of stagnation'.

This stagnation was not reflected in military expenditure when Brezhnev sought to capitalize on the apparent decline of the USA and the economic disarray in Europe. During this period the Soviets spent twice as much of their GNP on defence as the USA.[67] The sick, underfunded agriculture sector lurched from crisis to crisis into the 1980s. Between 1983 and 1988 the Soviets imported food and consumer goods annually within the range of 14–18 million roubles.[68] Today, the citizens of the CIS are faced with a fall in their standard of living of 1 per cent per annum,[69] inflation of 20 per cent per annum and shortages, even rationing, of basic goods.

> Shortages, not only of basic foodstuffs but also of consumer essentials such as soap, detergents, toothpaste and even school exercise books, are universal: the latest official statistic is that out of 276 so-called 'cultural, everyday and household articles', 243 are either available irregularly or are not on sale at all.[70]

All of this is destined to worsen before it improves as the CIS switches to a market economy, although this move is not a foregone conclusion. There is a prospect of the line of the former Iron Curtain becoming one of a number of poverty lines in the world: a line drawn between haves and have-nots whose crossing provides a worrying rationale for the mass movement of economic refugees. Given the increasing threat of paralysing anarchy and the escalating nationalities problems, the former USSR had little option but to exercise her principal foreign policy interests through bilateral and multilateral channels. The same is also likely to be true of the USA, but for different reasons.

In time, and for reasons about to be adduced, the United States will succumb to the changes now evident in world affairs. Realistically, there should be a dawning recognition of the merit to be found in adopting multilateral approaches towards political and economic burden-sharing, particularly in those areas where the United States is increasingly finding that she cannot act alone. The course of foreign affairs today emphasizes interdependence rather than independence. It would seem beneficial therefore for the United States to pursue a foreign policy founded not on confrontation but on co-operation, a policy which has been confirmed following the Gulf crisis.

There is a possible scenario that the United States will find herself squeezed between a post-1992 Europe and a Pacific becoming increasingly dominated by Japanese economic power. The East–West *rapprochement* will stress the fact that today the Europeans have less need of the United States and what some have regarded as her doubtful nuclear guarantee. While the Washington/Moscow climate is improving, that between Washington and Tokyo is deteriorating. On the surface, however, the USA was prepared to tolerate Japan's large trade surpluses for as long as Japan remained a strategic asset in support of the USA's role as a global power. Now that this situation is changing, often acrimonious attempts have been made to reduce Japan's trade surplus with the USA, which in 1989 had grown to $49 billion. Both states have thus far bumbled on in exasperating mutual dependence, but a firmer US line can only result in an emergent Japanese neo-nationalism. There are indications that, in time, Japan might turn to her giant, troubled western neighbour at the expense of the tiresome neighbour to her east. Such a scenario would foster the resurrection of the east is east and west is west syndrome. The key which will open any possible door to improved relations between Japan and the the former USSR lies in the future of the Kurile Islands.

The Soviets took possession of the Kurile Islands in the closing stages of the Second World War when Moscow unilaterally renounced its non-aggression treaty with Tokyo. What is in dispute are three small islands – Eterofu, Kunoshiri and Shikotan – as well as even smaller islands, or rather rocks, which make up the Habomai group. The Kuriles lie to the north-east of Hokkaido in the Sea of Okhotsk, lying astride the narrow sea route between Hokkaido and the Soviet island of Sakhalin. With the islands in Soviet hands they soothed a Red paranoia of encirclement, particularly of the important eastern naval port of Vladivostock. The Japanese have never accepted the loss of the islands through Stalin's opportunism and this has effectively prevented the signing of a peace treaty between the two states ending the Second World War.

In 1956 the Soviets proposed a compromise solution of handing back without strings the two smallest islands, Shikotan and Habomai, with the other two being the subject of negotiation once the peace treaty had been signed. Tokyo refused, and relations between the two states have remained frigid.

Trade in 1989–90 amounted to little more than 1 per cent of Japan's trading volume, and this is at a time when the Russian Far East region is desperate for an economic shot in the arm. Japan already demonstrated her regional independence when she restored credits to China in July 1990. A similar deal was half expected as an outcome of President Gorbachev's long-awaited visit to Japan in April 1991. If it had gone through, the resultant *rapprochement* would have accelerated the marginalization of US influence on the Pacific Rim. Everything hinged on Gorbachev's ability to outline mutually acceptable plans for the return of the Kurile Islands to Japan. For a state which entered into the unequal Treaty of Brest Litovsk, the return of the Kurile Islands is but a small concession. Indeed, the demise of the Cold War has rendered them less strategically relevant. However, by the time Gorbachev met Japanese Prime Minister Toshiki Kaifu, his domestic situation had so deteriorated that he was unable to deliver. The reconciliation has begun and the issue still remains on the agenda.

The failure of the right-wing coup in Moscow in August 1991 appeared to have strengthened Gorbachev's hand but his days in power were numbered.

But then, it could have been argued that the matter of the Kurile Islands falls within the jurisdiction of Boris Yeltsin's Russian republic. When at last, however, it seemed that the circumstances were favourable to formulate a solution to the long-standing Kurile question, the question is changing. Emergent democracy is beginning to impinge upon the new Commonwealth's foreign policy. Although the Kurile islanders would be manifestly better off under the flag of the Rising Sun, regional hostility to an accommodation with Japan is growing. History introduces its own potent influence.

It is possible therefore to suggest that the United States may at some stage readopt an isolationist policy. As a trading nation this cannot be a total isolation but will more resemble Britain's 'splendid isolation' at the turn of the last century. The burden-sharing exercise, so much a feature of the 1980s, will become a burden-shedding exercise in the 1990s. The USA's global power projection capability will become limited as the anticipated peace dividends are taken. In foreign affairs, the USA may choose not to become involved, perhaps just offering political support to collective security operations. Alternatively, where intervention really cannot be avoided, future policy will emphasize the employment of naval and air forces. The aim will be to deploy land forces only *in extremis*. (In 1950, Admiral Sherman and airforce General Vandenberg both believed that the North Korean assault into the South could be stopped by naval and air power alone.) What seems certain today is that multilateralism will prove to be a useful, more rational foreign policy mechanism in the 1990s than unilateralism. The current state of the US economy, now in recession, would certainly support this view.

Table 4 shows the United States' economic predicament. It has been forecast that the US national debt will increase to $13 (US) trillion by the end of this decade. Paul Kennedy recounts that the only other historical example which comes to mind of a great power increasing its indebtedness in peacetime is France in the 1780s.[71]

Recent economic trends in the USA indicate that the USA's indebtedness may not be as acute as Kennedy forecast. The 1990 trade deficit was $94.9

Table 4 US federal deficit, debt and interest, 1980–5
($ billion)

	Deficit	Deb	Interest on debt
1980	59.6	914.3	52.5
1983	195.4	1,387.9	87.8
1985	202.8	1,823.1	129.0

Source: Paul Kennedy, *The Rise and Fall of the Great Powers*, 681.

billion whereas the 1991 trade deficit was forecast as $25.5 billion. This goes to show that successful forecasting in today's frenetic international environment, even in the short term, will tend to be as much dependent upon good luck as good judgement. In summary, therefore, what has occurred in the 1990s is a parallelism of domestic influences impinging on the foreign policies of the two leading powers.

With Europe closing ranks in 1992, the outside possibility of an eventual Russo–Japanese economic alliance on the Pacific Rim and the United States with real economic problems, the USA seems unlikely to become a world hegemon. Nor does the existence of competing power groupings or the accelerating decline of the Soviet Union suggest that a superpower condominium seems likely. The logical conclusion is that it is beneficial for the significant and relevant medium powers to combine their interests in an organization that enjoys a position from which power may be exercised legally and multilaterally on behalf of the world body – the Security Council. But how is that to be achieved?

HOW?

ESTABLISH THE 'RULES OF THE GAME'

Many of the great human endeavours are guided by principles which have evolved and developed over time and through experience. The recognition and application of the relevant principles to any given enterprise are the essential first steps towards a successful conclusion. Naturally, success can never be guaranteed, but he who contemplates, for example, armed conflict and ignores the Principles of War[72] begins at a significant disadvantage: 'They are guides to conduct which have constantly proved successful in the past, and they serve as a warning that their disregard involves risks and is likely to bring failure.'[73] Among other well-known principles are Sir Robert Thompson's Principles for Defeating Communist Insurgency.[74] What should be understood about intervention principles is that they have to be applied to individual situations as they occur. Sometimes, indeed often, the principles may conflict and alternative sets of consequences have to be weighed.

A collator drawing up the principles which regulate any given enterprise is guided by the need for absolute stringency. The aim is to draw together a compact group of rules undiluted by subsidiary considerations such as, for example, capabilities or even lessons. Intelligence by itself is a capability but, arguably, can be 'grossed up' into a principle when joined by other factors which are themselves bricks in a total structure. There follows, as an illustration, the principle of the need to establish a simple and agreed unified command, control, communications and intelligence organization. Lessons obviously need to be heeded but these, in relative terms, are of less significance. An example of a lesson in an intervention context is the need, in most cases, to provide an opponent with the wherewithal to extricate himself from an undesirable confrontation. President John F. Kennedy achieved this in 1962 by trading space for time by reducing the radius of the Cuban 'quarantine', thus giving Khrushchev time to think. It is a lesson rather than a principle that aggressors who overreach themselves may need the offer of a ladder with which to extract themselves. That is not a new

47

lesson. C.E. Callwell wrote in 1899: 'To avoid desultory warfare the enemy must be brought to battle, and in such manner as to make his defeat decisive, but he should sometimes be left a golden bridge of eventual escape from the field.'[75]

The catalyst in this piece of work was the allied intervention in Russia's civil war of 1918–20. It was the basis of a book which set out in narrative form an account of Admiral Kolchak and the ill-fated allied intervention of 1918–20.[76] The motivation to go forward, to provide an academic dimension, was the author's realization that the mistakes made in Siberia were largely repeated by the Multi-National Force in Lebanon in 1982–4. The subsequent investigation to discover the principles of multilateral military intervention proved fruitless – there were none. Attempts, however, have been made in the past to formulate the conditions under which intervention might be justified.[77] No matter how justifiable intervention might be, it becomes a pointless exercise if it cannot succeed. It seems therefore that the first requirement in determining how multilateral military intervention might be achieved is to identify the rules of the game.

In 1918, the starting point of this analysis, the First World War had ended but the battle against Bolshevism had barely begun. Soviet Russia was assailed on all sides by a combination of foreign enemies and supporters of the old imperial order. The most dangerous threat faced by the Soviets from the converging armies came from Siberia in the east. There, the ambitions of the White soldiers led by Admiral Kolchak fell in with the revised aspirations of the former Allies, Britain, France, and the United States. Also in the east was a 70,000-strong army of freedom fighters determined to fight their way home; a legion of trained soldiers formed by the Czechs who had been prisoners of the Russians. Above all, there were the hidden ambitions of the Japanese, fulfilling their plan to achieve greater presence on the mainland of Asia. It was this background which provided the basis for the author's original study of multilateral intervention.

There is an admitted flaw in the logic which draws examples from 1918–20 to support the use of the offices of an organization which had its origins in 1945. It is possible to argue in defence that much of the attraction of the Russian intervention is that among the fourteen states either involved in the intervention or engaged in the war against Russia were all of today's significant world powers. Additionally, such study does not invalidate the legitimate lessons that arise, but in order to close the logic gap, additional post-Second World War examples will be adduced where possible to emphasize the validity of the nine basic principles of multilateral military intervention. These principles will be found to include some which are simply good military practice while others are highly political, of which perhaps the chief are the need to operate within the law and to maintain consensus. The degree of relevance of each of these individual principles will vary according to the circumstances of each different intervention.

The selection and maintenance of the aim

Of the ten Principles of War, only one is given any priority and that is one which in this context has equal political relevance: the selection and maintenance of the aim. For the majority of those engaged in conflict in Russia in 1918, the Armistice was assumed to have heralded the end of an intervention justified principally but not exclusively to keep open the Eastern Front. Most of the Allies, however, held on in Russia until 1919–20, while Japan did not leave until 1922. They had different reasons for remaining, including the existence of a political desire to curb Bolshevism, economic factors, and rivalry, most notably between the United States and Japan in the Pacific. That the Allies had separate national aims was unfortunate. Trotsky said that if the Allies could have acted together, the Revolution would have been defeated. Their failure to maintain even their original national aims had long-term political consequences.

The legacy of the intervention was to provide a rationale, or rather excuse, for some of Stalin's excesses as well as extending the Cold War. As recently as 1987, Soviet President Mikhail Gorbachev wrote: 'It is true to say that post-revolutionary development underwent difficult stages, largely due to the rude meddling of imperialist forces in our internal affairs.'[78] It seems that interventions in other states' affairs require a public declaration enunciating the political and military aim of the venture.

In 1950 the UN Security Council took the opportunity provided by the absence of the USSR to give the USA a mandate to lead collective military action against the invasion of South Korea by the North. The initial aim was to force North Korean troops back over the border, which coincided approximately with the 38th Parallel. Having satisfied that requirement, General Douglas MacArthur's aim was then changed by the UN to that of reuniting Korea and, accordingly, he drove on to the Yalu river which separates North Korea from China. The newly created Communist Chinese state reacted with a massive military intervention, which swept away the UN forces in front of them. Comprehensive defeat was only narrowly averted but the change of aim and the resultant suspicion raised in the minds of the People's Republic's leadership resulted in an extension of the war by three years. It is possible that a clear definition of the mission of the UN forces could have exercised a restraining influence when MacArthur's forces experienced an easier than anticipated advance northward.

The absence of a multinational aim in Siberia accounted for the irrelevance of the small, uncoordinated national contributions. In the case of the United States, the problem was more severe. The source of that problem was an *aide-mémoire*,[79] typed personally by President Wilson as a guide for the conduct of US affairs in Russia. George Kennan wrote:

That it was, even at the time it was presented to him [General Graves, GOC US Troops, Siberia], utterly inadequate to its purpose, that it was still further out of date by the time he arrived in Siberia, and that within two months after his arrival it had lost all conceivable relevance, seems never to have occurred to him.[80]

The fundamental problem was the serious schism which opened up between the State Department and the Military. Graves thought the *aide-mémoire* required him to be neutral, a stance which benefited the Reds. But, according to the future General Eichelberger, 'our consular representatives were pro-White, anti-Red and, in most cases, anti-Graves'.[81]

Operate under the auspices and co-ordination of a valid and supportive international organization

The Allied activities in Russia provided an overwhelming justification for the co-ordination of their multilateral military intervention by an international organization. It was unfortunate that the 1919 Paris Peace Conference was preoccupied both with the post-war settlement and with the establishment of the League of Nations. The absence of the United States and the Soviets from the League of Nations was one of that organization's principal weaknesses and not one which affects the United Nations. If states do become conditioned to operating under the auspices of a valid and supportive international organization, such as the United Nations, it seems logical that the inability to supply that essential support might prevent fruitless interventions being launched. The Multi-National Force, Lebanon of 1982–4 is a case in point. The United Nations therefore has a useful function to perform as a safety net.

Establish a simple and agreed unified command, control, communications and intelligence organization

Command is the authority for the direction, co-ordination and control of military forces. It embraces three broad activities which contribute to an activity's overall effectiveness – operational decision-making, management and leadership. The command problems experienced by the Allies in Russia are indicative of a vexed and potentially difficult area that touches on national pride and, in some areas, a natural expectation to command. An international agreement for the Vladivostock region placed the signatories' contingents under the command of the Japanese General Otani. The American General Graves refused to obey;

> In the afternoon of September 2, I called upon General Otani and, in a very few moments after I met him, he asked me if I had instructions that he was to command American troops. I told him that I did not have such instructions, but on the contrary, I had limitations placed on me as to the use of American troops that would make it necessary

for me to give all orders for future movements. He said that he had been notified by the U.S. State Department that he would be in command.[82]

The subsequent decision by the Allies to appoint the French General Maurice Janin as commander of all troops in Siberia forestalled the planning and training initiatives already taken by an *in situ* British general, Alfred Knox. Janin was still in France at the time of his appointment and the whole of the command process went into limbo while the Frenchman made his laborious progress into Siberia via the United States and Japan. When he arrived, the White Russians refused to accept his authority. The intervention proved to be a highly charged political affair.

That the United Nations is a political rather than a military organization was reflected in the command structure established for the Congo in 1960–4. The Secretary-General, Dag Hammarskjöld, was responsible to the Security Council for the organization of the peacekeeping forces. Hammarskjöld appointed as the chief of operations a Swedish businessman and initially, as force commander, a Swedish general commanding up to 23,000 troops from thirty-five different countries. Of the civilian direction of operations which were becoming increasingly warlike, Michael Harbottle wrote that it was 'understandable, maybe, but the meld did not work and much disagreement was generated'.[83] As one senior officer in the United Nations Force in Cyprus (UNFICYP) said, 'soldiers can be diplomats but diplomats cannot be soldiers'. Perhaps the command structure might have worked if something Moltke wrote had been heeded: 'Political considerations can be taken into account only as long as they do not make demands that are militarily improper or impossible.'[84]

While it may be laudable for a state to demonstrate political support for an enterprise, it is often the case that putting troops out on the ground is not the best medium in which to demonstrate that support. The viability of the entire military operation could be imperilled by a commander's obligation to embrace small national contingents whose function, level of training and experience are not in harmony with the environment in which they are required to operate. In civil employment, a management recruitment consultant is guided by his client's very precise job specifications. That approach needs to be replicated when troops are offered for interventionist roles. Expecting the nominated overall commander to take all-comers and slot them into an order of battle is not only prejudicial to the development of a sensible command and control regime, it can also be a recipe for disaster. The Charter does give to the Security Council the right to ask of a state those assets the Security Council requires.

Command and control in the Congo was greatly complicated by the number of nations supplying contingents to ONUC (Opération des Nations Unies au Congo). A general rule that can be identified is the lesser the

51

number of contingents, theoretically the simpler the task. The country of origin of the multinational force is an associated factor, as has been identified by General Gustav Hägglund: 'battalions from small countries from different parts of the world can never reach the same level of military professionalism as a single nation or unified European force'.[85]

Dilution can spell disaster even in unilateral acts of intervention. President Carter's preoccupation with achieving a representative ethnic mix and role of glory for all the US services in the 1980 Iran hostages venture contributed to its failure. The other serious error was to exercise the detailed command and control of the operation from the White House. From here, orders cascaded down through subordinate headquarters, thereby attracting a series of delays before reaching the forces directly responsible for the conduct of the operation.

When it became obvious that the 1983 Grenada and the 1982–4 Lebanon interventions had been similarly frustrated by the two same factors of command and control, some forward thinking in the Pentagon conceded that reform was overdue. No longer was it desirable for the single services to enjoy an independence which so often cultivated unhealthy competition and conflicting aims. However, these good intentions floundered on a combination of single service traditions as well as the presence of powerful parochial lobbies in Congress determined not to interfere with the independence of the individual services. One concession to have emerged so far from the logic of change in the command process has been alteration of the status of the Chairman of the Joint Chiefs of Staff Committee, from spokesman to the executive head and principal military adviser to the president. It is therefore possible to delegate the responsibility for operational command to the senior officer on the spot, as occurred in respect of the US naval force deployed to the Gulf in 1986.

It was the Goldwater-Nichols Department of Defence Reorganization Act of 1986 which placed combat formations in unified and specified commands. The act confirmed that the Chairman of the Joint Chiefs did not exercise military command over any combatant forces. This streamlined the chain of command, which now runs from the president to secretary of defence, directly to the unified and specified combatant commanders. This is not to say that a dotted line for communications does not go through the Chairman of the Joint Chiefs of Staff, nor that the single services do not still retain more autonomy than is militarily sensible. What it does mean, however, is that the lessons of Lebanon have been learned and that the commanders of the Unified Commands established in Saudi Arabia and Incirlik, Turkey, enjoyed considerable freedom to operate as they saw fit. This militarily desirable state of affairs arose through a combination of what the Goldwater-Nichols Act provided and what the leadership was prepared to concede.

The American experience, therefore, validates the principle that the chain of command must be kept simple and, in that respect, operational control with minimal political interference in military matters should be developed down to the lowest level at which it can sensibly function. It is at this level that co-ordination between the representatives of co-operating states can best be mapped out. It is also at this level, in coalition operations, that the importance of having the right personalities in the right places will become self-evident.

It is rather an elusive aspiration to believe that in time of peace there could be an uninhibited exchange of intelligence relating to intervention issues between former Cold War warriors. That had only selectively come to pass within the military structure of NATO, whose intelligence comes from member states. Intelligence that is freely made available risks not only the compromise of sources but also the devaluation of the intelligence. Bilateral and other sharing of certain secrets will of course continue. It is the crisis which serves as the catalyst, drawing together national interests and thereby polarizing those aspects of intelligence relevant to the circumstances. If, for example, the aggressor state deploys a weapon system supplied by a state whose national interests are threatened by that system, then the supplying state (as has happened in the past) could pool technical information aimed at minimizing the efficacy of the weapon system.

The self-evident, residual suspicions from the Cold War would preclude efficient centralization of intelligence data within the agency of any one state. The enterprise would be more gainfully served through an international organization dealing direct with the operational headquarters through the means of the myriad of available communications systems.

The separated national islands of command, control, communications and intelligence as well as the micromanagement of national activities from capital cities, as occurred in the Lebanon intervention of 1982–4, is the quintessential validation of the principle of simplicity and devolution. The passage of information and sharing of intelligence were abysmal, as was the demonstration of an understanding of the situation patchy in those few areas where it did exist.

There is a further dimension to communication and control in addition to the consideration of own and enemy forces' capabilities. This particular dimension has been the source of recent bitter acrimony, distrust and accusations of irresponsibility. It is a sensitive area which requires sensible management and mutual understanding. It was in 1904 that the fact of this problem began to be confirmed although the seeds had been evident in the Spanish–American and Boer Wars. In 1904, during the course of the Russo–Japanese War, Lionel James, the thirty-two-year-old *Times* correspondent, filled the 300-ton chartered steamer *Haimun* with radio equipment and made the first live broadcast, describing the Japanese attack on Port Arthur. The relationship between the media and the military would never be the same again.

Although this revolutionary change was inevitable, it was the manner of the change that was regretted by the truly professional war correspondent. Thomas Cowen of the *Daily Chronicle* was one of the reporters accredited to the Japanese general headquarters.

Men like Archibald Forbes and Dr Russell could not have brought the profession of war correspondent to this pass; but there have been so many less worthy men in the business in recent years that it is done to death. The authorities cannot discriminate or can only do so occasionally.[86]

Douglas Story, reporting from the opposing Russian lines echoed this sentiment:

Those of us who take our function seriously, who realise that war correspondence is as much a profession as that of the soldier or the engineer, resent the intrusion of the callow sensation mongers vomited from a hundred yellow journals.[87]

Much of the intelligence available on the situation in Manchuria and Korea was to be found in the London newspapers, which were avidly read both by the Russians and by the Japanese. The London *Times* of 29 February 1904 provides a case in point when describing the Japanese landings at Chemulpo, now known as Inchon:

The Japanese disembarkations during the last few days have been confined to supplies, the transport corps, and ponies of which there are 4,500. The total number of troops landed is 20,000 including the Twelfth Division and part of the Second Division. Another disembarkation, believed to be on a small scale, is taking place on the coast immediately south of Haiju whence the troops will advance, parallel to the Peking road, thus effecting a gain of five days' march. It is supposed that 8,000 troops, with a few guns, are now advancing beyond Seoul to Pyongyang.

The report in *The Times* prompted the Japanese to apply stringent controls over their bevy of foreign and domestic correspondents. The editor of one Japanese newspaper was arrested and tried for passing on information to an enemy. He had made an unauthorized report of a Japanese victory. The Russians did not impose such tight controls. According to the official German history of that war, 'The Russian press frequently stabbed out something worth knowing.'

Multilateral activity today merely exacerbates this problem. Controls, or the loyalty rein, can be applied to an individual national or pool of reporters but there will be variations in standards of control among disparate nations unless the whole media policy is controlled from the centre. A multilateral military organization that does not have a media plan and a specific media spokesman takes unnecessary risks in alienating one of the positive means of maintaining consensus within the sending states. The reverse can be true, yet by and large the media is controlled by responsible people. It is the immediacy of the means of passing information which is central to the problem, and that refers to the extraordinary developments in television news. It is reported that in Britain, 69 per cent of the population depend on television for their main source of the world news; 18 per cent depend on newspapers and 11 per cent on radio.[88]

What exasperates commanders is the reporter who steadfastly insists that the release of a particular piece of military information is in the public interest. More often than not, there is no reason for the public to be denied information. The machinery has to be in place and sensible decisions have to be made. 'Our presence is not by grace and favour,' wrote Sir David Nicholas, formerly of Independent Television News, 'we are the delegates of the public.'[89] It is not unknown that 'public interest' can be interpreted as to mean first, 'in the reporter's interest' and secondly, in the media's 'commercial interest'. There is a need here to recognize that a sensible balance has to be struck. A pool system of reporting may not be fair or even satisfactory, but the soldiers' right to survive transcends the public's need to know. The requirements of military security have to be balanced against the public's right to know.

Plan the force extraction concurrently with the planning of the force insertion

The lessons from both northern Russia and the intervention in the Dominican Republic indicate that the plans for extracting the force, when, where and how, need to be determined, if only in outline, at the same time that the insertion of the force is planned. Britain had to re-enlist demobilized soldiers and ship them to Russia in order to provide a force level sufficiently strong to permit a break-clean to occur. It would be beneficial for the Security Council to have an understanding of what results can be accepted as success. Intervention differs from peacekeeping in so far as there can be no publicly declared 'sunset' clause.

Uncertainty is a critical, variable factor which will impinge to a greater or lesser degree upon preliminary plans drawn up for the force extraction. The impact of uncertainty upon disengagement plans can be minimized through international co-operation, combined planning, the establishment of agreed aims and missions and, above all, by effective decision-making.

Establish an effective *cordon sanitaire* around the target area.

Cordon sanitaire is but another closely related name for the word 'quarantine', used by the Americans in 1962 in the Cuban missile crisis and 'interdiction', used also by the Americans in 1990 in relation to the Iraq/Kuwait crisis. While not entirely synonymous, they all mean much the same thing – blockade. Yet blockade in international law can only exist in war, hence a political reluctance to use the word. The term *cordon sanitaire* is preferred here because it is abstract and not so clinical as the physical action associated with the installation of a blockade. *Cordon sanitaire* would include other non-physical measures of coercion so that it is the leading edge of sanctions. Sanctions are a means by which the international community demonstrates its concern. They are a mechanism intended to reverse the situation responsible for their implementation. So much misunderstanding and so many prophets of doom have been associated with previous attempts at sanctions that it would be beneficial to examine this one area in some more detail.

The effectiveness of a *cordon sanitaire* depends not so much on the strength of the military ring surrounding the target state as upon the quality of the international agreement which gives the operatives their rules. The enabling resolution is most important. If it concedes too much to satisfy every possible national sensitivity it will be a fudge and will be practically impossible for the international organization's agents to put into effective action. The story is apposite of the camel being the outcome of a committee whose task was to design a horse.

In the past, a subjective approach to a decision whether or not armed conflict or war existed between two or more parties depended upon a declaration from the parties concerned on whether or not they were at war. The Covenant of the League of Nations possessed the power to impose sanctions on states which were at war. The 1931 Manchurian incident is one of those conflicts which is sometimes quoted to illustrate the impotence of the League of Nations. That is a simplification because, in that case, sanctions could not have worked. In a move to sidestep possible sanctions, Japan maintained that she was not at war with China. China, not wishing to turn off the tap of economic and commercial support from the United States, found it beneficial not to declare war. On the basis of the prevailing law therefore, the League of Nations was unable to impose sanctions on either Japan or China.

It is true that sanctions have often failed, but it becomes that much more important to understand why in order to cast around for a possible remedy. Sanctions against Italy in 1935 and, more recently, against Rhodesia in 1965, did not work. The reason was the same: the presence in the equation of a strong and secure state that was able to dilute attempts at sanctions. Now that there is a new-found collegiality among the principal states, it should in theory be easier to establish an effective *cordon sanitaire* around a target area. Iraq is particularly susceptible to the imposition of sanctions. If sanctions cannot be made to work there, it seems that they could not be made to work anywhere. There are important humanitarian issues to consider and these are examined in the second part of the book.

A blockade will work where there is the power, resolve and resources available to make it work. Liddell Hart said of the Royal Navy's function in the First World War that it was to 'win no Trafalgar but it was to do more than any other factor towards winning the war for the Allies'.[90] Liddell Hart was writing in 1930, at a time when he was attempting to influence future policy through economic pressure rather than through the resurrection of the British Expeditionary Force. There was, however, truth in what he claimed, that the Royal Navy had been a most effective instrument of blockade, as was confirmed by Keith Feiling when summarizing British sea power:

> which by blockade deprived Germany of war material, filled her home front with conviction of defeat, convoyed the food and coal which alone could keep France and Italy in the war, carried millions of American troops safely, took the means of victory to Palestine and the Balkans, and finally set up that desperation which appeared in the Germans' shattered discipline, even during their tactical victories at Amiens and the Marne.[91]

The blockade had weakened German resolve rather than destroyed it. People were hungry and malnourished, but not starved. The extent of the influence of the blockade only became really apparent at war's end, when German statisticians estimated that half a million civilian deaths through influenza and typhus were directly related to the deprivation resulting from the British blockade.[92]

It was from this example that the Allies in Russia in 1918–20 had learned of the validity of containment. The blockade of Russia was simply a rearranging of the blockade that had been applied against Germany. The intention was to deny the Soviets the resources with which to pursue their revolutionary campaign. It was in 1916 that President Wilson had complained through his country's London ambassador, of the effect the Royal Navy's European blockade was having on the USA's trade with neutral Holland. The Foreign Office responded with an interesting example of diplomatic *touché*. During the course of the American Civil War, the Union had established a blockade around the Bahamas and Mexico prejudicial to Britain's economic interests. Britain protested, but the response was a dismissive justification of the Union's rights to impose a complete blockade at a time of war. It was a copy of that same Union document which was returned to Washington in 1916. Woodrow Wilson had cause to be even more ill at ease in 1918 at war's end because of his reluctant complicity in occupying and imposing economic measures against Russia, a foreign country with which the United States was not at war.

States have different levels of vulnerability to blockades. To what degree a state is vulnerable requires an analysis of its assets, its political standing, leadership and geographical considerations. Among the evaluation of the state's assets would be factors such as economic strength, imports/exports, domestic production (particularly food and water), and the size of stock-piles (raw materials, fuels, food, water and medicines). The level of support a targeted state and its leadership enjoys, internally and externally, is important but not of paramount importance, particularly to an autocracy or dictatorship. Geography is significantly more important because it is this study which will identify the state's vulnerable or pressure points against which sanctions should be targeted. The battle is not only physical but also psychological, being aimed at the leader and the led. What is hoped for is the kind of capitulation that affected Ludendorff and his associates in 1918. That had been achieved over four desperate years. In the short and medium term, blockades can very often just heighten the resolve to resist within the target country.

It is rather obvious to say that the more effective the degree of contain-ment, the more likely the intervention is to succeed. The classic defeat of an insurgency occurred during the Malaya campaign. The narrow border separating Malaysia from Thailand should be set in comparison with Vietnam's long and difficult borders. An example of a legitimate and successful intervention was seen during the Falklands campaign. The naval, and later, a total exclusion zone provided the British forces with a credible and ultimately effective *cordon sanitaire*. These are of course ideals but are indicative of the area in which to proceed in order to deny oppo-nents the wherewithal to wage war. These are also factors in the decision-making function which considers the viability of military intervention. An effective arms control policy would have ensured that the Iran/Iraq War burnt itself out very much sooner than it did.

Maintenance of consensus

In circumstances where military power is deployed in support of purely political goals, that military power is highly susceptible to political change. 1919 was a critical, highly charged confrontational year between the ideol-ogies of capitalism and Communism. The fact that the war had ended the previous year raised the cry, 'What are our boys doing in Siberia?' It was a cry which was repeated at home, in Russia by the Reds, and also among the intervening forces. This reluctance and outright hostility at being involved in other people's wars arose from three separate sources: from among the public in the sending state; from among the Reds in the target state; and among the interventionist forces.

If intervention is to succeed it requires a green light in three areas. First, the need for home support is self-evident. Secondly but less easy to define (and it would be a mistake to try to lay down a rule), is what proportion of support is required in the target country. That green light judgement will have to form part of the conflict analysis related to the target state and consideration of the means available. Lastly, there is the matter of the support of interventionist forces. The troops that have the requisite mental attitude and military spirit to endure danger and long periods of separation in a war with possibly no national interest require a special quality. They will need to be convinced that their endeavour is in support of the *bellum justum*, the just war. The success of the enterprise will be influenced by three factors: the length of time involved in actual fighting; the prospects of success; and (particularly important among conscript armies) the casualty rates.

History is groaning with examples where the interventionists' opponent is better able to tolerate casualties than the intervening forces. The 'home team' is imbued with a higher level of resolve than the 'away team'. It can be argued therefore, that from the outset the intervenor begins at a significant disadvantage. The domestic problem of war casualties is not so much the number but the pointlessness of them in the public's mind. It is therefore a principal aim of the opposition to inflict unacceptable casualties upon interventionist troops. A Gurkha captain in India's intervention force in Sri Lanka said: 'Things would be different if we were fighting for our country but here it's difficult to explain to the troops why we are in it at all.'[93] Psychological defence is an important factor in a protracted intervention. The best psychological preparedness will be found within traditional regiments which are part of formations that have lived, worked and trained together.

It is of critical importance for the intervenors to keep the three lights green for the duration of the intervention. Should one or more flicker to yellow, immediate remedial action should be taken. If the situation does not respond to remedial action – and remedial action could be political, financial, military measures or just a straightforward public relations exercise – then steps need to be taken to investigate disengagement. The maintenance of international unanimity can be of considerable importance. If a key actor, for example, experiences a yellow or red light in the area of public consensus, which resists attempts to convert to green, it may well influence other states and the whole viability of military operations. The validity of this green-light theory can be tested against what happened recently in Vietnam, Afghanistan and the Falklands. The Peninsula War of 1808–14, provides a more historic perspective. One significant complication which occurs within a multilateral force is that nations do not have the same level of tolerance to the setbacks that will surely arise.

Agree and adhere to national contributions

Morale in multilateral intervention may be affected by a perceived lack of equity in the scale of support provided by the parties. If one party is seen to be doing most of the fighting and suffering most of the casualties and paying most of the cost then such a multilateral intervention will tend to be difficult to sustain other than for a short period. The highly trained 70,000-strong Czech Army in western Siberia, properly encouraged and motivated by Supreme Ruler Kolchak, could have tipped the balance in the Whites' favour. Their growing disillusionment and disaffection with the war was due to the realization that they had taken on the brunt of the Whites' fighting. This was something they were grudgingly prepared to tolerate until reinforced by the long-awaited British and French troops. When it became evident that the small numbers of British and French soldiers which trickled into western Siberia were there for political, not military, purposes, the Czechs began their anabasis eastward and out of Russia's civil war.

However, the certain recrimination and loss of morale caused by inequity will need to be balanced against the reality that the fewer the number of contingents involved in a multilateral intervention the better. Political impediments will prevent some states from allowing their troops to occupy front-line positions. To take this point to its ultimate conclusion, it shows overwhelmingly the need to establish in the United Nations the planning machinery to consider such contingencies. Peacekeeping has on occasions been a close-run thing due to reliance on *ad hoc* measures. If intervention, a considerably more complex exercise, is to succeed, it cannot expect to rely upon the *ad hoc* and 'hot plan'.

Operate within the law

With the exception of Korea 1950, all UN peacekeeping activities have been at the request of what has been taken to be the constitutional government of the target state. (In the case of Korea, it was the United States, working speedily through the offices of the Security Council – the Soviet representatives, Malik, was absent – which acted on South Korea's behalf.) There are circumstances within the intervention scenario where that invitation may be absent, the UN acting in the interest of broader international security principles. The crucial importance of the observance of municipal law and the operation of a sensible civil affairs or 'hearts and minds' policy cannot be overstated. The behaviour of the Japanese in the Russian Civil War, for example, within their own Siberian area of responsibility in terms of both cruelty to the Russians and overt support of two of the most sadistic of the Siberian atamen, made them in effect the best recruiting machine the Reds could have hoped for.

A multilateral military force deployed at the behest of the United Nations draws its international legality from the Charter of the United Nations. The Geneva Conventions which all potential sending states have ratified will apply. Participation in a multilateral operation does not affect legal undertakings negotiated nationally. The behaviour of troops deployed in an interventionist role and their observance of municipal law must be exemplary. Sir Robert Thompson's second principle in *Defeating Communist Insurgency* is the requirement of the government to function within the law. That is equally true of forces operating on behalf of the UN:

> There is a very strong temptation in dealing both with terrorism and with guerrilla actions for government forces to act outside the law, the excuses being that the processes of law are too cumbersome, that the normal safeguards in the law for the individual are not designed for an insurgency and a terrorist deserves to be treated as an outlaw anyway. Not only is this morally wrong but, over a period, it will create more practical difficulties for a government than it solves.[94]

Military intervention is the last resort of a collective security machine

It should be initiated only after the available satisfactory intelligence and detailed conflict analysis have revealed that the putative operation affords significant benefit to world or regional order. Above all, when a positive decision to intervene is made, the force must be properly resourced. It is not good enough to determine whether an intervention is justified. The interventions undertaken this century will have been considered justified by those responsible for the dispatch of interventionist forces, yet most have failed because they could not succeed and should not have been attempted. Other coercive measures should have been examined (as required by the UN Charter) or the conclusion reached that a satisfactory result could not be achieved. Many future conflicts will simply be tolerated in 'difficult' regions due to the sheer inability of other forces to form effective coalition operations.

The US consul at Archangel, Felix Cole, predicted that the 1918–20 'intervention will begin on a small scale but with each step forward will grow in scope and in its demands for ships, men, money and materials'.[95] Poor and loose planning were responsible for the dispatch of contingents ill prepared and ill equipped for a climate and expansive terrain which served to emphasize their unsuitability and insignificance. The key lies in drawing the correct balance between proportionality and sufficiency. The highly competent chief of staff of the US Army, General Peyton C. March, had justifiable misgivings concerning the presence of US troops on Russian soil. 'The sending of a little handful of men like our expedition' was, he said, 'a military crime'. March loyally supported Graves throughout his difficult time in Siberia. In his view, had Graves not been so dogged, it would have needed '100,000 men to get them out alive'.[96] Apropos Vietnam, another crucial lesson was relearned in the most tragic of circumstances. Britain's refusal to support the United States in Vietnam strained the special relationship. But military intervention is much to do with selecting winners and Britain since 1945, with one or two exceptions, has the best record among the medium and superpowers of selectivity, and therefore success. It is essentially a matter of evaluation, of looking very carefully before leaping.

In the case of Professor Ullman's escalatory model in which the third stage involves comprehensive military intervention, states do of course have the option to abort their further progress into the quagmire at stages one or two. It is easier said than done, however, to abandon the approach to a problem which impinges, or is perceived to impinge, upon national interests, when the initial objectives which spawned the original intervention still remain in place. The escape from this slippery slope requires astute decision-making and firm leadership in order to effect disengagement before full-blown military intervention is joined. Historical precedence shows that states are invariably drawn like lemmings into the third, critical stage, only being released from self-inflicted agony by a change of government.

UTILIZE THE UN's LEGAL MECHANISM

The cause of the proponent of the observance of international law in international relations is handicapped by the existence of frustratingly imprecise and ambiguous law. The rules relating to the use of force and self-defence, the *jus ad bellum*, are contained in Articles 2(4) and 51 of the Charter. These articles state that the use of force is, except in the extremest of circumstances, illegal, yet international law then provides a quite separate body of rules, the *jus in bello*, to relate to conflict when it does occur. The problem with Article 51, to be examined in some detail, is that it is both vague and uncertain. Consequently, a state is left free to offer a plausible justification of self-defence for any force it might choose to exercise.

The legal provisions which exist within the UN Charter establish an enabling mechanism for the legitimate conduct of multilateral military intervention. There are, however, two distinct threads. The first, which derives its authority and legality from Security Council Resolutions, is precise law which leaves little room for misinterpretation. The second thread, wound around Article 51, introduces an element of permissiveness and it is in this area that the law suffers from unintended elasticity. As this legal examination unfolds, the benefit of basing military intervention on the judgement and authority of the Security Council will become apparent. Additionally, as mentioned earlier, the Security Council avenue provides a useful safety net. When the authority to proceed cannot be obtained, it would indicate the existence of varying degrees of political misgivings, if not open hostility. The signal conveyed to the potential intervenor by the absence of this Security Council endorsement could mean that military action should not be contemplated, or the use of other coercive measures should be investigated, or even that no action is possible. The European Communist parties responded to Brezhnev's claim that the Afghanistan intervention was a form of foreign aid to a counter-revolution by remarking that his argument should have been tested at the United Nations.

Until 1945 there was no comprehensive international prohibition of the unilateral resort to force. It was the UN Charter which extended the 1928 Pact of Paris to introduce to international politics the concept that such unilateral resort to force by states was legally and morally wrong. Article 2(3) of the Charter of the United Nations set as one of the conditions of membership that: 'All Members shall settle their international disputes by peaceful means in such a manner that international peace and security, and justice, are not endangered.' It has been broadly recognized that only two exceptions are permitted: force used in self-defence when an armed attack occurs, and armed action authorized by the Security Council as an enforcement measure.

The two articles in the Charter which are relevant to the subjects of the use of force and self-defence are the aforementioned Articles 2(4) and 51. Article 2(4) is emphatic law not solely limited to the prohibition of war but covering all types of force and threats: 'All Members shall refrain in their international relations from the threat or use of force against the territorial integrity or political independence of any state, or in any other manner inconsistent with the Purposes of the United Nations.' Article 2(4) should be read in tandem with the more open-ended Article 51. This latter article provides a limited form of permission for 'the inherent right of individual or collective self-defence if an armed attack occurs'. It is incumbent upon states to report to the Security Council the nature of the measures that they have taken or propose to take under the umbrella of Article 51. The onus, however, still remains with the Security Council 'to take at any time such action as it deems necessary in order to maintain or restore international peace and security'. The decision therefore to indulge in self-defence is always subject to international review in the Security Council, or as happened in the Nicaragua case, it could be reviewed by a judicial tribunal. With the exception of Great Britain, states are not yet ready to have such questions resolved judicially by the International Court of Justice (ICJ).

It might be surprising to read that the meanings of self-defence and armed attack remains under discussion. Attempts have been made in the past to justify the use of force as self-defence to protect vital national interests, foreign nationals abroad and the observation of humanitarian principles. The truism implicit in the well-known aphorism 'where you stand is where you sit' can be found in the assertion of a respected US international lawyer. There is in the United States a college of opinion which holds the view that the failure of the United Nations to establish the collective security regime described on page 7 imposes limitations upon Articles 2(4) and 51. Their view is that the articles were all formulated on the understanding that a collective security machine would be established. The failure to introduce collective security measures therefore means that 'it does require that concepts like "self-defence" and the prohibition on the use of force against the "territorial integrity and political independence of states" be reasonably construed to enable the law-abiding states to defend the civilised order.'[97]

When the body of the law surrounding Article 51 is investigated, what is found is confusion, dissention and chicanery. This is symptomatic of a UN Charter which is caught between a nineteenth-century concept of sovereignty and a mid-twentieth-century view of humanity and universalism.

It was presumably the existence of an 'inherent' right of self-defence which accounted for the absence of any such mention in either the Covenant of the League of Nations or the 1928 Pact of Paris. Article 51 was drawn up in its present form to preserve the 1941 Chapultepec Treaty,[98] and similar treaties such as the Pact of the Arab League, principally to reassure the underdeveloped countries that their arrangements for mutual self-defence in the event of an armed attack were not considered illegal under the terms of the Charter. Recognition of the existence of the customary right of self-defence can also be found in the judgment arising from Nuremberg and the Far East military tribunals.

The permission for states to undertake individual or collective self-defence has been subjected to some elasticity to accommodate anticipatory (pre-emptive) self-defence. Thus far, the only circumstances when it has been considered legitimate to use force is the use of limited or minimum force within the restraints imposed by two factors, proportionality and necessity. If a state reacts by the use of excessive or disproportionate force it forgoes the right to the justification that its action was in accordance with international law. Additionally, if the use of force is not within the scope and ambit of legitimate national aims it would debar any claim of necessity.

The *locus classicus* of anticipatory self-defence arises from a planned rebel attack on Canada from the USA pre-empted by British forces in the so-called Caroline Incident of 1837. Daniel Webster, the US Secretary of State, set out his understanding of anticipatory self-defence in a note to Britain in 1842. There were three components: it must be a wrongful act which poses actual or imminent threat to the security of the state; the necessity for self-defence is instant, overwhelming and leaving no choice of means and no moment for deliberation; and the action must be proportionate to the harm threatened.[99]

What separates anticipatory self-defence from other forms of self-defence of course is that the delict, the actual armed attack, has not occurred: 'The right of self-defence lies against conduct by states which is delictual as being in breach of a duty established by International Law.'[100] As is so often the case, international law is less than clear and there are a number of differing interpretations of what the founders of the Charter intended.

Professor Henkin is among those who believe that the drafters of the Charter did envisage that states could undertake measures of self-defence in an emergency but only when an armed attack had occurred. The benefit of self-defence being dependent upon an actual armed attack is that such an attack 'is clear, unambiguous, subject to proof and not easily open to misinterpretation or fabrication'.[101] The Henkin viewpoint reflects a Cold War rationale yet one which is no less relevant today. In a nuclear environment it is undesirable for states to initiate a first strike 'under the pretext of prevention or pre-emption'.[102]

The dissenting view of Oscar Schachter indicates the scope that states do enjoy to pick and choose a justification for their action, claiming that it does fall within the law. Schachter points out that, during debates in the Security Council, delegates had referred to the precedent of the Caroline case as an accepted statement of customary law. It is on the basis of these statements that the continued validity of the 'inherent' right to use armed force in self-defence prior to an actual attack is upheld. The one limitation conceded is that anticipatory self-defence is only admissible 'where such an attack is imminent "leaving no room for deliberation" '.[103]

A third, more fundamental line of argument maintains that the reference to 'armed attack' included in Article 51 at the time of its hurried drafting was intended to be merely illustrative, not restrictive. 'In other words, it was to furnish an example of circumstances in which the right of self-defence existed, not to reduce the scope of that right.'[104] In the Nicaragua case, the ICJ upheld the requirement for an armed attack to have occurred before a second state can respond but did not have to decide on the issue of whether anticipatory self-defence is lawful.

There is a common yet erroneous view that a state remains domestically immune within its borders from the physical attention of other states. This is generally true, but the Charter makes one important exception. The domestic jurisdiction clause within the Charter is Article 2(7).

> Nothing contained in the present Charter shall authorize the United Nations to intervene in matters which are essentially within the domestic jurisdiction of any state or shall require the Members to submit such matters to settlement under the present Charter.

There is a 'but' and it is a significant 'but':' ... but this principle shall not prejudice the application of enforcement measures under Chapter VII'. This article therefore permits the UN to intervene in such matters as the violation of humanitarian principles when they occur within a sovereign state's boundaries. Article 2(7) has rarely been implemented. Arguably it was the basis for the UN involvement in Rhodesia, but more recently it has been invoked in Security Council Resolution 688 designed to protect Iraq's Kurdish and Shia populations.

Within the United Nations' two-tiered structure, decisions which emanate from the Security Council are binding and have the force of law. Those resolutions which arise from the General Assembly, however, do not enjoy the force of law. This means that declarations such as the Declaration on Friendly Relations between Nations remain entirely advisory.[105] The Declaration is a highly moralized attempt to prohibit all forms of intervention and coercion through its non-intervention resolution. Looked at critically, it could be deemed to be unrealistic, and for that reason is not generally taken seriously.

The military enforcement powers provided in Chapter VII have only been exercised on two occasions: in Korea in June 1950 and in the Gulf in 1990–1. Immediately after military action in Korea was approved in November 1950, Dean Acheson, the US Secretary of State, and Trygve Lie, the UN Secretary-General, needed some sleight of hand to introduce the Uniting for Peace Resolution to overcome the problems associated with the return of the USSR to the Security Council. Under that new resolution, by a two-thirds majority the General Assembly has the authority to sidestep the veto and sanction enforcement measures. Today it is improbable that the Security Council will again permit the General Assembly the opportunity to decide to authorize such measures.

The utility of multilateral security action under the auspices of the Security Council, thereby avoiding the legal doubts arising in alleged cases of self-defence, can be most advantageously illustrated by reviewing the post-1945 incidence of self-defence. It comes in various guises: collective support, intervention by invitation, protection of own nationals, and for humanitarian motives. The examples are to be found in state practice, from whence international law derives its force.

What undermines the Security Council's and International Court of Justice's judgments on claimed acts of self-defence is a view taken by some states, notably Israel, that they fail to take account of military necessity. The Security Council suffers from the same weakness so apparent in the League of Nations: it lacks the enforcement means to give bite to its deliberations. However, it has to be conceded that the UN is not a court but a political assembly making political judgements. In terms of anticipatory self-defence, there is a dearth of bona fide incidents from which to indicate a clear definition in state practice. Most actions have been of the clinical strike type and therefore fall outside the scope of this study.

There was a superficial examination of a case for collective self-defence during the thirteen days of the 1962 Cuban missile crisis. It proved not to be a serious consideration. If the USA had no right to individual self-defence then neither could their orchestration of the Organization of American States provide legitimate collective rights. When no individual right exists, it is not possible to bind together a number of states in the hope of securing a justification for collective action.

Both the USA and the former USSR have frequently used as their justification for military intervention an invitation from the target state. Intervention on behalf of either side in a civil conflict may well interfere with the rights of peoples to self-determination. Admittedly, self-determination is a concept which had clear application in colonial days, but today, its meaning is less distinct. If military force is deployed to impose restriction on the political independence of the target state by restraining the opposition, then such action is contrary to Article 2(4). The attraction of intervention by invitation, such as occurred in the Philippines in 1989, is that when military force is employed to put down a coup or to restore law and order there is, arguably, no violation of Article 2(4).

> There is good reason therefore to place a heavy burden on any foreign government which intervenes with armed forces even at the invitation of the constitutional authority to demonstrate convincingly that its use of force has not infringed the right of the people to determine their political system and the composition of their government.[106]

The words 'at the invitation of the constitutional authority' are important. Past cases indicate that the intervening state has frequently recognized as the constitutional authority whomsoever it chose.

Armed intervention to protect nationals is a long-standing and often bogus justification. Among both the real and contrived examples of nationals being in danger have been the real interventions of the Belgian action in Stanleyville in 1961, the Israeli rescue at Entebbe in 1976, and US attempts to release hostages in Iran in 1980. Contrived or bogus interventions include the Anglo-French invasion of the Suez Canal in 1956, the US intervention in the Dominican Republic in 1965 and Grenada in 1983. Despite the dissimilarities that exist between these examples, it is evident that states do regard the rescue of own-nationals as a form of self-defence. The Entebbe rescue comes closest to a formula identified by Professor Bowett which supports such intervention when the original delict is contrary to international law, when there are no alternative means, when the danger is serious and imminent and counter-measures are proportional to the original delict.[107] Rarely, however, are delicts against individuals the result of action taken by established governments. With the exception of the Mayaguez action, the Iranian hostages episode, and the recent incident with Iraq, all other cases affecting nationals have been terrorist inspired.

There is a good deal of literature which upholds the right of humanitarian intervention, yet there is arguably only one positive example in state practice. That was the 1991 humanitarian intervention in support of Iraq's Kurdish minorities. The 1971 Indian intervention in Bangladesh, the 1978 Vietnamese intervention in Cambodia and the 1979 Tanzanian intervention in Uganda may have had residual humanitarian aims but they were not the *raison d'être* for the interventions. It may well be that the way forward in humanitarian intervention is to base the action on respectable argument. In these circumstances a state would forgo its normal sovereignty by conduct found to be so odious as to mobilize a counter-action by a consensus of right-minded states. Alternatively, action could be taken through the organs of the United Nations. Such a proposal would have been unthinkable a few years ago but in 1989 the UN's Assistant Secretary-General in the Office for Research and the Collection of Information, James O.C. Jonah, believed that the changing international atmosphere, the growing rapport between superpowers and the increased harmony in the Security Council meant that 'it is not inconceivable that the Security Council may contemplate military action to ensure that humanitarian assistance is delivered safely to a targeted civilian population in jeopardy'.[108]

The above statement is one of the very first in which a senior representative has discussed the UN's preparedness to consider undertaking some of the responsibilities given to the organization in 1945. If the UN does move towards the adoption of a legal collective security mechanism, the rationale for states to arm themselves to the hilt will be undermined. In addition, states will be spared the need for doubtful expositions of a state's rights to use force, as was evident in the State Department's Meeker Memorandum, which referred to the Vietnamese war.[109]

An effective legal adjudication of the Vietnamese War is complicated by argument as to where, exactly, the factual baseline was to be drawn. There are at least three distinctly separate analyses to describe the origins of the war. Case One envisaged a civil war in South Vietnam between the South Vietnamese government and the Vietcong. Within this case are two threads. The first is of an illegal North Vietnamese intervention on the side of the Vietcong which prompted a counter-intervention by the USA on the side of the South Vietnamese government. The second thread has an intervention of doubtful legality by the USA in support of the South Vietnamese government, to which the North Vietnamese counter-intervened on behalf of the Vietcong. The second thread does not come close to what actually happened.

Case Two, if it could have been argued to be correct, would preclude the legitimate intervention by any third party. In this case, there had been a civil war in a unified state of Vietnam between the North Vietnamese regime, including the Vietcong, and the South Vietnamese regime. The peace movement in the USA identified themselves with Case Two. Indeed, there is collateral support in the Geneva Final Declaration, arising from the 1954 ceasefire, which was couched in terms of one independent state of Vietnam with elections to be held in 1956. The South refused to co-operate in national elections because south of the 17th Parallel there existed a minority, but nonetheless significant, Communist party whose votes, when added to a 98 per cent Communist vote in the North, would have produced a strong Communist regime throughout the whole of Vietnam. Meeker argued that the South had no need to hold elections, for that would have been tantamount to handing the country over, contrary to the southern majority's wishes.

Case Three, the analysis Meeker supported, recognized North and South

Vietnam as separate states by 1964. The North attacked the South contrary to Article 2(4) and the USA intervened to assist South Vietnam as a form of collective self-defence. The Meeker thesis is valid if South Vietnam was a separate legal entity by 1964. There is in the margin sympathetic evidence to support an argument of two Vietnamese states. The history of the region would be more likely to support the case of a divided Vietnam than, for example, a divided Korea, which had previously been one nation. It is also true that the South had been operating as an independent state and had attracted considerable international recognition. Nevertheless, it is the Geneva Final Accord (to which the USA was not a signatory), which envisaged one Vietnam after the elections scheduled for 1956.

Which of the three cases is legally safe is difficult to pronounce with absolute certainty. In Meeker's preferred Case Three, international lawyers are divided as to whether the right existed for the USA to intervene on behalf of South Vietnam. One who argued against the USA intervention maintained that it could not be condoned, for to do so would be endorsing a recipe for widening conflicts. Case Two is the weaker case to argue, for although it was intended that Vietnam should be a unified state, unification had not come about, principally due to the South's obstruction. Circumstances tend to support the validity of the first thread of Case One: that what had occurred was an illegal North Vietnamese intervention on the side of the Vietcong, prompting a counter-intervention by the USA at the request of, and on behalf of, the South Vietnamese government. But a legal counter-intervention should not have taken the battle either north over the 17th Parallel or into neighbouring states. The question immediately raised is whether that judgement takes account of military necessity. The subsequent Allied operations in Iraq were deemed to have been necessary to achieve the aims enshrined in Resolution 678.

The study of international law relating to military intervention does, in the main, reveal attempts to observe the principle if not the letter of the law. On other occasions, the failure to observe international law has drawn states into a vortex of ill-advised commitment and consequent ignominious failure. Justice is an important notion in international affairs yet it is a concept of legality which is subject to differing interpretation. Regrettably, before the Aspen declaration, nowhere in the First World had the principle of international law been afforded lower public esteem than in the United States. Although the Third World countries are generally opposed to that traditional international law which is tainted by a perceived imperialist and colonialist past, they are nevertheless acquiescent towards the 1945 laws embodied within the Charter. This is largely a reflection of self-interest in keeping in touch with other countries: 'For this reason, the newly independent countries have all taken an affirmative attitude towards international law itself, and many of them have constitutionally recognised its validity.'[110] In view of the foregoing, therefore, the Third World expects an equality of states within the law. It is admittedly imprecise to describe the Third World as though it is a compact bloc, but this tradition has been established through common usage. It could be argued that the Second World's merging with the First means there is no longer a Third. Notwithstanding this digression, the use of illegal force in world affairs will increasingly become counter-productive.

> When governments break the law, it does nothing to encourage others to respect it. As the nation with the most to lose from international anarchy, the United States has a vested interest in promoting international law, not destroying it. [111]

RESTRUCTURE THE UN'S MILITARY ORGANIZATION

The military organization which exists today within the UN is a compromise arising from the Security Council's inability to implement what was the intended collective security regime. The MSC does still exist and does meet, yet until August 1990 it had been little more than a luncheon club. The Secretary-General takes his formal military advice from his solitary military adviser, currently a Ghanaian major-general. General Dibuama has a minuscule staff, which does not enjoy the benefit of so much as a planning cell. This is at a time when the UN has mandated eight new and far-flung peacekeeping operations over a four-year period. A strong military representation within the United Nations has been anathema to what emerged to be its international Whig traditions. In consequence, the peacekeeping function has climbed like a funicular railway, the cogs of imaginative improvisation and perpetual crisis within the tight bounds of Chapter VI.

There have been suggestions that the moribund MSC should be reinvigorated to use its offices and expertise to assist Chapter VI peacekeeping operations, particularly in those areas where it is recognized as being weak, namely in intelligence, logistics and transportation. There are also more fundamental roles for the MSC in relation to formulating Standing Operating Procedures (SOPs) and standardizing intervention doctrine and training. It might be assumed that the modern United Nations, that is, united in peace, would embrace a plan which would tap the Security Council's reservoir of military professionalism. The principal objectors however have resided within the Third World, resisting any move perceived to enhance superpower involvement in world affairs. The Soviets proposed a wider use of the MSC in relation to peacekeeping activities but that suggestion was met with coolness by the other permanent members of the Security Council, emphasizing what has been a long-term reluctance and even hostility elsewhere to the permanent members of the Security Council becoming involved with the peacekeeping function.

There is an unwritten law that the permanent members of the Security Council demonstrate their impartiality by not joining peacekeeping operations. That rule has been selectively broken by Britain in Cyprus and Namibia, France in the Lebanon, and the United States, the Soviet Union and China in the Middle East. Generally, peacekeeping has been the province of the small and non-aligned states: it has been a useful area in which to keep their armies up to the mark short of actual conflict. For Canada it is one of her primary defence functions. The Irish Republic and Scandinavian countries have also been prominent. What has evolved is a club of protectionist peacekeepers who are also placekeepers intent on maintaining these positions. Peacekeeping should continue to be operated in the main by the traditional donor states, where the presence of the peacekeepers has the consent of both parties and where lethal force is to be used only in self-defence. In addition, there is no reason why the MSC should not be available to offer the Secretary-General advice on Chapter VI operations when requested.

There are circumstances where peacekeeping may be required to be conducted with the consent of only one host state – what the Soviets described as preventive diplomacy – or with the consent of both host states but in circumstances where the violence and risk thresholds are unacceptably high for the traditional donor states. A case in point would be a peacekeeping operation maintaining the divide between a rehabilitated PLO and Israel in Palestine. Valerie Yorke sets out the criteria for such an International Guarantor Force (IGF) as follows: 'the IGF would need contingents that were both militarily capable of fulfilling the tasks, and recruited from states politically willing for their men to fight and suffer casualties and politically acceptable to Israel, Palestine and Jordan.'[112]

The Finnish General Hägglund, Force Commander of (UNIFIL) United Nations Forces in Lebanon in 1986–8, recognizes this wind of change:

> Peace-enforcement should not necessarily be opposed; it simply requires different forces and a completely different concept. An intention to deter and enforce requires forces which are as frightening as possible. For this kind of mission great-power battalions, professional soldiers and all the means at their disposal are preferable.[113]

It is therefore illusory to believe that a general representing a non-aligned country would hold much credibility on his own to determine the fortune of, and advise the Secretary-General on the deployment of, superpower forces. The fact is inescapable that something does need to be done to upgrade the UN's organization to match the capability to the threat. The Charter of the United Nations provides in part its own solution in the form of the MSC and the quantity and quality of forces at the Security Council's disposal. The pedantic argument that the MSC should not involve itself in peacekeeping because it has no mandate can best be met by the observation that the UN Charter is totally silent on the whole concept of peacekeeping.

71

In the light of the changes which are imminent in the military organization of NATO and with the demise of the Warsaw Pact, there is an implicit obligation on the part of the UN to ascertain whether that organization can now take up its intended lead with the formation of a collective security regime. The UN Charter establishes the theory that interventionist activities may be legally sanctioned and even initiated through UN headquarters. If force is to be applied at the behest of the UN it surely needs a dedicated military staff to provide the necessary planning, intelligence, communications and resource management. It is incongruous to maintain fully staffed headquarters in a Central Region where it has been agreed that minimal prospects of general conflict exist while the one organization empowered to deploy forces is embarrassed by a poverty of military support staff. Some of the anticipated peace dividend arising from trimmed NATO and Warsaw Pact headquarters could be beneficially deployed to the UN headquarters as contingency planning staff. Military reforms have to be implemented concurrently with political change within the Secretariat. There is an overwhelming need for the addition of a new political office to draw together the decision-making process, which is currently dispersed throughout the UN building. If such a measure is not adopted, the UN is unlikely to rise to the many new challenges the organization is expected to resolve.

It is proposed that the UN should adopt a two-tier structure to operate its military activities. Uncomplicated peacekeeping under Chapter VI should continue, where possible bolstered by the availability of the MSC to advise the Secretary-General when requested. There is the option that the MSC could take up the responsibility for Chapter VII action and Chapter 'VI $\frac{1}{2}$', drawing advice from representatives of the traditional peacekeeping donor states. The value to be derived in running Chapter VI and Chapter VII action together is in satisfying the intellectual tradition within the UN. There will still be a requirement to work with the selfsame administrators who thus far have balanced Chapters VI and VII military operations. There is also a role for peacekeepers to play in intervention actions as observers and advisers on such matters as the Geneva Convention and the Laws of Armed Conflict.

DESIGN A STRATEGY

The time for a new military strategy of peace for the world based on the UN in general and the Security Council in particular has never been more propitious. Since the 1960s there has been a steady erosion in the effectiveness and the stability of those regional military organizations which owed their origins to the sterility of the UN. The Warsaw Pact, SEATO and CENTO have folded, ANZUS has lost NZ and NATO is reeling from the effects of Arbatov's promise to 'deprive you of your enemy'.

NATO finds itself in a quandary following the disappearance of the Warsaw Pact. Long will be the debate within the NATO countries to identify a suitable, credible threat in order to extract funds from cynical governments to resource reduced force levels. Something of these circumstances was foreseen in 1973:

> For many Western taxpayers, the military are on their way to becoming latter-day remittance men, given a small slice of the family income on condition that they go off and pursue their unsavoury activities quietly where they will not embarrass decent folk. [114]

Where a real threat does not exist, there is a tendency to manufacture one. Indonesia suits Australia's purposes as the necessary focal point upon which the political and military minds justify their force structure and forward deployment in northern Australia. The absence of a threat will pose a continuing greater problem for NATO's military rather than political side. The capacity for member states to train sensibly for general war, which all indications reveal to be extremely improbable, will be bedevilled by the severest of resource restrictions and training impediments derived from economic and environmental sources. These restrictions could also, over a period of time, influence an effective response by NATO's member states to an out-of-area crisis. Commanders will struggle to maintain both credibility and morale. For them, this apparent absence of a threat is rather like playing football without goalposts. The enterprise may well lack aim as well as direction.

NATO's own rules currently forbid out-of-area operations. Military action can be valid only if the proposed use of force satisfies the criteria of credibility and legality. This is not to say that in international law, the member states of NATO and the former Warsaw Pact should not undertake multilateral military intervention in or out of area but rather that they should only do so as a UN surrogate under the authority of the regional arrangements embodied in Article 53 of the United Nations Charter. Without that authority it might appear that NATO is attempting to impose the north's Brezhnev Doctrine upon the south. Historically such measures have proved counter-productive.

NATO does have much to offer. The organization's troops are trained to the level required to counter conventional, nuclear, chemical and biological threats and she enjoys a sophisticated in-being communications, command and control structure. After overseeing forty-one years of peace in Europe, NATO's capacity in this area should not be understated. Such a role is open to any designated military or political organization. The Commonwealth, which spans the First/Third World divide, seems well placed to play a positive role in a proactive field.

Inis Claude wrote that: 'NATO is not a collective security system added as an afterthought to the United Nations, but a new type of alliance'. [115] It is a distinctly separate and regionalized alliance. The Europeans have in the past endeavoured to maintain the regional distinction whereas the Americans have more than once attempted to take NATO outside the NATO defensive region. 'Division within the alliance regarding the use of military force has tended to place the United States on one side and most of its allies on the other,' wrote former deputy to the president's national security adviser, Robert Hunter.[116] He went on to forecast a continuation of this trend of the United States to seek assistance 'from European states and perhaps also other countries in meeting out of area challenges'. There is then an implied warning that: 'Increasingly, resistance on the part of its allies is likely to have a negative impact on US domestic opinion.'[117] The American position has now shifted to conform with the European Position. The terms 'in' and 'out of area' no longer represent a helpful distinction. Issues arising outside the NATO area will play an increasing role in NATO defence considerations.

A strategy for multilateral intervention capable of responding to an immediate crisis designed within the aegis of the United Nations would on first consideration appear to be a forlorn hope. It is possible, however, to circumvent the routine sloth of the UN's bureaucracy by keeping the decision-making within the Security Council. Key decisions would have been agreed prior to any military-orientated crisis arising.

Under this proposed new strategy, the world would be divided into regions. Within each region would be a predetermined and stocked Forward Operating Base (FOB). The purpose is to minimize the movement of assets by having a proportion of logistics and materiel already in-place. A FOB could be any one of the US, British or French garrisons worldwide such as Panama, Cyprus or the Ivory Coast. Alternatively, for small operations, a FOB could be seaborne, centred on carriers and Maritime Prepositioning Ships (MPS). A suitable commander is nominated and agreed by the Security Council for operations in a predetermined region supported by a FOB. Thus the scope for squabbling and recrimination is minimized. 'If we had had one single commander,' said a British officer of the MNF in Lebanon,

> we could have changed the face of what happened in Beirut. But I would not have been happy if the force commander had been an American because they could have got us into trouble. They really had no idea what was going on. Their policy seemed to be to wait in their sandbagged frontiers of freedom for something to happen and then respond with massive firepower.[118]

The prior nomination of commanders would go some way towards informing representatives of sending states of what was likely to be 'going on'. In 1918 the celebrated General Graves was preparing the 8th US Division for service on the Western Front when he was assigned to Siberia.

'I have often thought it unfortunate,' he wrote, 'that I did not know more of the conditions in Siberia than I did when I was pitchforked into the mêlée at Vladivostock.'[119]

On a national level, the United States has implemented such a plan. It has established a number of Unified Commands composed of US combat forces from two or more services with broad and continuing missions, and which are normally organized on a geographical basis. For example, the United States Central Command (USCENTCOM) whose headquarters is located in Florida, is responsible for possible tasks within most of the Middle East. What is proposed is the internationalization of the US system to improve the credibility of such a concept as well as both its acceptability and its operational feasibility.

There is no question of having standing forces permanently under UN orders. Troops will be multi-roled, probably specialist forces, tailored to fit the intended environment. Their own status and the rules of engagement will be determined prior to the launch of an operation in support of the actors within a given region. Rogue states will not be pre-identified, for such detailed contingency planning would be unworkable. Planning will be in abstraction and in co-operation with neighbouring states, with UN forces offering a higher level of power projection to combat a mutual threat.

The MSC would be the focal point for this planning and liaison. A change of title might be of benefit to appease Third World sensitivities; possibly the UN Military Planning Group (MPG). Their function would be to match suitable force structures, logistics and materiel to possible tasks, recommend regional commanders, establish a communications and control system and, not least, build up a military intelligence bank for each designated region. Which command and control regime emerges has much to do with the level of the conflict and the time available (which will be a reflection of the pre-planning achieved in relation to the target area). Thus, options could be the establishment of an international headquarters or, *in extremis*, the delegating of military command and control to one of the major, participating nations in a UN-sanctioned intervention.

RESOURCE ALLOCATION

The outline strategy thus far enumerated will require resourcing, of which the key areas for consideration are troops to tasks, funding and equipment.

Troops to tasks

The assessment of which troops and in what quantities can be made available to intervene in given regions is dependent upon a number of factors: their type and equipment; level of training and quality; the political agreement for them to operate in specific regions; their acceptability within a specific region; and linguistics.

The launch of an intervention will be subject to reaching agreement within the Security Council. It is in the political field that China, with her leadership of the Third World, can make her most significant contribution. Political and legal clearance is the first step in the deployment of forces. Those forces would invariably include representatives from the superpowers and the medium powers. There is some scope for risk reduction in the deployment of the troops, whether it be at the point of conflict or in the less vulnerable support or logistic functions. It would seem certain that irrespective of where their forces were deployed, sending states might normally expect some form of terrorist retaliation.

Troops fall into two general categories: professional and conscript. The scope for deployment of these two groups is entirely different. British and US forces are all professional, the French are mixed, and the 'Warsaw Pact' are mostly conscripts. The French Force d'Action Rapide (FAR) is a 47,000-strong force with a European and out-of-area mission. A parliamentary decision is required to deploy French conscripts on interventionist operations, so FAR comprises 60 per cent professional, mainly elitist, troops. These troops, however, are dispersed throughout every unit and sub-unit. In extracting the regular component, there is therefore a very real risk of administrative chaos and the formation in the theatre of war of *ad hoc*, unfamiliar, unrehearsed and uncoordinated units. The ending of the Cold War will lead to a re-evaluation of the numbers, role and purpose of the conscript in France and elsewhere. A French government official explained the French public sensitivity towards casualties among conscripts. 'There is a tendency in France to accept the death of professional soldiers, for that in the curious public logic is part of the risk involved in their employment. If conscripts get killed that would be a much more serious matter.'[120]

The spectre of Indo-China and Algeria is ever present in French minds. There would need to be very sound reasons for France to commit more than 1,500 men, their equipment and money to an interventionist operation. It was noted that France offered to intervene in Romania in December 1989.

It might be assumed that deployment of troops from the former Warsaw Pact countries, notably the Soviet Union, would be uncomplicated. That assumption, however, would fail to reflect the impact of the Afghanistan factor on public opinion. The *matrushkas* of this once so-called evil empire would so raise the political temperature on the announcement of the first significant conscript casualties that keeping the forces in place would be extremely difficult. The former Soviets will be able to exercise greater flexibility once they increase the proportion of professionals within their armed forces. In 1991, 60 per cent of its 2-million-strong army were conscripts, none of whom were permitted to serve within a 200-mile radius of their home town. The new Soviet Union is now moving towards a smaller, defence-orientated, professional army.

There does appear to be a military conundrum. It is represented by a past defence posture which involved massive, armoured forces facing a stable situation and a clearly defined threat compared with today's heavy reductionist influences whereby the situation is distinctly unstable and the threat imprecise. However, the sources of today's instability do not require a large numeric force commitment. The threat, or what exists as the threat, cannot be addressed by massive armoured forces. The emphasis is upon multi-skilled, professional forces with comprehensive high-tech support to confront a turbulent rather than a warlike future. It is this fact which marginalizes the future use of conscript or reserve forces. We now have a highly complex threat or rather risk scenario where what have passed as conventional military responses have become largely redundant.

The type and quantity of professional troops available for out-of-area operations is difficult to forecast since it is the current universal subject of debate. It is the area which will be weakened the least in the climate of reduction and in some cases, notably Britain, it has been strengthened. President Reagan greatly enhanced the force projection capabilities of the US Special Operation Forces (SOF). Specialist forces were expanded and, under the amazingly ambiguous description of 'Low Intensity Conflict', five light infantry divisions were formed for intervention tasks. One, the 82nd Airborne Division, was in action in Panama. A US State Department official in Moscow summed up the core problem of this wealth of strategically mobile forces for use in intervention: 'The US is among the most capable but least politically palatable.'[121]

Equipment

Few states have sufficient equipment with which to launch even a modest unilateral intervention. The United States is an exception although she, in common with the other states, suffers a severe shortage of merchant shipping for strategic sealift. 'Shipbuilding in this country,' Admiral William J. Crowe said in congressional testimony, 'and also the capacity of our merchant marine ... is dismal. It is a disaster. The maritime industry ... needs an infusion. It needs help. It needs resurrecting ... it is a national problem.'[122]

An effective co-ordination of assets could apportion equipment to tasks. For example, the United States, the United Kingdom, France and Russia have amphibious capabilities. There are sufficient resources here to cope with one or more over-the-beach operations, although it is extremely unlikely that more than one operation will be going on at any given time. Each state has a quantity of strategic aircraft and invariably they have conditions whereby they are able to call on the services of their national carriers. There is a shortage of heavy lift aircraft. France has none but did arrange the use of USAF Galaxies to support their joint intervention with Belgium in the Shaba capital of Kolwezi in 1978. The same exercise was repeated in the 1991 Zaire intervention. The Russians are introducing their heavy lift Condor to supplement the primary aircraft in their fleet, the Il-76 Candid jet transport. The transportation of one Soviet-style airborne division requires 639 Candid aircraft, which is twice the number the Commonwealth possesses. 'The Soviet Union is prepared to provide its share of logistical and transportation support for UN forces,' wrote Ambassador Aleksandr M. Belonogov, Permanent Representative of the USSR to the UN, 'and it has already done so by airlifting UN observers into Namibia.'[123]

The allocation of warships, fighter aircraft, satellite and other communications can be made from a pool of adequate, national resources. Factors to be weighed in such a deliberation would include role specialization, commonality of equipment and the level of interoperability of the forces who possess the required equipment. Again, it is a matter of making these essential assessments and attempting to secure agreement in an environment of calm consideration.

Finance

The five new [peacekeeping] operations authorised since April 1988 have increased the peace-keeping budget from a little over $200m in 1987 to about $850m in 1989 [more than the UN's regular annual budget]. If contemplated operations in Cambodia or Western Sahara come to fruition, the annual peacekeeping budget could reach $1.2–2bn.[124]

The UN has been beset by financial difficulties since the early 1960s when peacekeeping operations precipitated what has since been an ongoing crisis. There has not been a standardized system for funding UN peacekeeping operations. Some have been financed from the UN's regular budget, others by the parties involved, while others have been subject to special assessments.

It is necessary to separate proposed intervention funding from peacekeeping. The recurring problem with the funding of past peacekeeping operations is that detractors – those who have refused to pay their assessed dues – have by their action emphasized the fact that the financial support of peacekeeping is political. No state can rationally fund an activity that runs contrary to its national interest. In theory, such an objection should not prevail when the Security Council has drawn up a Resolution for intervention action. Intervention, however, is many times more expensive than peacekeeping and the difficulties must not be minimized. It is the single most important issue to be resolved by the UN.

The principal danger is that the permanent members of the Security Council might underfund and thereby threaten the enterprise at its outset, as occurred in the Namibia peacekeeping operation. There is no standard solution to the financing of UN peacekeeping and peacemaking operations.

The establishment of a rolling fund and an insurance system have been suggested, but in essence, funding will relate to the circumstances peculiar to each individual conflict. The contesting states might be 'invited' to share the burden or, perhaps, in other circumstances, multinational corporations might be involved. Every one of these proposals is fraught with political or idealistic difficulties. There are of course other paymasters outside the Security Council, such as Germany and Japan, currently debarred from intervention activities by their interpretation of the Basic Law or *Grundgesetz* and Article 9 of the Japanese Constitution respectively.

The West German constitution confines the Bundeswehr (German Army) to a defensive role within NATO's boundaries. Japan still functions under the Constitution imposed upon her by the United States at the end of the Second World War. Article 9 declares that the Japanese people renounce for ever the use of force as a means of solving international disputes. Although Japan has the third largest defence budget in the world (at just over 1 per cent of GNP), Article 9 does quite specifically forbid Japan to maintain land, sea and air forces. The rationale for the 247,000 members of the Self-Defence Forces is identical to that of the Germans, emphasizing the exclusivity of the defence function. In fact, it seems possible to interpret both sets of laws quite liberally, even to the extent of justifying physical intervention where the political will was of that mind. It is a possibility that, where it is in those two states' national interest, financial support will be forthcoming. Both states gave financial support to the 1990–1 Gulf operation. There will be a political penalty. No longer can it be assumed that Japan and Germany will wish to be passive paymasters. They will expect to be brought into the political decision-making from the beginning.

SUMMARY

States can and do act either independently or collectively in their own national interest. A state can still act collectively for selfish reasons and altruistically for unilateral reasons. The manifestation of collective action may not always represent totally fair action due to the fact that it impinges on national sovereignty. The UN's future success will depend to a large degree upon the influence of the local actors. Some will feel that they, or others, are being shabbily treated. But this proposal does not set out to be utopian panacea for all ills. It is just not possible to formulate a perfect international system to operate within an imperfect international environment. What the reader has been offered is a necessarily compressed solution to attempt to bridge what are often irreconcilable differences. Powers acting collectively will still appear to some to be unjust and far from ideal beings.

What the UN can achieve by taking up the responsibilities intended by the original drafters of the Charter in developing a new collective security system is to introduce an element of equitability, rationality and legality to interventionist operations. It is the unique circumstances of the 1990s which make it possible to respond to the 'why' and 'how' challenge put down over fifty years ago by E.H. Carr. The conditions for establishing a new collective security regime have never been more opportune. What is now required of the politicians is to demonstrate the 'will'.

Part II

POSTSCRIPT

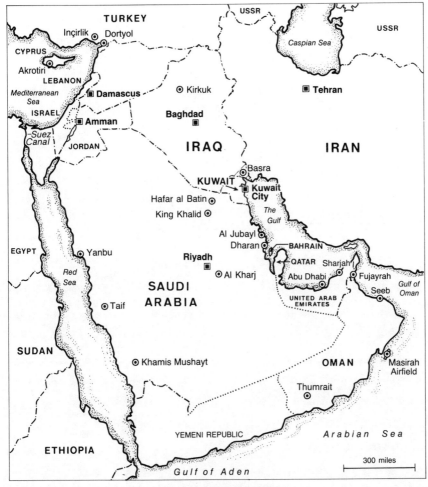

Map 1　The Middle East

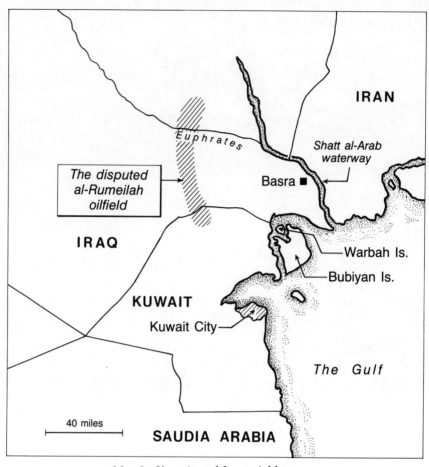

Map 2 Kuwait and her neighbours

INTRODUCTION

At the time the foregoing was being written and discussed there arose a persistent academic demand for an illustrative scenario. That desire to put the picture in a frame was deliberately sidestepped because the factors affecting and influencing military intervention are so diverse that it would be a mistake to attempt to suggest a template scenario. Some time after this concept had been drawn up, however, the Iraq/Kuwait crisis arose. It seemed a reasonable exercise or concession in lieu of a scenario to relate the theory to the actuality. Iraq's invasion of Kuwait was notable for two reasons. It was the first post-Cold War crisis and it was also the first occasion in the UN's history that one member state had claimed to annex the territory of another member state.

Having said that, it has to be recognized that Iraq's invasion of Kuwait is not, for our purposes, an ideal comparator. The original delict, the attack on Kuwait by Iraq, was not military intervention. No state gave credence to Iraq's claim that its action was taken in direct response to an appeal for help in consolidating a local coup. The USA's Permanent Representative at the UN, Ambassador Thomas Pickering, said at the time of the Iraqi blunder:

> Instead of staging their *coup d'état* and installing this so-called provisional government before the invasion, they got it the wrong way around. They invaded Kuwait and then staged the *coup d'état* in a blatant and deceitful effort to try to justify their action.

Kuwait had been subjected to an uncompromising invasion by the overwhelming power of a foreign state. Nor was the military response to Saudi Arabia's call for assistance by land and air a recognizable form of military intervention. The intervention only occurred once the predominantly US armed forces crossed over the border into Iraq and Kuwait. The pre-emptive deployment of this large force was a form of preventive diplomacy. On the other hand, once the United Nations Security Council authorized the use of force in implementing the naval embargo, that most decidedly delineated the maritime operation as a military intervention.

'The objective,' explained the *Times* editorial of 13 August 1990

> is therefore quite different from the operation in Saudi Arabia. It is aggressive, the enforcement of an economic sanction against Iraq to bring about a change in the political and military status quo. The means are the strangling of the Iraqi economy, the cessation of oil revenues, the exhaustion of the people, even the toppling of Saddam.

After a thumbnail sketch of the origins of the conflict, the concept outlined earlier will be tested against what is an admittedly untidy and not entirely apposite armed attack and its immediate consequences.

Not for the first time has a state decided upon the perceived benefits of a short, victorious war to resolve internal problems. In terms of miscalculation, none this century was more severe than the decision of imperial Russia to fight Japan in 1904. Iraq, however, on two occasions within the space of a decade has come close to challenging that inauspicious distinction. Saddam Hussein, the ruler of Iraq, is no stranger to miscalculation. In 1980 he mobilized his state's 17 million people to fight what he also thought would be a short, victorious war against the traditional enemy and regional rival, Iran. So flawed was his strategic perception that his attack was launched on the premiss of a two-week military operation. Eight years later, with Iraq's economy in ruins and his long-suffering people devastated through the loss of hundreds of thousands of lives, Saddam (the name means 'he who confronts') Hussein and Ayatollah Khomeini agreed to abide by Security Council Resolution 598, which drew to a close the bloody Gulf War.

Iraq's situation in 1990 was more parlous than it had been in 1980. The nation's strangely incongruous, even anachronistic leader – he has likened himself to Nebuchadnezzar and the Kurdish leader Saladin, while others have preferred comparisons with Hitler, Stalin and Ceausescu – was faced in 1988 with rebuilding the nation's economy. In his crusade against Iran, Saddam was generously supported by other Arab states who feared both Iranian regional expansionism and what they saw as the increasingly virulent Islamic fundamentalism. Collectively they made over $30 billion as loans. One such financial backer of Iraq was Kuwait, who made loans available to the value of $15 billion. At war's end, the more placid of Arabia's autocrats became concerned by Saddam Hussein's malignant narcissism, dangerous rhetoric, the use of institutionalized violence and his undisguised quest for leadership of the Arab world.

Arab nationalism had emerged as the ruling Iraqi Baath Arab socialist party's battle cry. The pan-Arab concept of Baathism, shared with opponents Syria, is to abandon the inherited, artificial borders and draw its strength from one unified Middle East homeland. It is not by chance that Baghdad lies in the centre of this proposed new superstate. Baghdad grew to be seen as the centre of an imaginary Arab nation. There was therefore no difficulty in adducing a curious logic that the war against Iran was not simply Iraq's war but the entire Arab nation's war. An extension of that logic would argue that as the sole fighter for Arab interests against Iran, the debts owed to 'brotherly Arab countries' had been repaid in blood. No other measure could have been more certain to turn off the financial tap serviced by the majority of Saddam Hussein's erstwhile Arab supporters.

At this point in time, therefore, the portents for Saddam succeeding in what may have been an ultimate aim of leading a unified Arabia against Israel did not appear propitious. In 1985, Iraq's Gross Domestic Product (GDP) was $46.8 billion. This was over twice that of Kuwait, yet up to 50 per cent was squandered on weaponry, the principal supplier of which was the USSR, closely followed by France. In addition, Kuwait's population of 1.9 million was eight times less than that of Iraq. The source of Iraq's problem is her almost total dependence on oil; her anticipated export income in 1990 was expected to be in the region of $16 billion, with oil accounting for 95 per cent of that total. The value of Iraq's exports normally exceeds her imports by a factor of $10 billion per annum yet that apparent surplus has to be set against servicing a foreign debt of up to $80 billion. Efforts were made at the end of the Iran/Iraq War to reduce Iraq's dependence on oil and diversify its interests through industrialization. Such a long-term strategic plan did exist in the Iraqi leader's mind but it would require both time and money, neither of which were available to the impulsive and overconfident Saddam Hussein. The invasion of Kuwait crippled any prospect of success of the important capital projects upon which Iraqi hopes of becoming an advanced industrial society were based. The western support upon which these projects' continued development depended simply evaporated.

Kuwait was a British protectorate from 1899 to 1961. In 1961 the minuscule 11,000-square-mile state secured its independence from Britain but almost immediately, on 25 June 1961, came under threat of invasion from Iraq's Abdul Karim Qasim. Only positive intervention by the Arab League, Britain and Iran prevented Iraq from gobbling up territory that had been in the ownership of the Kuwaiti al-Sabah family for over two centuries. In 1961 it had only required the deployment of one British brigade in a form of preventive diplomacy to forestall Iraqi ambitions. Kuwait was claimed by Iraq as having formerly been hers throughout the currency of the Ottoman Empire, allegedly as a province of Basra.

Iraq eventually backed off when, in 1963, a coup occurred in Baghdad. Iraq accordingly fully recognized the 'independence and complete sovereignty of Kuwait with its boundaries' as had been drawn up by the senior British envoy in the Gulf in 1922. It is said that Sir Percy Cox, bored and boiled by two days of deliberations in the burning sun at Uqair, settled the matter by drawing a red line between what is now Iraq and Kuwait. There soon followed another Baghdad coup and a resumption of claims for Kuwaiti territory, particularly the strategically placed Warba and Bubiyan islands. The 1963 joint Iraqi–Kuwaiti statement recognizing the independence of Kuwait was rejected in recent times on the grounds that it had never been put before the Iraqi National Revolutionary Council. Setting aside Iraq's acquiescence until 1990, it remains a fact that under international law boundary agreements are final unless changed by the express wishes of all the parties directly involved. That has not prevented the dispute from rumbling on. The then Iraqi Foreign Minister, Tariq Aziz, stated that the boundaries today were the work of imperialists: 'In 1930, Kuwait city was no more than a collection of mud huts.'

Iraq's fixation on securing access and egress into the Gulf is as intense as was imperial Russia's determination to secure warm-water ports. Iraq's attack on Iran was justified in part to seize exclusive use of the Shatt al-Arab waterway. But no less important is the land boundary which separates Iraq from Kuwait. It runs through the al-Rumeiliah oilfield, one of the world's richest oil-producing regions, believed to hold $750 billion in reserves. Most of the field lies in Iraq but it was Iraq's unrestrained exploitation of the field during the war with Iran which prompted Kuwait to exploit the field also. A unitization agreement would appear to be an essential prerequisite in relation to oilfields which straddle borders. 'The borders of the Gulf countries,' said Mohammed Heikal, a prominent political commentator in the Arab world, 'sprang from the British genius for creating situations which would provide reasons to keep returning.' This view was not universally accepted among Arab writers.

If Saddam had confined himself to limited objectives, such as the contested area of the oilfield and the strategic islands,[125] he might just possibly not have stirred the hornets' nest. Indeed, the following evidence suggests that the United States also might have accepted that move as a *fait accompli*. The central message of the invasion was aimed not at America but at the Arabs[126] and the core of that message was the removal of the al-Sabah family from Kuwait city – *pour encourager les autres*. Tariq Aziz heatedly responded to Saudi criticism by saying:

> The economic situation in Iraq was so bad that it had no other choice than to resort to such methods. It had reached the stage where Iraq no longer had faith in promises that Gulf states would help it out of its crisis.

After the divisions brought about by the Camp David accords, Kuwait aligned itself with the moderate interests in the Middle East under the leadership of Saudi Arabia. Pragmatically diplomatic, it was the only Arab state until 1985 to have diplomatic relations with both East and West. That undoubtedly proved to be a good insurance policy. During the Iran/Iraq War, Kuwaiti territory and oil tankers came under attack from Iranian missiles as reprisals for supporting Saddam Hussein's regime. It was as a result of these attacks that in the last year of the then Gulf conflict, the US Navy escorted Kuwaiti tankers and the Stars and Stripes became, for a short while, a flag of convenience.

Kuwait, which is essentially a city-state, continued to flourish under the paternal autocracy of the al-Sabah dynasty, owing its wealth almost entirely to oil. Kuwait and Iraq produce 20 per cent of the world's oil supplies. Only 40 per cent of Kuwait's population is indigenous to that state and it is only bona-fide Kuwaitis who enjoy the full benefits of the state's wealth in terms of social and welfare support. Nevertheless, with a GDP of $19 billion, the per capita income was extremely high, in the region of $13,000 per annum. The significance of that statistic on Kuwait's neighbouring Arab states is of economic importance in terms of customs dues and homeward remittances. Forty-eight per cent of Kuwait's *Gastarbeiters* were Arabs, mostly Palestinians, Jordanians and Egyptians. Menial tasks were undertaken by Asian helots but the most significant grouping, as events would prove, were thousands of westerners employed for their special skills such as civil engineering.

Before the Gulf War, the OPEC-imposed production restrictions and the fall in oil prices had served to reduce oil income. Kuwait had, however, already diversified into the financial market with financial reserves prior to the invasion estimated at $80 billion, which meant that for the previous four years the state had derived more through foreign investments, managed in the main by the secretive London-based Kuwait Investment Office (KIO), than she did through the sale of oil. Meanwhile to the north, the lionized leader of Iraq was struggling with the real problems of balancing the demands of the state's growing band of significant creditors. Finance was not his only problem

Of all the characters that fifty-three-year-old Saddam Hussein is said by his behaviour to resemble, there is arguably one other whose characteristics he partially shares – Mao Tse Tung. There existed in Iraq (and still exists in some areas) a strangely anachronistic Saddamist cult of personality resembling the fawning adulation of Mao. 'The media maintain a non-stop drumfire of adulation which strains the rhetorical powers of even the Arab language,' wrote Anthony Parsons:

> Massive, hideous statuary bestrides the avenues and, most bizarre of all, huge billboards representing Saddam in different costumes and postures line not only the streets of cities and towns but march at regular intervals deep into the countryside. There is something for everyone: Saddam the dauntless warrior, Saddam the Kurdish chieftain (a touch of irony there), Saddam in Arab robes, Saddam the dreamy academic, Saddam the captain of industry, Saddam the jovial uncle.

A reason for this unusual Arab behaviour lies in the need to maintain the cohesion of a modern Iraqi state which had its origins in an untidy post-First World War settlement. The newly created, artificial state of Iraq brought together for an uneasy relationship the Kurds of Mosul, the Shias of Basra and the Sunnis of Baghdad. Shias represent half of Iraq's population, with Sunnis and Kurds accounting for approximately a quarter each. Saddam Hussein is a Sunni and therefore represents a minority in Iraq. Prior to the latest war, Shias and Sunnis had lived in relative harmony. The war against Iran served to strengthen tribal links but an equilibrium of fear was maintained by the 80,000-strong Amn Al Kass, Iraq's secret police led by Saddam's son-in-law, Hussein Kamil. Ever since Saddam Hussein became president in July 1979 order had been maintained through terror and also through a battle waged principally against the autonomy-inclined Kurds. Among the 1.5-million membership of the Baath party is a hard core of 50,000 activists and informants. They are Iraq's own version of the Red Guard, whipping up revolutionary zeal, idolizing Saddam and serving as the front line in the identification of opponents. In Iraq, power is maintained through the barrel of a gun.

Although outwardly there appeared to be calm in this police state, there was an underlying disaffection among the educated class. There has been a discernible objection to inexplicable and permanent disappearances, to the inability to engage in political dialogue with foreigners, as well as to the lack of personal economic fulfilment. What the revolution in Eastern Europe proved was the close linkage between economic aspirations and political liberalization.

The greatest internal threat to Saddam Hussein came from the Army, particularly the officer corps, who have had to concede power to their president and subordinate themselves to the Baath Party. Today Field-Marshal Saddam masquerades in military uniform pretending not to be what he has always been, a professional civilian. As a young man, he failed to gain entry into the military academy and has never been a soldier. The anticipated short 1990–1 war promising big benefits appeared to be a solution to re-engage the 300,000 demobilized, unhoused and unemployed veterans of the war with Iran. But unpopular as the al-Sabah family may have been, the Emir's people were first and foremost Arabs: this was different from fighting the traditional enemy, Iran. The Egyptian semi-official newspaper *al-Ahram* reported the execution of 120 Iraqi officers for refusing to go to war against Kuwait, just as those before them, who had engineered seven assassination attempts and at least one failed coup, were similarly disposed of. The Army remains the president's Achilles' heel and it was his vulnerability here that seemed certain to be exploited by the intelligence agencies of the growing number of countries opposed to his rule.

This is not to say that elsewhere within the Arab world there is not an element of respect for an Arab leader who will stand up against Israel and the West. There is significant support throughout Arabia for the Palestinian perception that here, at last, in Saddam Hussein is a rare Arab leader, capable of taking the lead in regaining Arab territory seized in 1967 and obliging Israel to comply with Security Council resolutions. 'Hussein awakened the desire in every Arab soul for a glorious Arab stand,' the Jordanian newspaper *Ad Dustour* reported. 'His combative tone awakened every Arab's longing to respond to his nation's enemies with language not used for a long time.' The war served to confirm that the ideology of Islam is a powerful, uniting force for the Third World. Not since Nasser had any one single Arab leader attracted such widespread support or generated such genuine enthusiasm. Saddam Hussein remembered what Nasser had done in 1967 when he had associated himself with the Palestinian cause. Then, as now, the Palestinians would be the worse for the experience.

The outrage felt in the West by the hanging of the Iranian-born *Observer* reporter, Farzad Bazoft, was in contrast to Iraq and her supporters' dismissal of the protest as evidence of a western conspiracy. The support of Libya's Colonel Gadaffi is predictable, yet even he condemned the invasion of Kuwait. Less predictable at first was the acquiescence of Jordan's soldier-king, Hussein. He was in an extraordinarily difficult position. His virtually oil-barren nation is an economic colony of Iraq[127] and his people, over 60 per cent of whom are Palestinian, applauded Saddam Hussein's direct action and use of the big stick. The King's was a very difficult tightrope to walk, for if he had fallen the whole conduit of Jordan's territory would have brought Iraqi interests right up to Israel's eastern border. It is a tightrope the old-Harrovian, ex-Sandhurst monarch has balanced upon for over thirty-eight years. The region's geo-strategic realities are not lost upon him. President Bush's insistence that the King should decide on one side or the other represented a curious misappreciation of King Hussein's position. Israel's Foreign Minister, Moshe Levy, said on Israeli radio on 3 August 1990 that 'The movement of Iraqi forces into Jordan would represent a real and immediate threat to Israel.'

Through some massaging of genealogy, Iraq's leader, the son of a Takriti peasant, has been determined to be a descendant of Hashemi, a descendant of Mohammed. There is therefore some nebulous claim of a relationship between Jordan's and Iraq's Husseins. Strangely, however, there was a genuine political and personal rapport between the two leaders.

At what stage Saddam Hussein decided on a short, victorious war against Kuwait, both to solve his nepotocracy's dramatic economic problems and to resolve the long-standing territorial issues in addition to bonding his disparate tribes, is not yet clear. It was, however, on 17 July 1990 that the first perceptible move against Kuwait (and the other Gulf states) was made. Saddam Hussein claimed that the Gulf states had used 'a poisoned dagger' to stab Iraq in the back by depressing the price of oil and exceeding OPEC production quotas. There was some truth in that claim but it hardly amounted to a *casus belli*. The next day, at a meeting of the Arab League, Iraq's Foreign Minister Tariq Aziz claimed that Kuwait had stolen $2.4 billion of Iraqi oil and, furthermore, had laid out defensive positions on Iraq's soil. Kuwait rejected the allegations. Claim and counter-claim continued for four days until 22 July 1990, when Tariq Aziz arrived in Cairo to attend an emergency Arab summit.

Kuwait insisted that the problem should be resolved by the Arabs without foreign involvement. Meanwhile, the Baghdad newspapers claimed that the Kuwaiti foreign minister was an agent of the USA. The tension in the Middle East had already caused oil prices to rise as Iraq had wished. Iraq was still not satisfied, insisting that OPEC should force the price even higher. On 24 July, 100,000 heavily armed Iraqis deployed on the Kuwaiti border. Western observers determined that the troops' function was to intimidate, not to invade Kuwait. Indeed, Saddam Hussein promised that they would not invade Kuwait. President Mubarak of Egypt, believing Saddam, indulged in urgent shuttle diplomacy in Baghdad, Kuwait and Jeddah. OPEC agreed to raise the price of a barrel of oil to $21, but still Iraq was not satisfied.

On 1 August 1990 the talks in Jeddah between Kuwait and Iraq collapsed. Kuwait refused to accede to Iraqi demands for Kuwaiti territory. At 2 a.m. local time on 2 August, to the embarrassment of western intelligence analysts,[128] 30,000 Iraqi troops led by the elite Presidential Republican Guard Corps and *coup de main* heliborne detachments invaded Kuwait. According to Baghdad radio, their *Anschluss* was in response to a call from young revolutionaries who had mounted a coup attempt. Kuwait's 23,000-strong armed forces were taken completely by surprise and only in some areas was there sporadic fighting. Other than isolated acts of armed resistance, which would continue throughout the early stages of the occupation, Kuwait city had been subdued in just thirty-six hours. The sixty-two-year-old Emir escaped to Saudi Arabia in a helicopter, but his younger brother, Sheikh Fahd, was killed fighting on the steps of the Dasman Palace. Kuwait means 'small fortress'; against a large, surprise Iraqi attack, it did prove to be a too small and too unprepared fortress.

A Transitional Free Government announced that the Emir and his 'stooges' had been deposed. Saddam compared the Emir with the fabulously rich, sixth-century BC King Croesus. He was the 'Croesus of Kuwait and his aides became the obedient, humiliated and treacherous dependants of foreigners'. It was the thus far unknown new government's intention that

the interim free government, after securing necessary stability in the country will hold free and honest elections [which would be a novelty in both Iraq and Kuwait] to elect a new assembly which represents the people and will decide the form of government and other basic issues.

The 'token institutions' established by the al-Sabah family were denounced in a 'pot calling the kettle black' statement which declared the Kuwaiti institutions to be 'nothing but a cover for nepotistic and despotic rule. It was widely reported at the time that the Iraqi 'stooge' leading the nine-member Transitional Free Government was Colonel Ali Hassan al-Majid.

Not only was he prime minister, commander-in-chief and defence and interior minister but exiled Kuwaitis claimed (vehemently denied by Iraq) that he was Saddam's son-in-law. (He was removed from office in November 1990 and re-emerged after the war, in March 1991, as interior minister.) Ali Hassan al-Majid was formerly the Iraqi local government minister. It is also believed that he was responsible for crushing the 1987-8 Kurdish rebellion when he was serving as the senior Baath party member in Kurdistan. 'Brother Arabs in Kuwait,' the appeal continued, 'the free interim government of Kuwait greets you and calls on you to support the uprising of your free brothers. You are our relatives. What is ours is yours and our tasks are your tasks.' There were words of reassurance and good intent towards the thousands of resident foreigners, subject to them behaving. If they did not, they would be hit with 'an iron fist'.

Before the thirty-six hours had elapsed it had become apparent to Saddam Hussein that again he had blundered and had made a serious miscalculation in attacking Kuwait. He had gambled on a near-certainty that the world would accept the *fait accompli* of the invasion. Iraq's *al-Jumhuriya* newspaper advised that 'the imperialist forces should accept the fact and acknowledge it no matter how bitter it tastes in their stinking mouths'. Not only did the imperialist forces not accept the fact, neither did the Soviet Union, who had an in-being treaty of friendship and co-operation with Iraq. Almost as surprising was the condemnation emanating from a majority within the Arab League, which extinguished Saddam Hussein's hopes of a pan-Arab state. All these threads culminated in the Security Council censure of Baghdad by their Resolution 660.

Iraq has enjoyed only two years of peace during Saddam Hussein's presidency. One of the results of the years of war was to limit Saddam's freedom to travel abroad. Besides, autocrats are by nature loath to leave their power base too often and instead surround themselves with minders, who limit access to the president. This meant that Iraq's president was the least internationally streetwise of the Arabian leaders for, first, he had totally failed to register the important growth in world interdependence which had by chance coincided with the end of the Gulf War and secondly, if he had noticed the ending of the Cold War, he had failed to grasp its significance in terms of the potential for superpower co-operation. Absolutists are not surrounded by outspoken, impartial advisers who give balanced judgements. His foreign policy representatives had become diplomatic neuters. The consequences of giving Saddam advice he did not want to hear had often proved to be fatal. Foreign minister Tariq Aziz was (wrongly) reported to have been executed for opposing the invasion. The fifty-three-year-old politician is a Christian with a degree in English literature and is well versed in the nuances of western politics. Outwardly, however, he behaved as an obedient party *apparatchik*, aware of both the quality and tone of advice required.

Prior to the conflict, Saddam Hussein drew his military advice from a committee of three generals. One, who came from the Mosul area, was not thought to have any influence. Of the other two, one came from the city of Takrit and the other, said to be the second most powerful man in the state, was the fifty-year-old Brigadier Hussein Kamil Hassan al-Majid Takriti. Saddam Hussein's cousin and son-in-law, he is also a representative of the Takrit mafia. He was in charge of the high-profile Iraqi weapons development programme operating under the umbrella of the Military Industry Commission (MIC). He was also thought to be the president's successor and policy adviser but, conscious of his own and colleagues' need for personal security, he would in all probability have given the president an inflated assessment of Iraqi forces' capabilities. Hussein Kamil fell from power in November 1991 after a power struggle with Ali Hassan al-Majid, who succeeded him as defence minister. The prospect of a military schism existing outside the fractured clique was highly probable, for Iraq's professional officers would have been acutely conscious of their army's capabilities and prospects of military success against the growing Allied forces. The professional military were doubtless aware of the concept of air–land operations developing in the West and the significance that concept had for possible conflict in the Middle East. The thought of a divide between Saddam Hussein and the military, however, was not universally held. A conclusion following the Iran/Iraq war was that

Iraq won the war through its own efforts and skill, and a substantial amount of credit for this must go to the Iraqi military. The officers adopted the doctrine needed to take the offensive and then drilled their troops to bring them to a high level of proficiency. Overall, the Iraqi officer corps is professionalized and obviously has pride in its accomplishments. There is virtually no sign that the Iraqi army is estranged from the regime; if anything it appears to be its mainstay.[129]

Saddam's decision to take direct command of Iraq's armed forces against the Allies would not have been greeted by his generals with universal approval. The poverty of his strategic prowess did not deter him from interfering in earlier military affairs. In 1986, for example, a series of battlefield disasters obliged a quorum of generals to face up to him and insist that his further meddling in the war would lead to an Iraqi defeat. So parlous had the military situation become that Saddam had to accede and back off but he never forgave, and every member of the group of generals which confronted him disappeared. By drawing together the military and political leadership, Saddam Hussein accentuated the possibility of a military coup. It might have been a sensible military appreciation to give up Kuwait in order to save Iraq. But, due to his own personal involvement, Saddam Hussein was firmly committed to retaining Kuwait.

It was from 1988 that the 'Ceausescu-ization' of Saddam Hussein became most apparent. Historically his country had been the centre of world power and the seat of a dozen empires. He harked back to these past glories of Iraq rather than becoming aware of the changes that had occurred around him. In the past, if he had a supply problem with one state he could always rely on finding another state willing to sell him what he wanted. When the USSR refused to release weaponry for the duration of his occupancy of Iranian territory, he turned instead to France and other western states. Saddam could pick and choose among the western and Warsaw Pact countries so long as he could offer them political, diplomatic and economic benefit. At a stroke, his invasion of Kuwait made him dispensable.

The Soviet newspaper *Rabochaya Tribuna* was unimpressed by Iraq's claim that the intervention had been by invitation. They had, of course, seen it all before: 'We have learned how to send in troops in response to an appeal or in order to block possible foreign interference.' The paper concluded that the 'crime' had been committed because Baghdad 'does not want to pay the bills from the Arab countries which helped it during the conflict with Iran'. The more authoritative Soviet news agency, Tass took the view that Iraq's deliberate aggression was 'to resolve at one go all its acute political and economic problems: to boost the price of crude oil, to get from Kuwait $2.4 billion in compensation and to write off its $15 billion debt'. With these strong words had come the suspension of Soviet arms supplies to Iraq. When Moscow was faced with the choice between supporting a wayward friend and damaging her new image as a responsible actor in foreign affairs it was clear that Iraq was expendable. There was also evidence in both Moscow and Washington of a guilt complex for their part in nurturing the monster. All along, however, Moscow attempted to keep a bridge open to Baghdad.

Saddam Hussein enjoyed western support during the struggle with Iran in which Iraq suffered equally with Iran. Nevertheless, Saddam went on to claim victory, and it was a victory of sorts because, in neutralizing Iran, he had opened up the prospect of marching on Kuwait without the fear of intervention by his eastern neighbour. Although Saddam's inability to grasp the finer points of strategy led to his failure in achieving the military objectives against Iran, he enjoyed the support of both superpowers and most of the Arab world. In taking Kuwait, Saddam possessed the strength to achieve his military objectives but this was at the expense of the alienation of both superpowers and most of the Arab world. His political foundation had crumbled. There was to be no political victory and in his dalliance, while the United States and Arab forces reinforced Saudi Arabia, he also let slip the military initiative. This would not herald an immediate collapse, for despite domestic deprivation, cruelty and excesses, the settling of the account with the rich in Kuwait had restored some of the pride of the suffering Iraqi population.

Kuwait was the first domino to tumble in a long-term strategy designed to end in a triumphant final act with a victorious showdown with Israel. Saddam calculated that such an aim was indeed achievable. Iraq had proved to be a useful sponge for international weaponry, goods and foodstuffs as well as being a beneficial target to divert the attention of what had become an obsessive western phobia of a volatile, virulent and unstable form of Iranian fundamentalism. The western aim had been to neutralize Iran through the willing surrogacy of Iraq. At the time, the USA would have clutched at any straw that promised to assuage the humiliation suffered during the siege of the American Embassy in Tehran. The irony is that Saddam Hussein posed a far greater threat to moderate states in the Gulf, and therefore to Gulf security, than was ever posed by the Ayatollah Khomeini.

The support of Saddam came at a price. The USA shrugged off the twin Exocet attack by an Iraqi Mirage F1 on the USS *Stark* with the loss of thirty-seven lives in order to preserve a trade agreement and keep Saddam sweet. He was a man who enjoyed a charmed and unrealistic life in international politics. His abysmal record on human rights and acts of genocide were overlooked by the West so as not to cause waves at a time when Security Council Resolution 598 was being seriously considered. One US senator, Claiborne Pell, Chairman of the Senate Foreign Relations Committee, attempted to have sanctions imposed on Iraq as a protest against that country's human rights record. The Reagan administration intervened to squeeze the sanction move out. Iraq remained the beneficiary of a kind of deceptive support which was only good for as long as it suited the power brokers. Saddam's sabre-rattling was discernible from a speech in Amman on 24 February 1990, but as the rhetoric grew both louder and more frequent, governments were warned by their advisers not to over-react. The journalist responsible for a strong, anti-Saddam broadcast on the Voice of America on 15 February 1990 was sacked. Iraq's name was not to appear on the list of the most persistent violators before the UN Commission on Human Rights even at a time when Amnesty International and the Washington-based Middle East Watch loudly accused Iraq of the most grotesque violations of human rights. The Iraqi's also induced a number of developing countries to do a deal so that Baghdad would not be criticized.

With such a record, the judicial murder of the alleged spy Farzad Bazoft was already preordained. The execution, in Iraq's eyes, emphasized their superiority. After implementing diplomatic action, the British government worked hard to ensure that the trade links between the two countries had not been irreparably damaged by the justifiable public outcry of protest. In 1982 Iraq became Britain's biggest Middle East customer after Saudi Arabia and, in the two years since the earlier Gulf War, British export credits amounted to £690 million. It now seems that the Export Credit Guarantee Department has lost hundreds of millions of pounds. It was immediately following Saddam's worst chemical attack on the Kurds that Britain doubled Iraq's exports credit guarantee. The London *Times* of 3 August 1990 commented: 'Observers believe that episode convinced President Saddam that, as long as Iraq had money to spend abroad, all avowed concern for human rights in the world would remain hypocrisy.'

False signals emanated not only from London but also, and more importantly, from Washington. At the time when Iraq mobilized on the border, Congress had enacted a series of unilateral economic measures against Iraq. The Congress initiative was to be opposed both by the State Department and by the White House, who wanted to 'keep the dialogue open'. They saw in sanctions a weakening of the USA's leverage on Saddam Hussein, something which was not in the USA's foreign policy interests. The day after the Under-Secretary of Commerce, Dennis Kloske, testified in the House that he had recommended more stringent controls on the export of US high technology to Iraq, he was dismissed. The immorality of the Iraqi regime had been regularly exposed by the Middle East Watch and openly acknowledged by the most recent State Department review of human rights violations.

Business considerations, however, relegated these widely held moral objections to the giving of unproductive lectures. On 15 June 1990 the State Department's assistant-secretary of state for Near Eastern affairs appeared before the Senate Foreign Relations Committee to justify the administration's appeasement of Saddam Hussein. Trade sanctions against Iraq were not the way forward because, according to the State Department's representative, 'our competitors in Canada, Australia, Europe and Japan would step in quickly to fill the breach'. Iraq was an important US export market, taking US $1 billion of agricultural products each year, including cattle, chickens, eggs, tobacco and 23 per cent of the nation's total rice output. Two months later, during a committee hearing in the House of Representatives, the Democrats blamed the State Department for pursuing a policy which, they felt, might have encouraged Iraq to invade Kuwait. It had been a 'policy premised in fiction and fantasy'. The BBC World Service broadcast a statement, by Assistant-Secretary John Kelly to Congress, that there was no treaty obligation with Kuwait which would require US forces to defend Kuwait.

The State Department's Near East bureau was not the only source from which Saddam Hussein might have claimed to have misinterpreted signals emanating from the USA. He warned the US ambassador, April Glaspie, that he would take whatever steps were necessary to halt Kuwait's economic war against Iraq. Allegedly speaking on the instructions of Secretary of State Baker, Ambassador Glaspie said, according to the Iraqi transcript, that the USA had 'no opinion on the Arab–Arab conflicts, like your border disagreement with Kuwait'. The *Washington Post* emphasizes the similarities of the presumed, diplomatic *faux pas* between Kuwait and what had happened in Korea. The attack on South Korea by the North was said by some authorities to have been triggered by the State Department's exclusion of Korea from within the USA's defensive perimeter. According to the *Washington Post*:

> The substance of Miss Glaspie's recorded remarks closely parallels official US positions stated in Washington at the same time, in which other state officials publicly disavowed any American security commitments to Kuwait.

Later, the hapless Miss Glaspie explained to the *New York Times*: 'Obviously I didn't think and nobody else did, that the Iraqi's were going to take *all* of Kuwait.'[130] What she may have intended to signal to Saddam Hussein was the alleged State Department's official position that there was no fundamental objection to Iraq taking Warba and Bubiyan islands. Interestingly, Secretary Baker did not resign, as Foreign Secretary Lord Carrington did after the Foreign Office misread Argentine intentions towards the Falklands.

April Glaspie made no further public statements after her *New York Times* interview until she appeared before the Senate Foreign Relations Committee in April 1991. The administration had not wished to divert the attention of the anti-Iraq coalition. She told the committee that the Iraqi transcript had been edited to such a degree that it was 'disinformation'. She said that Saddam had been made aware of Washington's intention to defend its vital interests in the Gulf and of its support for the sovereignty and integrity of the Gulf states. Was this a classic case of plausible deniability? April Glaspie left her critics with a simple choice of 'Saddam's words or mine'.

State Department exasperation over Israeli intransigence sent a false message to Baghdad that the State Department, whose attention was also held by troubles nearer home in Trinidad and Liberia, had adopted a more *laissez-faire* attitude towards a client so despised by Iraq. What these unintentional, small fragments of international body language added up to in Baghdad was the mistaken, cumulative view that indecision and hesitancy was a sign of either weakness or uninterest, or both. All that this appeasement had achieved was the feeding of the Thief of Baghdad's megalomaniac appetite. He had come to the conclusion that the West would not be prepared to suffer the quantity of casualties that would be required to stop his ambition. He boasted to April Glaspie that 'Yours is a society which cannot accept 10,000 dead in one battle.' It would transpire that the shoe was on the other foot when 'the mother of all battles' suffered a severe miscarriage.

But the diplomatic and economic appeasement, which had been a feature up until 2 August 1990, was set aside. The United States, the Soviet Union, Britain and the rest of Europe had all suffered the consequences of the appeasement of Hitler. They remembered their history and determined to stop Saddam Hussein's attempt at Arab hegemony in the 'Rhineland' of Kuwait.

If Saddam's former clients were at fault for what had come to pass it was the fault of not making their intentions clear. Mention has been made of similar misconceptions arising in the minds of the aggressors in Korea in 1950 and the Falklands in 1982 when they too had misread international body language. The time to have 'drawn the line in the sand' was on 24 July 1990, and the place to have drawn it was the Iraq/Kuwait border in front of the 100,000 massed Iraqi troops. It had been an error of judgement not to have convened a meeting of the Security Council to warn off Iraq and to have backed that warning with the precautionary move of significant force into the Gulf. In such a situation, it would have been possible to initiate the Soviet concept of preventive diplomacy whereby a force would be established on the Kuwait side of the border with the permission of Kuwait. The force might arguably have forestalled Saddam Hussein, but such an action is more certain to succeed in less cut-and-dried circumstances. Preventive diplomacy should be seen as a trip-wire deterrent by which violation is linked to certain retaliation. A discreet US 'short notice exercise' was held in the Gulf 600 miles south of the Iraq/Kuwait border, but it failed to intimidate Saddam. Judith Kipper of the Brookings Institution said: 'I think we have enough experience of the Iraqi approach to protecting what it says are its interests to know that if Hussein puts troops on the border he is not bluffing.' Saddam's *bête noire*, Senator Claiborne Pell, claimed that had President Bush (and presumably Reagan) responded to previous Iraqi crimes, Saddam Hussein might have got the message that his lawlessness would not be tolerated. Pell likened Saddam to 'the Adolf Hitler of the Middle East. Like Hitler, he is emboldened when there is no reaction to his outrages.' A week after the invasion of Kuwait had occurred, President Bush admitted:

If history teaches us anything, it is that we must resist aggression or it will destroy our freedoms. Appeasement does not work. As was the case in the 1930s, we see in Saddam Hussein an aggressive dictator threatening his neighbours.

Years before, George Kennan described the influence of the foreign Czech army in Russia in the context of a post-Russian Revolution environment:

Had the Corps succeeded in making its way through the vast tinder-box of central Siberia during the Spring of 1918, striking no sparks and raising no crucial issues as it went along, this – rather than what actually occurred – would have been the true wonder.[131]

The same was true of the Gulf. The concern uppermost in the minds of leaders in many state capitals was the influence their own and other forces could exert upon the political and economic life within the ethnic and religious tinderbox of the Middle East.

Saddam Hussein learned an important lesson from the 1967 Six Day War and from the ease of destruction of the Osiraq nuclear reactor. Subsequent builds within Iraq were of special, hardened facilities. In some years, up to 50 per cent of GNP had been allocated to defence. Three hundred super aircraft bunkers were among the protected facilities that this money acquired in a multimillion-pound British contract. The concrete and steel shelters were built on eight new air bases, three of which were in the north of the country. The roofs were made of steel, above which was a four-feet-thick layer of reinforced concrete below a deep sand covering, which provided both camouflage and additional protection. The doors, protected by a concrete and sandblast wall, were made of two-feet-thick steel and concrete and weighed 40 tons. The one or more aircraft in each shelter were thought to be virtually immune from damage. Events would prove that they were not.

The interregnum from the time when the Iraqi Army so unwisely marched into Kuwait until the separate Allied operations coalesced into the American-led Operation Desert Storm had lasted five months and thirteen days. Throughout that period, the search for a diplomatic solution had run parallel with a slow-working, but what might nonetheless have been an ultimately successful, embargo. Three quite separate sets of positions emerged. First it became increasingly evident that in no circumstances would Saddam Hussein relinquish his hold on Kuwait. He, as Stalin and Hitler before him, was prepared to defend his position in his capital from a secure bunker, fighting to the last Iraqi. Secondly, there was a genuinely held desire for a peaceful settlement based upon Iraq's unconditional withdrawal from Kuwait. This was principally a European goal but Europe had been weakened through being marginalized by Saddam Hussein's dismissive treatment and also through its ill-concealed divisions. It is a truism of international relations that coalition governments rarely respond positively in crises by strong and uncompromising foreign policy. It was during the course of this diplomatic phase that Europe's aspirations to be seen as a political force in the world took a decidedly backward step. 'To be brutally frank,' admitted Jacques Delors with unusual candour to the European Parliament on 23 January 1991, 'public opinion sensed that Europe was rather ineffectual.' Finally, there were also within the equation others who, while prepared to mouth the utterances of diplomacy, had private hopes that Saddam Hussein would indeed decline to withdraw from Kuwait.

One of the conditions for Iraq's withdrawal leading to 'peace and security in the area' was an Allied guarantee that Iraqi territory would be spared subsequent military action. A number of opposing states took the view that this would be little more than an exercise in papering over cracks, of postponing an inevitable conflict and one which, in time, could but increase the potential of the magnitude of Iraq's destructive force. Among the states to hold such a view were Israel and certain Arab states within the Allied coalition. On Wednesday, 16 January 1991, less than twenty-four hours after the expiry of the United Nations deadline, the air and naval onslaught went ahead.

The intervention proper to liberate Kuwait had begun. Facing each other on the Saudi–Kuwait border were an estimated 1.2 million servicemen from Iraq and the military representatives of seventeen states who had contributed to the coalition land order of battle: At 440,000, the US force level had grown to three-quarters as many as there had ever been in Vietnam. In addition, contributions from other Allied states exceeded 265,000. There were erroneous reports that over half the Iraqi Army – 500,000 – were deployed in or in support of their defence of Kuwait. Subsequent assessments suggest that figure may have been exaggerated. The combined strength of the forty-two divisions facing the Allies probably numbered 350,000. Nevertheless, this conflict was big in every respect. The first air attack was of three hours' duration, and in that one period aircraft and the $1.3 million Tomahawk Cruise missiles had delivered with great accuracy 18,000 tons of high explosives on pre-selected Iraqi targets. This tonnage was equivalent to that dropped on Hiroshima and was twice that required to destroy the German city of Dresden. Air power made the highly successful hundred-hour land campaign possible.

It might seem curious, therefore, that the facing up of such powerful forces would not have led to a declaration of war. The legal state or condition of war can only exist where one or more states makes an unequivocal, non-rhetorical war declaration. Saddam Hussein's call for a jihad or holy war does not fall within that category. It was the involvement of the United Nations which acted to ensure that a state of war between Iraq and others would not exist. Unlike in Korea, the Allied troops in the Gulf were not put under nominal UN command but there is no doubt that they had the UN's authority to take enforcement action to oblige Iraq to comply with those UN Resolutions relating to Kuwait. Whether or not war has been declared does not absolve parties of the armed conflict from their freely entered-into obligations under the 1949 Geneva Conventions and the body of international law.

What this crisis demonstrated was the need to investigate the means by which the United Nations would be given positive and credible command functions and an overall higher visibility. That requires the construction of the requisite political and military architecture. Given that the Allied offensive against Iraq and occupied Kuwait was under the UN umbrella, it seems a curious oversight not to have informed the UN Secretary-General when the attack was launched. There was a suspicion among some of the Allies that the UN was being manipulated and used selectively in order to achieve the undeclared aims of the Pax Americana. What irked a number of Europeans was the consistent and unilateral lead taken by the Americans in the decision-making process.

What follows is not intended to be either a political or a military record of the Gulf crisis. It is the validation of the foregoing theories and principles against the events in one admittedly very large and highly significant military intervention. The 1990–1 Gulf crisis is not an ideal model either to evaluate intervention principles or to argue for a convincing, comprehensive re-evaluation of defence policy. The Gulf War was unique. So unambiguous and exceptional had been Saddam's aggression that a repetition is unlikely to be permitted. At the time of writing, however, as a contemporary and topical event it is the best model available. The format to be used in this examination will be through the use of the 'Why' and 'How' structure introduced earlier.

WHY?

INSTABILITY IN LARGE PARTS OF THE THIRD WORLD

The invasion of Kuwait by Iraq on 2 August 1990 was the most positive manifestation of the latent instability in the Middle East succumbing to the unequal pressure and boiling over. Few would disagree that when the crisis was finally resolved, the Middle East would in some respects not be the same again. It is true that the war largely restored the status quo *ante bellum*, but political realignments will be confirmed, autocracies will come under the microscope and pressure will be sustained to resolve the outstanding problem of the Israeli occupation of Palestinian land.

Throughout the currency of the Gulf crisis, Israel had been encouraged by the USA to maintain a low profile. It was from such a position that she observed, to her alarm, the unanimous adoption by the Security Council of Resolution 681. The terms of the Resolution roundly condemned Israel's treatment of the Palestinian population in the occupied territory. What was conceded was the prospect of the oft-discussed Middle East conference, now perceived as the first essential step towards resolving the Arab–Israeli dispute. Saddam Hussein had latterly conspired to link the resolution of the Kuwait problem with a satisfactory solution of Palestinian claims, the hope being that self-inflicted defeat in Kuwait might translate into victory in Palestine. This initiative was a ploy to save his own skin, but the promulgation of Resolution 681 could be seen as Saddam Hussein winning a point. The US administration, however, steadfastly maintained that there was no linkage, insisting, according to Ambassador Pickering, that the conference would be held 'at an appropriate time', as indeed it was, in Madrid.

The Middle East is strewn with political minefields and bear traps awaiting unwary foreigners. The Kuwait crisis demonstrated the kind of fragility that can exist in the relationship between host and donor states. Outlooks, customs, religions and conventions can be very different and, over a period of time, can become the source of serious friction. Israel has shown that she pays little heed to UN initiatives. Meanwhile, Yasser Arafat's highly acclaimed recognition of Israel's right to exist as a state and the renunciation of terrorism was utterly marginalized by the subsequent PLO alignment with Saddam Hussein. Certainly, it helped to take the pressure off Yitzhak Shamir's hard-line, right-wing government. If that now means that the Israeli government will feel less constrained in annexing the West Bank into a greater Israel settled by incoming immigrants, then serious instability will remain a continuing feature in the Middle East. However, the big political surprise to have emerged after the Gulf War is the position taken by President Bush as the honest broker between the Israelis and Palestinians. Having set aside Israel's previous favoured status, there is now an outside prospect for a compromise solution to the Palestine problem. As a result of his uncompromising anti-Israeli position, it is not difficult to understand how a man as undeniably hideous as Saddam Hussein can command a broad cross-section of Arab support and admiration. The Israeli/Palestinian ulcer proved to be a welcome sore left unattended for too long upon which Saddam Hussein, with characteristic opportunism, unjustifiably yet effectively focused. A political solution here which will guarantee Israel's security as well as Israel's compliance with Resolution 242 would go a long way towards achieving regional stability.

During the course of the Gulf crisis the issue of weapons of mass destruction, nuclear, biological and chemical (n.b.c.) emerged as requiring urgent, international consideration and legislation. The majority of the well established nuclear-exporting states belong to an organization known as the London Suppliers Club (LSC). The LSC acts as an informal control mechanism overseeing the export of nuclear information and materiel in much the same way as missile proliferation is overseen and partially controlled by MTCR. The LSC writ runs only within the domains of respective members. In July 1990, for example, Washington blocked the shipment to Iraq of a $15 million titanium alloy furnace which could have been used within Iraq's nuclear and ballistic missile research programme. In the following month Washington and London co-operated in a move which stopped Saddam Hussein acquiring nuclear trigger devices. These states are powerless, however, to stop the apparently harmless sale of dual-technology machinery, the purchase of specialist components from low-key sources (such as South Africa, Switzerland, Austria, Liechtenstein and Argentina) and the employment within potential rogue states of high-technology mercenaries.

The bombing of the Osiraq nuclear reactor in 1981 prompted the diversification of Iraq's special weapons interests. Iraq's Military Industry Commission (MIC) headed by Saddam's cousin and brother-in-law, Brigadier Hussein Kamil Hassan al–Majid Takriti, had as its primary function the construction of a nuclear bomb, through no less than-three separate projects. Kamil established bogus engineering organizations as subsidiary front companies to the MIC. Among these were the State Organization for Technical Industries (SOTI) and the Industrial Products Company (IPC). Agents of the state, operating from within these organizations, established a worldwide network which trawled the high-technology industry for the specialist machinery and parts demanded by the nuclear programme. It proved to be a relatively simple matter to buy high-technology, dual-purpose machinery (machinery designated for peaceful purposes but convertible to military use), and to secure the all-important export licences. In the case of the more difficult, more sensitive components and bomb parts, these were procured from less scrupulous, often smaller states.

What the Iraqis had done, therefore, in a cleverly complicated procurement operation, was to buy the individual pieces of their nuclear puzzle throughout the world, to be assembled secretly in Iraq. This accounts for the wide variation in the estimates of exactly how close Saddam Hussein was to making a nuclear bomb. Evidence is available that Iraq had bought the necessary technical know-how to build a bomb, but equally important is the ready availability of sufficient uranium 235 as well as the means of delivery.

Twice a year, the Vienna-based International Atomic Energy Authority (IAEA) monitored developments within the restored Osiraq plant inside the Tuwaitha nuclear facility. The Tuwaitha research institute, twelve miles to the south of Baghdad, was one of 922 declared nuclear facilities which appeared on the IAEA's inspection schedule. The inspectors monitor both the quality of fuel produced and the degree to which it is enriched, to ensure that the uranium is not upgraded from civilian to military use. This series of prearranged inspections has been going on since 1978 and, as recently as March 1990, the inspectors found no evidence of Iraq's diversion from its civilian nuclear programme to the military. This apparent confirmation of Iraq's adherence to their Nuclear Non-Proliferation Treaty obligations was in direct contrast to Saddam Hussein's obsessive and confessed intention to obtain nuclear weapons. The principal weakness of the IAEA inspection process is that it only inspects declared nuclear installations and has a very limited prerogative to initiate random inspections.

The uranium Iraq recovered from the stricken Osiraq site in 1981 would have been declared and, as known stock, was therefore embargoed from military use through IAEA monitoring. Efforts to import weapon-grade fuel are not thought to have been successful. In 1984 Iraqi agents offered several Italian criminals £30 million for 74lb of plutonium in what transpired to be an elaborate hoax. But fortune smiled on Saddam Hussein when mineable deposits of uranium were discovered in the Chiya Gara mountains in Kurdistan, close to the Turkish border. The indigenous Kurds were uprooted and the opencast mine became enclosed within a Restricted Area.

The mined ore, known colloquially as yellow cake, is militarily useless until it has been refined through a cascade of thousands of centrifuges which separate the approximately 25 per cent volume of radioactive uranium 235 from the inert uranium 238. The *Sunday Times'* 'Insight' of 16 December 1990 revealed how a German scientist had, unwittingly, helped

Iraq perfect the all-important centrifuge technology. Not for the first time had Germany been embarrassed by revelations of entrepreneurial industrial activity. The giant chemical laboratory built by a Düsseldorf company at Salman Pak ten years ago was claimed by the company to have been a contract to equip a university's laboratory. German companies played a crucial role in building Gadaffi's chemical factory at Rabta, Libya, and the range of Scud missiles was extended through the use of machinery provided by a German company with the benefit of government export credits. The resources of Bonn's secret services were reported to have been concentrated upon the investigation of illegal exports to Iraq. As a result, almost sixty German firms were investigated for selling high technology and arms to Iraq and, in August 1990, seven people were arrested on suspicion of having sold poison-gas equipment to Iraq. Germany remains ultra-sensitive to claims that Germany supplied Iraq with a nuclear, biological and chemical potential; Bonn's figures indicate that only 0.2 per cent of Saddam Hussein's weaponry originated in Germany. The percentage of German industrial support made available to Iraq has not yet been fully quantified. Speaking on Radio Luxembourg, Herr Genscher said that: 'Germany recognized at an early stage the danger of the Iraqi leadership under Saddam Hussein, which is why, unlike other western states, we did not approve arms sales to Iraq.'

In 1988 Brazil took a firm constitutional line by prohibiting the development of nuclear weapons. Despite being a significant conventional arms manufacturer, with arms sales representing an important component of her export market, Brazil now claims to sell arms only for defensive purposes. President Fernando Collor de Mello has admitted that, in the past, Brazil supplied nuclear technology to Iraq. Brazil, like Argentina, is not a signatory of the Nuclear Non-Proliferation Treaty but, according to her president, has now renounced 'all such efforts'. In addition, the Brazilian foreign ministry appealed to twenty of her nationals engaged as high-technology mercenaries in Iraq, to cease work 'for patriotic reasons'. The freelance Brazilian engineers were thought to be helping Iraq develop a short-range missile similar to the Brazilian Piranha. The team was alleged to have been headed by a former director of the Brazilian Air Force's Aerospace Technology Centre, Brigadier Hugo Piva.

The web of Iraq's arms intrigue stretched around the globe, often with fatal consequences. In March 1990 Jonathan Moyle, a twenty-eight-year-old ex-RAF officer and editor of *Defence Helicopter World*, was found dead in his hotel room in Santiago, Chile. It is believed that Moyle was investigating the interface between Iraq's arms buyers and Chile's giant armaments company, Industrias Cardoen SA. The Canadian supercannon designer, Dr Gerald Bull, head of the Space Research Corporation, was also murdered in March 1990 in his Brussels flat. He had been in the forefront of supercannon development and had been actively assisting Iraq. He designed, for example, their excellent, South African-made G-5 howitzer. Reports at the end of September 1990 said that Iraq had one assembled and one disassembled 350mm cannon, capable of firing rocket shells over 200 miles. No less than eight nations provided components for the superguns. Some of the parts of a giant 1,000mm cannon, declared to be oil piping and therefore granted a British Department of Trade and Industry export licence, did reach Iraq but the exportation of follow-on parts of the barrel were blocked at Teesport, the port of departure.

The final component to be examined in the troika of weapons of mass destruction is the 'b' in 'n.b.c' – biological weapons. Immediately prior to the invasion of Kuwait, Britain's Foreign Office warned academics to be on their guard for increased interest by Middle East students in research into the types of bacteria suitable for use in biological weapons. These include anthrax, cholera and typhoid. Bacteriological weapons cannot be employed as discriminately as the quicker-reacting chemical weapons and for battle-field use are regarded very much as a double-edged weapon.

The urgent need for an arms transfer control regime for the Middle East is one of the more obvious lessons arising from the 1990–1 Gulf crisis. The recipe would need to include something similar to the European disarmament agreements plus the establishment of an organization to regulate strategic exports, a Co-ordinating Committee Controlling Middle East Trade, a COCOM (ME). Unless such controlling initiatives are taken, instability will continue to be an unwelcome feature in parts of the Third World.

THE NEW COLLEGIALITY AMONG THE PERMANENT MEMBERS OF THE UN SECURITY COUNCIL

Collegiality is the product of a symphony of national interests. It is debatable whether there might have been so much co-operation in the Security Council had there not existed, to a greater or lesser degree, concern among the permanent membership about their contribution to the creation of the monster, Saddam Hussein. The binding factors which were evident in this the most recent Gulf crisis were not evident, for example, during the concurrent discussions of the General Agreement on Tariffs and Trade (GATT). Collegiality is therefore related to circumstances tempered by the unanimous convergence of the national interests of the important players. GATT is an organization with a worldwide membership of over one hundred states and so it is infinitely more difficult to orchestrate unanimity. It is, in theory, a simpler matter to achieve unanimity in the UN Security Council with its five/four vote than, for example, in the EC with a membership of twelve, NATO with a membership of sixteen and CSCE with a membership of fifty-two.

Some would have it that the collegiality was contrived, being merely a mask behind which Bush and Baker pursued their national interest. That view is too simplistic. Certainly, from a credibility and 'sales' point of view, it would have been infinitely preferable to have seen rather more of the Secretary-General of the United Nations and rather less of the heavier hand of the senior representatives of the United States administration. In the early stages in the crisis, when visiting South America for example, it is true that the Secretary-General appeared to have opted out, even though that was not his intention. At the point of time when the Gulf crisis flared up, however, it was only the United States which possessed the power, the determination, the will and the bag full of rewards with which to achieve unanimity or something closely approaching unanimity. There is a widely held view that from now on, the United States' capacity to influence will decline, whereas, given the will and the necessary machinery, the United Nations' capacity to influence could well increase.

Now, for the first time, the United Nations was performing as the drafters of the Charter had intended. Most striking of all was the rapport established between the two former belligerent superpowers. The bilateral Helsinki talks did not produce from Gorbachev the promise of Soviet troops to reinforce Security Council Resolutions but he did not rule out the possibility that force might have to be employed. The Helsinki Joint Declaration laid to rest traditional ideological feuding: 'We are determined to see this aggression end, and if the current steps fail to end it, we are prepared to consider other ones consistent with the UN Charter.'

Even those who might have cynical regard for the United States' methods would nevertheless be prepared to applaud the fact that it was the United Nations forum which was taken as the venue for the mobilization of an international response to the problems created by Saddam Hussein. The presence in one place of the representatives of 179 states or republics creates the ideal environment for the conduct of international business. Moreover, despite internal and external pressures, the collegiality among the permanent members of the UN Security Council remained more or less intact. That China, flag-bearer of Third World interests, did not veto the Resolution authorizing the use of all necessary measures to expel Iraqi troops from Kuwait, came as a relief, yet her abstention is unlikely to have been without strings. China was not the sole state to have obtained possible concessions from the United States in exchange for maintaining solidarity against Saddam Hussein. Manipulation in these circumstances did not present an overwhelming moral quandary, because the logic that aggression should not be permitted to succeed is both straightforward and also well-nigh universally supported. The Gulf crisis had represented a financial loss in one way or another to the majority of world actors. The trade-offs achieved by those states holding the trump cards were a beneficial form of damage limitation.

What was seen within the United Nations throughout the course of the crisis was a continuation of the collegial trend noted earlier. The UN confirmed its position as the key international institution. France would not have been drawn into the Gulf except under the aegis of the UN. It had not been a perfect display but when dealing with the separate aspirations of less than perfect actors, the ultimate result had nevertheless been a source of great encouragement for internationalists. 'No longer,' declared George Bush, 'can a dictator count on East–West confrontation to stymie concerted UN action against aggression.' But how had the other relevant regional organizations fared? The following review of tortuous and even indifferent responses to the threat casts the United Nations as the undisputed leading international organization.

At the onset of the crisis there had been a universal pause within the external international order to allow the Arab states themselves to achieve an Arab solution to the crisis. There did exist a valid need to find a truly 'Arab solution'. Among the anti-Saddamist Arabs there was a common belief that they must at all costs avoid being tarred with the brush that it had been they who had reopened the door to the Middle East to admit western imperialism once again. It did not work. What the crisis achieved was to underline the deep divisions within Arab ranks due to their separate interests and separate aims. Arab unity must remain a myth for as long as there remain such fundamental divisions between the haves and have-nots, and republicans and monarchs. Political life within the Arab League had always been manifested by a constant struggle for power and pre-eminence among faction leaders. As long as that rivalry continued, there could be no Arab unity and there would be no effective regional role for the Arab League to play.

The subsidiary Arab regional alliances' performances were no more collegial. Saddam Hussein's Arab Co-operation Council (ACC) was finally certified dead. Egypt and Iraq were never the most comfortable or co-operative of bedfellows and now, by way of confirmation, they found themselves as adversaries. The African Maghreb Union, comprising Algeria, Libya, Tunisia, Mauritania and Morocco, was torn asunder. Algeria failed to be impressed by either the invasion of Kuwait or the western response to the invasion. Libya, surprisingly, took a more or less neutral position. Tunisia was less coy and supported Iraq, while pro-western Morocco not only favoured a return to the status quo *ante bellum* but, despite considerable domestic opposition, also dispatched troops to Saudi Arabia. The Moroccan troops were more enthusiastically received than their fellow military Muslim brethren from Pakistan. Pakistan intended sending a 5,000-strong armoured division to the Gulf; it was Islamabad's hope that the requisite armour would be supplied by Saudi Arabia. Not only was this initially refused but Pakistan's influx of manpower had reached only 2,000 when the Saudis said they did not want any more. When it seemed that non-Arab Muslims were to be denied a role in the Gulf and hence access to important financial preference, Riyadh relented. A force of 12,000 Pakistani troops was eventually accepted but its mission was confined to the defence of the kingdom and it was not permitted by Islamabad to take on an offensive role against Iraq. This arrangement reflected a recognition first of Saudi Arabia's shortage of manpower yet prevalence of targets and, secondly, of the restriction placed on the employment of Pakistani troops through a prevailing anti-western sentiment in Pakistan. General Mirza Aslam Beg, the army commander, claimed that the western powers and Zionists had a mission to neutralize those Muslim countries which could not be defeated militarily and to divide others by encouraging them to fight one another. Pakistan's wider attempt to arrange a role for the Organization of the Islamic Conference (OIC) was rejected by most Arab states and also by the USA.

On the face of it, it might have been assumed that a greater degree of unanimity would have existed within the United Arab Emirates (UAE). The Emirates, together with Saudi Arabia, Kuwait, Oman, Bahrain and Qatar are members of the Gulf Co-operation Council. The GCC's collective security force was in effect a division of two brigades, one of which was Saudi and the other made up from representatives of the other five states in the GCC. The mission of the two brigades was to forestall the very misfortune that befell Kuwait. In fact, only lip service had been paid to the raising and sustaining of the Gulf's so-called Peninsula Shield. It had been intended that the 10,000-man force would be the best-equipped rapid-reaction force in the region, yet the promised modern equipment never materialized. Moreover, only 4,000 troops were allocated to the task. It was understandable, therefore, that this force never managed to get to its starting line to face up to the threat posed by Saddam's 100,000.

The reason why Peninsula Shield never became a credible protector was the mistrust which pervaded the relationship between kings and emirs. These were leaders whose past conflict resolutions had been achieved by the open chequebook, not by the gun. The less than fulsome support of the concept of a modern, well-equipped and professional quick-reaction force – a modern Glubb Pasha-style Arab Legion – floundered because it represented something that could be turned against its sponsors. The source of concern of the smaller royal states was not fear of the Saudis but fear from within the seven member states of the UAE.[132] The resignation of Chedli Klibi, Secretary-General of the League of Arab States, had been the final, exasperated recognition that the League had failed to fulfil its function and rise to its biggest ever challenge in settling inter-Arab disputes.

Nowhere equalled the European Community's speedy political response to the invasion of the Gulf. The EC's condemnation of the Iraqi invasion and the call for a blockade preceded the Security Council's action. This zeal and enthusiasm was the continuation of a dynamic wave of political activity which had experienced new levels of success following progress with European monetary union and political integration. Unfortunately, what the Gulf crisis did was to erect a wall which the EC obligingly ran into. When a unified response was demanded, Europe indulged in its customary pursuit of purely national and often fractured aims while the United States was barely restrained from describing as gutless the unwillingness in some quarters to provide troops or reasonable financial support, or both. What the Gulf crisis had demonstrated quite convincingly to Europe and the EC was the definite linkage of economic and security policy. Yet the EC has no security machinery. On 7 March 1991 Jacques Delors, President of the European Commission, admitted in London:

The Gulf War has provided an object lesson – if one were needed – on the limitations of the European Community. It is true that giant steps have been taken along the path of economic integration, and the last two years have seen advances on foreign policy co-operation. But the Community's influence and ability to act have not kept pace.

There are some opportunists in Europe who recommend that the way in which the EC should overcome its security shortcomings is to subsume the WEU. The WEU is Europe's sole defence forum and comprises nine of the twelve EC members, excluding Denmark, Greece and Ireland. Neutral Dublin would possibly resist any move in which the EC absorbed the militarist WEU on the expiration of the Union's treaty in 1998. So too might such a step deter future neutral EC aspirants such as Finland and Sweden from joining. What could be achieved in a totally balanced consideration of the need to defend the whole of Europe from all directions is the advancement of Turkey's fragile claim to join the Community. The United States would be unimpressed by enthusiastic European supranationalism overflowing into the realms of defence. That is the path towards isolationism, the seeds of which are already in place on both sides of the Atlantic. Any thoughts that the EC might generate a new security regime are, at the best, premature.[133]

It took the WEU two weeks to put its act together. Although it is closely linked to NATO it benefits by not suffering NATO's geographical limitations. It has, however, no integrated military command. The WEU took over where it had stopped during the previous Gulf crisis by co-ordinating the embargo activities of the naval ships offered up by the six participating WEU states. The WEU also undertook the co-ordination of naval intelligence. In addition, in consultation with allies, the WEU divided the sea approaches to Iraq into national areas of responsibility. This co-ordination and support function was as far as the currently configured WEU could go, since it is not structured to orchestrate a European response for war. When the shooting war started, of the Europeans, all but the Royal Navy ships stayed well clear at the southern end of the Gulf.

After France's last-minute attempt to take a unilateral negotiating path suffered the same arbitrary rejection as that experienced by Javier Pérez de Cuéllar, she ended a Gaullist tradition by placing her Gulf troops under US operational control 'for specific times and specific missions'. Prime Minister

Michel Rocard explained to the National Assembly that the liberation of Kuwait would mean that 'in order for Kuwait to be freed it may prove necessary to destroy military targets in Iraq'. In a vote which, at the time, ran contrary to public opinion, only 43 deputies out of the 568 present voted against committing France's 10,000 troops to possible combat in occupied Kuwait. The opposition Gaullist party had voted with the government but its leader, Jacques Chirac, commenting on the European Community's response to the crisis, 'deplored [its] ineffectiveness and total lack of credibility'. But the crisis had created some positive movement. Italy's eight Tornados in Dubai were assigned to operations in Kuwait. In addition, the Netherlands considered the dispatch of troops and reached the same conclusion as the French, putting her two frigates under US control. Germany sent ships to the Mediterranean and had some political difficulty in deploying a squadron of Alpha jets to Turkey. That was the sum of the new movement in Europe, a Europe without a command structure and with the WEU only able to provide an elementary co-ordination of defence activity. Herein lies a possible future role for NATO, perhaps in association with the WEU's current studies into the role member countries may play in developing future security relationships.

Although NATO was not directly involved in the conflict, claims that it is 'an obsolete organization' and 'a victim of its own success' are also premature. It has enjoyed the political consensus of its member states and this momentum can, and should, be sustained. NATO possesses a quite unique and enviable international command, control and force structure which it would be utter folly to discard. The premiss must begin with the machinery in existence. The machinery needs to be adapted to respond to changed circumstances to produce what European security now requires. The creation of the Allied Command in Europe Rapid Reaction Force (ACERRF) is indicative of the acceptance of the need for change. What is certain is that the machine is too valuable to be destroyed by political Luddites. NATO's contribution to the Gulf War effort has been understated. The Organization supported Turkey and guaranteed the sea and air lines of communication. The standardization of the way in which significant NATO powers approached the armed conflict greatly facilitated the management of the potentially fraught areas of command, control, communications and intelligence. What may well emerge as a result of NATO's mating dance and her possible future employment as a UN surrogate is not a bona fide NATO force but rather a grouping of independent NATO member states operating out of area in pursuit of shared national interests.

By threatening the West's oil supplies, Saddam Hussein has shown that the NATO members need to think about new ways to protect their interests beyond the limits of an area which was established on the basis of historic criteria. Moreover, NATO members have the collective capacity to offer their expertise and professionalism to the United Nations for the benefit of broader international security interests. On 20 September 1990 Manfred Wörner, NATO's Secretary-General, told a NATO conference in Brussels:

Looking to the future it seems obvious that we have to draw lessons from the current crisis. The main question is: should the alliance as such play an increased role in dealing with regional conflicts which directly affect the security of its members? I believe we all have to think carefully about that.

The Gulf War demonstrated that states will need to be more aware of, and pay more attention to, the risks that emanate from outside Europe. That NATO does not regard itself as obsolescent was apparent from the upbeat London Declaration of 6 July 1990.

What is sadly true of most European states is that politically it really does not matter greatly whether they take as their shield CSCE, EC, WEU or NATO. The umbrella provided by such an organization is no more likely to encourage a state to take action prejudicial to that state's national or public interest. Addressing the thirty-sixth session of the North Atlantic Assembly in London in November 1990, Manfred Wörner, who favours a more flexible and imaginative NATO approach, admitted to there being

A widespread feeling that some Allies and the Alliance can and should do more. After the Gulf crisis is over, there will be a debate – but I hope not before, as we must concentrate now on maintaining our well-established solidarity.

The launching of the formal Allied ground attack into Kuwait and Iraq at 1 a.m. on 24 February 1991 gave rise to the only major test of Security Council collegiality. At the time when President Bush ordered the coalition troops to advance, there had been a Soviet peace plan 'on the table'. The Iraqi response to the plan had been ambiguous, Kuwait's oil wells had been put to the torch, the infrastructure was being systematically destroyed and parts of the population had either been taken north as prisoners or summarily executed. This was the time for the Allied coalition to observe strictly the UN mandate and the twelve resolutions. That is precisely what the Soviet peace plan neglected to do. It had not addressed Iraq's war crimes, nor did it satisfy the UN's requirement that Saddam Hussein should not profit from the invasion and sacking of Kuwait. Certainly there was some vying for regional pre-eminence between the two superpowers. What had irked the US administration was that it had been they who had taken the political risks and suffered the slings and arrows of the campaign. At the eleventh hour there appeared to be a risk that they would be upstaged by the Soviets, who had had none of those risks but threatened to capture the political high ground with their own peace initiative. In the event, it did not happen. What the Gulf crisis so indelibly underlined was the confirmation of the continuing decline of Soviet power and influence.

The arrangements for ultimate peace required that the Soviets remain on-side and for the superpower rapport to be sustained. Beijing regretted the beginning of the offensive and Moscow also regretted that 'the instinct for a military solution won through'. Reading between the lines, it was apparent that the Kremlin, although bitterly disappointed at being marginalized, would keep in step with the Allied coalition as long as the campaign was of short duration. The Soviets had learned that Security Council resolutions freely entered into promised to be more difficult to disengage from. One veto from any one of the other four permanent members is sufficient to prevent change coming about.

A long-drawn-out war would have created difficulties for Gorbachev, difficulties emanating from what was then a strengthening conservative lobby. International relations is a series of wheels within wheels. What the Soviets had attempted and failed to achieve in 1991 was what the Americans had succeeded in doing in 1956 at the half-way point of modern Iraq's development. The Americans intervened in 1956 to prevent the Anglo–French coalition from putting down Nasser. President Nixon admitted later that the US intervention had been a mistake: Nasser's survival and the primacy of his will over the former imperialists enhanced his status as an unique pan-Arab leader. His followers went on to murder Iraq's royal family and in 1967 he considered Egypt sufficiently strong to challenge Israel for leadership of the region. There is some speculation that it had become an unspoken Washington aim that Saddam Hussein would not be permitted to emulate Nasser's example or be the trigger to set Israel once more upon the warpath.

THE FAILURE AND DIFFICULTIES IN ACHIEVING MILITARY INTERVENTION

This account, beginning with the move to the starting blocks for military intervention, must obviously be a record of difficulties rather than failure. Militarily, Saddam Hussein was certain to face defeat in the Allied effort to remove his forces from Kuwait. The only circumstances that could be envisaged whereby the putative military intervention could fail would be lack of resolve and substantial erosion of consensus within key sending states. The 1990–1 Gulf crisis is therefore an illuminating example of a situation fraught with problems and difficulties at a time when the outlook appeared so positive and favourable.

The UN had shown itself to be an important and effective international organization and, in view of its comprehensive display of competence, an even more important future role seemed likely. Saddam Hussein's invasion of Kuwait had been almost universally condemned. The international co-operative venture raised to make the point that aggression by one state against another must not be allowed to succeed had the significant benefit of political, military and economic support as well as the all-important aspect of the backing of international law. So how was it that a small, war-weary, virtually landlocked state of 17 million, of whom only 5 million were males over the age of fourteen, which had been the subject of twelve Security Council Resolutions (see Annex A), faced up not only to world-wide condemnation and opprobrium but also to the most sophisticated array of weaponry ever assembled? It is too simplistic to suggest that this was due to Saddam Hussein's stupidity. He had been stupid, but the capabilities of his ground forces were afforded considerable – in time, proved unwarranted – respect. The difficulties that arose are worth enu-meration in order to serve as a lesson for the future. There were two distinct paths towards the goal of defeating Saddam Hussein: by laying siege to, or by destroying, his citadel.

There is a rather obvious correlation between allowing time for diplo-macy to succeed and the impact which that concession is likely to have upon force structures. There are a number of related threads here. First there is the recognition that it is in the nature of the autocrat to gamble. In Saddam Hussein's case, he had nothing to lose by gambling. He had made a second grave military miscalculation during the currency of his leader-ship. If he had responded to UN Resolution 660 prior to armed conflict and withdrawn from Kuwait, his continuing leadership of Iraq would have been most unlikely. 'I have two options', Saddam Hussein explained to a senior member of the Algerian delegation to Baghdad: 'to be killed by US bombs or by Iraqi officers. In the first case I shall be a martyr, in the second a traitor. If I withdraw unconditionally from Kuwait, I shall certainly have to face the second scenario.' It is also true that some national elements within the Allied consortium would not have been prepared to allow Saddam Hussein the opportunity to withdraw, regroup and attack again as a wiser man with his improving weapons systems of mass destruction still intact. It is for this reason that one of the lessons of intervention – that of offering an opponent who had overreached himself a face-saving exit – in this case was, for some, not applicable.

Secondly, ethnic and national considerations dictated that diplomacy had to be given time to work. The Middle East is a great tinderbox capable of being fuelled from the world's largest reservoir of oil reserves. Damage inflicted upon significant extraction areas, Saudi Arabia as well as Kuwait, might well have driven the cost of oil towards $100 per barrel. Those who would suffer would be not only the economies of the leading powers but also a Third World already crippled by debt. A diplomatic solution offered the additional advantage of not triggering the anticipated worldwide ter-rorist backlash, some of the groups of which had relocated to Baghdad from Damascus. Among these were Abu Nidal's 300-strong Fatah Revolutionary Council and Abu Abbas's Palestine Liberation Front. Other pro-Saddam groups were the military wing of the Baath Party, the Arab Liberation Front, and a group which had specialized in attacks on aircraft, the Arab Organization 15th May. In the event, the terrorist backlash did not transpire, for which Syria claimed some of the credit.

A high proportion of states, among them many European, favoured the investigation of those avenues which avoided direct armed conflict, principally through diplomacy and by embargo. It was for this reason that almost four months would elapse by the time, on 29 November 1990, Security Council Resolution 678 authorized:

> member states co-operating with the government of Kuwait, unless Iraq on or before 15 January 1991 fully implements the foregoing resolutions, to use all necessary means to uphold and implement Security Council Resolution 660 and to restore international peace and security in the area; requests all states to provide appropriate support for the actions undertaken in pursuance of this resolution.

It was evident that the main body of those who subscribed to the ultra-cautious approach were those who had not provided ground forces authorized to 'use all necessary means' to force Iraq out of Kuwait. Blood is a more emotive commodity than political support or treasure, and action more fraught than rhetoric. The prospect of bitter recrimination arising between those who had supplied forces and those who had not was avoided due to the short duration of war and the low casualty rate.

During the course of this interregnum the Iraqi Army, which is highly competent in field engineering, built defences of Maginot length if not sophistication, and stationed what was believed to have been half their land forces on Kuwaiti territory. As the defences improved, the size of the opposing Allied force had to be revised upward. It is a lesson of coalition operations that the longer the delay in moving, the greater the response required. There is an association here with available strategic lift and also utilizing that lift early. An ideal solution lies in having a force and its equipment close to the problem – a forward presence. Future strategies will develop in a regional context and will attract credibility through having a potential collective security response close at hand. This obviates the problem which acknowledges the shortfall in strategic lift capability by being drawn into a conflict before the decision-making process has been fully exercised and plans fully collaborated. In such a situation the emphasis falls on the quality of peacetime intelligence and its early sharing between potential coalition states. The problems of Allied strategic mobility have already been highlighted as the Allies prepared for conventional war in an unconventional environment. With the increase in the estimate of the number of Allied troops required to breach the Iraqi ' Maginot' line, so too did the estimates of Allied casualties increase. Rejecting arguments that he should give sanctions more time to work, Bush replied: 'we risk paying a higher price in the most precious currency of all – human life – if we give Saddam more time to prepare for war'.

All this was, of course, bad news in the United States due to the striking similarities being drawn with the Vietnam War. In fact, there were very few similarities. What were perceived as similarities were the result of US domestic ignorance and alarm. Military folklore suggests that the attack is to the defence as three is to one. In effect, the Allied technological advantages, particularly their night-fighting capability coupled with air superiority, would serve as force multipliers, thereby considerably reducing the Allied numbers required.

The Gulf crisis demanded of the NATO members the consideration of a rethink of their military options and the means available of pursuing those options. Central to the tactical reappraisal was the abandonment of the traditional, defensive concept in favour of a high-intensity, offensive, break-in battle into Kuwait. Light units enjoy a high state of readiness but are lightly armed. Low-intensity conflict had come to be regarded as synonymous with light forces being deployed with light equipment. For the majority of subsequent interventionist circumstances this is still likely to remain the case, but the Gulf became an important exception, the scale of which left the Allies unprepared and slow to respond. It became a large-scale, limited war at the thick end of the intervention spectrum. Significantly, no role was found in the battle *per se* for the traditional British troubleshooters of the Royal Marine Commandos and the Parachute Brigade. British Gurkha troops, whose Indian counterparts had been the best of the bunch in the Congo, were, however, deployed to the support area.

There were two principal reasons why the Iraqi forces were given an appreciable degree of respect: their sheer size, and the chemical dimension. Reports of the military prowess of Iraq's 950,000-strong Army varied from the very good to the indifferent. Based on their performance against Iran in eight years of desert warfare, a number of truisms had emerged. Demographic factors showed that (in contrast to the Iranians) they were very careful not to suffer heavy casualties. They did not fight with distinction on Iranian territory but were much more tenacious in defending their own land. The defence of Basra in 1987 was conducted with great fortitude and courage. The armour and air wars, however, were not distinguished affairs. Much had been made of the modern Soviet T-72s, but these comprised a small proportion of the total armoured force in a predominantly infantry-heavy Army and too often were kept in the Republican Guard reserve. The more numerous and older models of Soviet tanks were fought as direct-fire artillery. Their ability to be used emphatically to change the balance on the battlefield was severely inhibited by the absence of radios. Such are the precautions that dictators perceive to be necessary. Iraqi airpower was not used at all boldly. During the Iran/Iraq War, large elements of the airforce were kept on Jordanian airfields beyond the range of Iranian fighters. What the Iraqis were most positive about was their preparedness to use chemical weapons in order to break a stalemate. Iran had not developed deliverable forms of chemical weapons. The Allies could, of course, match anything Saddam Hussein could produce. In January, Prime Minister Major made it clear that the coalition would have taken a very serious view of the use of any chemical or biological weapon by Iraq, and that forces in the Gulf had a wide range of weapons available but the need to use nuclear weapons was not envisaged.

Deterrence is predicated upon the existence of the rational actors on both sides. Saddam Hussein's proven unpredictability and irrationality meant that his capabilities and intentions had to be respected.

In June 1980 the Pentagon wargamed a study designed to investigate the effects of an intervention in which an opponent possessed chemical weapons. The wargame setting was a Saudi Arabia/Iraq environment. The conclusion reached was that US forces would be unable to win without neutralizing oil-production facilities, with all the unwelcome, attendant economic implications. The *New York Post* published the findings of the conclusions of a study team set up in 1982 to investigate the feasibility of operations in an intemperate climate under chemical conditions: 'airbase survivability is nil: heat stress reduces our forces to a glob. It would be a sweaty blood bath'. No seasonal differentiation was made but the overall conclusion was revealing. The report strongly supported the thesis that military action in the Gulf environment remains the last resort, particularly where there is the prospect of aims being achieved by non-military means, albeit over a longer period.

A number of reasons have been advanced for the Iraqis not employing their chemical weapons. Central to this was their conceding air superiority to the Allies. Aircraft and missiles were two of only three means available for the delivery of chemical weapons. The fact that so little of the Iraqi airforce chose to stay and fight gave the Allied airforce complete domination of the battlefields in Kuwait and southern Iraq. Artillery was the other means available for firing chemical weapons, but even in its conventional mode the Iraqi artillery proved to be indifferent. Their Forward Observation Officers (FOOs) were more often than not unable to locate the Allied forces and, when their guns did open up, they faced instant retribution from patrolling taxi-ranked Allied aircraft or from counter-battery fire. In that respect, elements of the Iraqi artillery found the Allied artillery to be more effective than the Allied air forces. The reaction was quicker, more concentrated and not weather dependent – cogent reasons for no Iraqi first use of chemical weapons. The Iraqis also knew that the Allied n.b.c. protection was superior to theirs and, in view of the wind and rain blowing in their faces, the use of chemical weapons by Iraq did not make military sense.

The Republican Guard were an important consideration in the war because they provided the backbone of Saddam's regime. Whereas the Guard were kept in reserve until the fourth year of Iraq's war with Iran, they formed part of the spearhead in the attack on Kuwait. After that, they went back into reserve to fulfil their primary function, which has been described as 'the army which watches the army'. For that reason, and for their complete dedication to Saddam, they have been likened to the Waffen SS. Certainly they enjoyed privileges not experienced by the mainstream of the Army. For example, prior to the invasion of Kuwait, Saddam Hussein delegated to his Guard commanders the use, without prior clearance, of chemical weapons and missiles. This concession was more widely extended during the course of the war.

There are some striking similarities between Napoleon's Imperial Guard and Saddam Hussein's Republican Guard. When formed in the late 1970s, the Iraqi presidential guard numbered only a few thousand. Napoleon's Imperial Guard was also, originally, a small, personal *corps d'élite*, inactive on the battlefield, enjoying a charmed and safe life until faced with the realities and expediencies of 1812. They were highly dedicated and utterly loyal to Napoleon. The early Iraqi presidential guard was Sunni, like Saddam's tribe, and was commanded by officers from Takrit. Just as 1812 had been an important milestone for the Imperial Guard, the expediencies of the Iran/Iraq War witnessed the expansion of the presidential guard into the Republican Guard.

Napoleon's Guard increased in size. In 1805 it had been 10,000 strong, by 1809 it was 32,000, and it had swelled to 120,000 for the advance into Russia. The Imperial Guard now consisted of the Young, Middle and Old Guard. It had been in 1809 that Napoleon had created the Young Guard, comprising the very best of the available conscripts. There was a contemporary argument that it was prejudicial to the overall quality of an army to cream off the best talent into an elite corps. From 1814, however, it ceased for the French to be a one-way process. Thirty thousand guardsman were commissioned and went back to bolster the line regiments, now made up of the very young and the very old.

Saddam Hussein took a leaf from Napoleon's book by recruiting all college student conscripts, irrespective of religion, into the Republican Guard. At the beginning of the war, the Guard had swelled to eight divisions, each of approximately 14,000 men. The three armoured divisions were established for 800 tanks, of which 500 were the most modern Soviet T-72s. There were four infantry divisions and one special operations division which served as a political commissariat spying within the service and maintaining discipline.

The Republican Guard was therefore the best trained, best motivated, best paid, best quality, and best equipped group of formations. It was as though the military talent of Iraq had been conveniently gathered in a clutch of baskets. Their destruction became a key Allied war aim, for their survival was regarded as synonymous with Saddam's. What had to be achieved was to crack their resolve in the same way that the cracking of the will of the Middle Guard at Waterloo had signified the end of Napoleon.

The Republican Guard did not live up to their reputation in battle. To what degree this was due to the unrelenting attention of B-52 bombers is not yet known.

Some twenty-eight states supported Resolution 660 by supplying land, sea or air components to the Allied effort. The problems presented by the assemblage of this disparate and unstructured force, not least in command and control, are covered in detail elsewhere. Absent from the line-up of troop-providing states was the Soviet Union. It is thought to have been an important foreign policy aim for the United States to co-opt the Soviet Union to deploy a token force, apparently to strengthen the Allied multi-national credentials. History was again repeating itself for, during the Vietnam War, the US administration had tried very hard to entice a token British battalion into Vietnam. They even went so far as to recommend the Black Watch; the regiment's pipe band had made a most favourable impression whilst playing at John F. Kennedy's funeral service in 1963. The British government, as circumstances were to prove, wisely declined. Soviet Foreign Minister Shevardnadze told Foreign Secretary Baker that the dispatch of Soviet forces to the Gulf was 'not under consideration and that this option is non-existent'.

The legacy of Afghanistan affected the Soviets even more profoundly than the legacy of Vietnam would affect the Americans. The Soviets were deprived of the option of some foreign adventure as a means of diverting attention from domestic problems. Both the Russian Federation and Russian Congress of People's Deputies appealed to President Gorbachev to keep Soviet forces out of the Gulf. The deputies went so far as to pass a resolution imploring Gorbachev not to permit the Soviet Union to be 'drawn into a military conflict which could have the most serious consequences for peace and stability on the planet'. Some questions were even raised as to the legality of Soviet support for Security Council Resolution 678.

A token Soviet presence in the Gulf would have been seen through as the transparent gesture that it represented. The Soviet difficulty was not only political but also military. It seems likely that the insertion of even a small-size formation could have posed potentially serious problems for Moscow. Among the conservative officers were many who were pro-Iraq. 'It is not easy for us, said a certain Colonel Valentin Ogurtsov, 'to move from full-fledged relations to zero'. Formations also mean conscripts. Soviet soldiery had become resistant to conscription, and draft-dodging was prevalent in a number of republics. In another unpopular war, coming so soon after Afghanistan, the prospect would have existed that the soldiery could have behaved as did their forebears in the Imperial Russian Army of 1917 by voting with their feet or, at least, sitting on their hands. Either way, it would not have made a positive contribution to the broader concept of Allied solidarity. In these circumstances, the political support of the Soviet Union sufficed.

The Gulf crisis confirmed what had been long suspected; that no one state would wish to bear the burden of the cost of military operations on such a large scale. That the economics of the deployment to the Gulf did not appear to produce insurmountable difficulties was due almost exclusively to the special circumstances relating to that particular environment. There were deep pockets both among the host nations and among those most heavily dependent upon supplies of oil from the Gulf. What had become evident was that the owners of these pockets would need to dig less deep if sanctions succeeded, thereby obviating the need for the perceived, expensive military action. The convergence of so many national interests is such a rare event that, in terms of economic support of a military enterprise, it should not be taken as a new norm in international behaviour.

The overwhelming evidence of the Gulf crisis is that, in time, the embargo would have worked. The hope would have been that domestic dissatisfaction would have swept Saddam Hussein away before the situation inside Iraq became too parlous. The benefit of hindsight, however, suggests that this would have been an over-optimistic hope. Time was something that the Americans did not have on their side. The real problems in achieving a successful military intervention had again come to the fore. Consensus on the home front was, at the time, on the wane and the keeping of troops indefinitely in the desert could also have affected morale. Time was a most important factor. If intervention is to become the necessary agent of a collective security regime, the ground needs to be prepared politically for a speedy, proportional and legal response. Having said that, the adage 'look very carefully before you leap' is something which needs to be written prominently in all areas where the decision-making process takes place.In this case, the decision to intervene was taken during a fortuitous meeting between George Bush and Margaret Thatcher in Aspen, Colorado on 2 August 1990. It was here that Thatcher said to the president: 'Don't go wobbly, George.' The position of the United States, and therefore of the Allies, was to a large degree preordained from the time troops deployed into Saudi Arabia with uncertain missions and aims. It was at that point that the clock had started ticking.

HOW?

THE PRINCIPLES

THE SELECTION AND MAINTENANCE OF THE AIM

The first question that multilateral governments must address is: 'What is our political and military aim?' Failure to take such elementary action is merely building up to the certainty of serious problems for the future. The initial American defensive deployment into Saudi Arabia, both big and fast, fostered at home and abroad the impression of a confused mission. This impression was encouraged by the comments of some senior military officials who, seemingly of the opinion that Christmas had come early in 1990, made graphic public statements as to what fate was going to befall Saddam Hussein. However, the American deployment into Saudi Arabia, justified to the administration on the grounds of apparently incontrovertible aerial intelligence, was an example of the lessons of history having been properly learned. Dribbling forces into interventionist-type operations failed in Russia in 1918–19 and failed again in Vietnam in the 1960s.

In attempting to manage a suitable international response to Saddam Hussein's aggression, the United States found that she had fallen victim to her own legacy of unilateralism and direct pursuit of her own national interests. At the very time that she needed to carry with her the permanent members of the Security Council and co-ordinate with allies an agreed international political and military aim, there arose in some quarters both within and outside the Security Council a not unexpected reaction of suspicion and mistrust. International spectators were, after all, confused. Were the Americans really making the point that aggression must not be allowed to succeed when they themselves had used force or the threat of force to secure their aims more than any other state post-1945? Conservative elements in Moscow were troubled by the American mobilization into Saudi Arabia. Significant US forces were encamped close to the Soviets' none-too-stable southern border. These forces were representatives of a nation which would be foremost among those least affected by a heavier

Iraqi hand on the taps of the Middle East's oil. Baker's round of capital cities was essentially a matter of Hobson's choice; no other state could have done it. There was no other machinery available to discuss future joint aims and intentions. Presentationally it left much to be desired because it handed to potential malcontents a propaganda stick with which to attack what represented, after all, an Allied effort. The manoeuvring could be construed, by those so desirous, as a single state soliciting international support for a national policy, something which could be avoided if the lead were taken more decisively within an international forum.

Setting aside doubts with regard to the reasoning for a positive show of significant force by the USA, the result was the right result for the Gulf scenario. History indicates that dictators cannot be appeased but ultimately have to be destroyed. Initially, America emphasized that her troops in Saudi Arabia were purely defensive, yet the associated rhetoric and hint of switching to the offensive, although at the time undeliverable, was nevertheless a sound concept. An early assault to restore the status quo *ante bellum* in Kuwait was militarily logical yet impractical and politically impossible due to the absence of international consensus. Environments dictate military possibilities. It is specialist troops and their light equipment which can be moved the fastest. In an entirely urban or jungle terrain, light troops could have engaged their opponents faster and to better effect than in a mixed desert and urban environment which, combined with the enemy's particular order of battle, dictated the need for slow-to-deploy main battle tanks and heavy artillery. Troops and pilots have to be trained for desert operations, they need to be acclimatized, and finally, time is required to build up adequate logistic and materiel stocks. It is therefore very fortunate that Saddam Hussein did not move on to Saudi Arabia after taking Kuwait. Had he done so, it is difficult to envisage in what circumstances the Allied coalition would have got off the ground.

Concurrent with the build-up of forces, attempts were made in the short term to find an Arab, political solution to the problem and, once that proved an impossibility, broad-based diplomacy was then given a chance to work. So, in the phoney war period, when fruitless attempts were made to find a political solution, Saddam Hussein used the time gainfully to strengthen the defences of occupied Kuwait. In consequence, Allied casualty estimates were revised upwards. This latter fact again underlined the different positions and political risks involved between those states providing simple political support to the aims of the intervention as opposed to those with both military and political commitments.

The Gulf crisis demonstrated that whereas the desirability of the declaration of a unified aim was obvious, it was difficult to achieve in practice. The reasons for this included the nature of the dictator Hussein, the differing perspectives of the local and remoter actors, and the inability among some of the latter to make their intentions absolutely clear.

121

The maintenance of a unitary aim against the moving target of Saddam Hussein at the same time as the backdrop of regional affiliations was undergoing a form of musical chairs was no simple task. The Iraqi president used all the tricks available to deflect the focus of the Allies away from the fact of the original delict of the invasion of Kuwait. His attempt to convert the annexation of another state into a Muslim-versus-infidel conflict faltered, not least because he did not have the credentials to call a jihad, or holy war, and because the Koran offers no solace for aggressors. Furthermore, Saddam Hussein's late conversion to Islam failed to convince majority Muslim opinion, who remembered the late Ayatollah Khomeini labelling the Iraqi leader 'an enemy of God'. He also failed in his attempt to persuade his old enemy President Assad of Syria to reopen the Iraqi pipeline in Syria. A new and unconvincing ruse was to link the future of Palestine to the invasion of Kuwait.

The most significant of Saddam Hussein's manoeuvres occurred on 15 August 1990, when he renounced Iraq's claims to the Shatt-al-Arab waterway and agreed to return Iranian territory occupied by Iraq. It had been his refusal to recognize Iran's rights to the eastern side of the river system under the 1975 pact with Iran which had been instrumental in leading to war. He took that domestic political risk not least because of the hope of easing the embargo but also because of a genuine need to redeploy 300,000 troops from the Iranian border to the Kuwaiti border.

Saddam Hussein's change of heart over the Shatt-al-Arab was much less significant than it first appeared. The waterway had become useless, silted up and made doubly hazardous through intensive mining. One estimate put the cost of reopening the waterway at $10 billion. Saddam Hussein's focus of attention had therefore shifted away from the waterway running south from Basra and into Kuwaiti territorial waters. The belief in some areas that after such an apparently humiliating capitulation there was equal scope for his voluntary withdrawal from Kuwait was based on a fundamental misconception of the pertinent circumstances.

He attempted to woo the financially strapped Third World with offers of free oil, yet treated their nationals trapped in Iraq and Kuwait abominably. Meanwhile, he maintained pressure against what he saw to be the weak links in the Allied alliance, namely the Soviet Union and France. He played the hostage card to the full. France remained unmoved by the cynical early release of all her hostages but the steady procession of politicians to the tyrant's door in Baghdad provided welcome levels of undeserved propaganda and credibility. There is a lesson here.

Military academics expect from their students single aims. In the exceptional circumstances where there are two genuine, procedurally linked aims, the ploy is to use the conjunctive phrase 'with a view to'. This sleight of hand cannot be employed in the circumstances surrounding the Gulf because of the presence, arguably, of no less than three aims, only two of which were capable of being declared. The declaratory aims, supported by a broad international consensus, were to defend Saudi Arabia, and using the words in the UN resolution, to effect Iraq's 'immediate, unconditional and complete withdrawal from Kuwait'. The demand that Iraq should leave Kuwait was supported by both the Arab League and by Iran, no doubt because of the latter's concern arising from Iraq's possible occupation of Warba and Bubiyan islands.

The suggested unspoken aim was the neutralization of Saddam Hussein, his war-waging capability and his power base. Put simply, the aim of forcing Saddam Hussein out of Kuwait, for some, did not go far enough. For the crisis to be permitted to end with Saddam Hussein still in control in Iraq, with his chemical capability intact and with nuclear research and development continuing unabated, would be little more than an appeasing fudge. Yet the overt declaration of an aim which involved the removal of not only a *de facto* national leader but also one who claimed with some plausibility to champion the Arab cause would be counter-productive. It could be argued that such a proposed action was disproportionate to the original delict. But again, would such a legalistic interpretation take account of political and military necessity? The removal of Saddam Hussein never formed part of UN Resolutions and President Bush made it clear that the USA was not after Saddam Hussein. But the man's subsequent behaviour in attacking Israeli centres of civilian population, the humiliating display of prisoners of war and the use of them as human shields all suggested that Saddam Hussein and peace in the Middle East were incompatible. Yet there were practical difficulties in accessing one whose position was secured through a reign of ruthless terror and who was protected by a cushion of trusted, chosen elite. Furthermore, the legacy inherited by those who topple a regime is the obligation either to replace it or to fill the vacuum themselves.

A letter dwelling on the important matter of proportionality and signed by Lord Gifford QC and others, appeared in the London *Independent* of 14 January 1991. The lawyers concluded that:

> The authority given by Resolution 678 to member states to use 'all necessary means' to secure Iraq's withdrawal after 15 January 1991 is not a blank cheque for the United States to pursue its own ends by its own means. The choice of means is legally subject to the same principle of proportionality.

The letter continued:

> The readiness of the US to go to war in these circumstances suggests that the upholding of the rule of law between nations is not its true objective. This suspicion tends to be confirmed both by its passivity towards the illegal acts of 'friendly' nations (which until recently included Iraq), and by its own activity in invading other nations such

as Panama and Grenada and removing their governments.

A response to Lord Gifford's assertions came from Christopher Green-wood, Lecturer in International Law at Cambridge University. His letter appeared in the *Independent* on 16 January 1991.

Lord Gifford invokes the principle of proportionality, but misunder-stands its meaning. That principle requires that any use of force must not go beyond what is reasonably necessary to achieve the aims set out in Resolution 678, namely the removal of Iraq from Kuwait, ensuring compliance wi h all the relevant Council resolutions and restoring international peace and security in the area. It does not require the international community to reject recourse to force simply because Iraq has put so many troops into Kuwait that resort to force would entail heavy loss of life.

The comparisons drawn between US action in Panama and Grenada and Iraq's invasion of Kuwait were further described as 'untenable':

I would not defend the legality of those actions [Panama and Grenada], but in neither case did the US annex the countries concerned, impose a reign of terror upon the population or carry out large-scale looting. Moreover, in each case, there was clear majority support for the govern-ment that took power following the US intervention, something that cannot be said of popular Kuwaiti reaction to the Iraqi invasion.

Forcing Saddam Hussein out of Kuwait and thereby bruising his ego might have produced a more dangerous and better-prepared Iraqi response in the future. It remained little more than an outside possibility that Iraq's dictator might not again have been permitted the opportunity to exercise his doubtful strategy. Soldiers and politicians who consistently fail have no future. Just as General Galtieri's Falklands failure brought democracy to Argentina, it was seen as an outside possibility that Saddam Hussein's failure could provide a platform for the introduction into Iraq of a more benevolent, less ambitious regime. But then, the assassination of Saddam Hussein did not necessarily mean that changes would occur among the hierarchy: there were other Baathists waiting in the wings who could have taken his place.

The authority for military action lies in the UN Security Council Resolu-tions and they form the basis for the establishment of war aims. There is therefore an immediate conflict between a vaguely written Resolution, so crafted as to satisfy various international political sensitivities and the precision that military and political aims demand. The debate which emerged between these two quite distinct requirements threatened to wreck the Allied coalition.

Security Council Resolution 678 legitimized the use of force in order to 'restore international peace and security within the area'. What this meant was subject to different interpretations. Douglas Hurd admitted that the phrase was 'a wide one' and it was one which Britain and the United States interpreted as a licence to destroy that part of Iraq's military and strategic capabilities supporting the illegal occupation of Kuwait. In Britain, this apparent extension of war aims threatened the bilateral consensus. The leader of the opposition, Neil Kinnock, struggled to maintain front-bench solidarity among a number of shadow ministers who uneasily walked the tightrope between loyalty on one side and conscience on the other. In the United States, the president's declaration of an intention of bringing Saddam Hussein to trial for war crimes implied to some the invasion of Iraq and presumably its occupation. There were in fact no such plans to go into Iraq. Such a proposal would have gone beyond a strict interpretation of the UN Resolution. Or would it? Would it be possible for the area to enjoy international peace and security with Saddam Hussein still at the helm in Iraq?

One man who thought the Allies were acting outside their authority was Jean-Pierre Chevènement, the French socialist defence minister and founder of the Franco-Iraqi Friendship Society. His resignation, because 'the logic of war threatens to distance us each day from the objectives fixed by the United Nations', removed some of the ambiguity associated with France's Gulf policy. Lower down the scale, Italy's naval commander in the Gulf, Rear-Admiral Mario Buracchia, also resigned in protest. An official in the Soviet foreign ministry said that Moscow had not changed its position but restated the government's position that the aim was to liberate Kuwait, not to destroy Iraq. 'There is some concern,' said Vitaly Churkin, 'that, should the hostilities continue to escalate, it could lead to the devastation of Iraq'. President Gorbachev added weight to the growing Soviet concern about the war's development when he said on television on 9 February 1991: 'the logic of the military operations and the character of the military actions, threaten to exceed the mandate defined by these [UN] Resolutions'. The principal Soviet concern was the perception of the similarities to be drawn between a weakened Iraq and a weakened Germany after two world wars. They feared the emergence of a power vacuum as a result of enfeebling Iraq. Iraq's border lies only 150 miles from the Soviet Union. These considerations, as well as Gorbachev's personal need for political success, accounted for the peacemaking initiative prior to the commencement of hostilities. The Soviets maintained a foreign policy aim of preserving the Baath party, if not the party's unpredictable leader.

An Allied offensive, mounted with the blessing of the Security Council and aimed at relieving Kuwait, did not attract excessive international fall-out. Some reaction was anticipated from the terrorist groups who had so promptly transferred their allegiance from Damascus to Baghdad. An Allied land offensive deep into Iraq would be more controversial. It was widely believed that the Iraqi troops would fight with greater determination than they would in Kuwait and that the human toll on both sides would be very high. In addition, it was unlikely that Iran would welcome an intervention deep into Iraq by the former imperialists. Saudi Arabia did not want the emasculation of Iraq. Nor did Turkey, a member of NATO, relish upheaval in Iraq for fear of the ramifications in Kurdistan.

It seems increasingly likely that the ultimate pacification of Iraq has to be achieved in the medium term through the same formula that brought peace to the 'north'. The Cold War was finally declared to be at an end after general regional peacekeeping linked to planned disarmament had succeeded. That must be the aim for the Middle East. Having achieved mutual disarmament and force reduction, the peace must be guaranteed through the significant actors in the United Nations giving support to regional organizations. This means, *inter alia*, that the Palestine problem is inextricably linked to a Middle East peace initiative. It requires that states give equal emphasis to Security Council Resolutions 242 and 660. To suggest that there is no association between the Gulf crisis and Palestine is the expression of a fond but myopic hope. Although a Palestine settlement is linked to the Middle East peace process, Kuwait was a quite separate subject. It was a straightforward case of naked aggression. To group a Palestine and Kuwait settlement together would only have served to reward Saddam Hussein by enhancing his status. It has to be remembered that the Cold War had made an earlier settlement of Palestine's problem a political non-starter, as could the occupation of Palestinian lands be argued, at the time it occurred, to have been a necessary defence in the face of threats emanating from neighbouring Arab states.

OPERATE UNDER THE AUSPICES AND CO-ORDINATION OF A VALID AND SUPPORTIVE INTERNATIONAL ORGANIZATION

The operation of the Allied coalition under the auspices of the United Nations removed many of the problems encountered in Siberia in 1918–20 and in the Lebanon in 1982–4. It is true that the cause in the 1990–1 Gulf intervention evoked more sympathy, particularly in the Third World, whose hidden veto will increasingly influence what can and cannot be achieved in international relations. The annexation of a member state by another was a precedent which they and the medium and superpowers did not wish to see established. It was this consensus and support of states which bestowed upon the intervention its validity and also its legality through the series of twelve Security Council Resolutions.

Towards the end of the Gulf operation international support for the armed conflict had begun to waver. It was particularly within the Third World that attitudes had begun to change to horror as the selectively transmitted television pictures conveyed images of the massive destruction inflicted on Iraq over a short period. While this action could be salutary in the case of potential aggressor states, the feeling of many small states apparently was that there was a lack of proportionality in the western response. Further destruction of Iraqi ground forces at Mutla Ridge, justified as militarily necessary, could probably not have been sustained politically. Had something similar occurred at the beginning rather than at the end of the operation, serious difficulties would have arisen. The eleventh-hour change of Third World attitudes probably influenced the Secretary-General. Coming from a Third World country himself, he may well have shared them.

The word within this generic heading, not used thus far, is 'co-ordination': 'The war is not a classic United Nations war in the sense that there is no United Nations control of the operations, no United Nations flag,[blue] helmet, or any engagement of the military staff committee,' said UN Secretary-General Javier Pérez de Cuéllar.

> What we know about the war, which I prefer to call hostilities, is what we hear from the three members of the Security Council which are involved – Britain, France and the United States – which every two or three days report to the Council after the actions have taken place. The Council, which has authorised all this [is informed] only after the military activities have taken place.

In different circumstances, different conditions and different places, such latitude might well prove difficult either to sustain or to replicate. The potential political penalties are so enormous that it might be that in the future no one state is prepared to carry such an awesome burden. The formal Article 42 route would have been ideally suited to the Gulf crisis but although the machinery was in existence it was not in working order. The UN was unprepared for the rapidity of the political change in Europe and hence the new possibilities in international relations. But the members of the Military Staff Committee did meet informally from August 1990 onwards to exchange information. There is no reason why, in the future, the Military Staff Committee representing the symbolic will of the United Nations could not co-opt other interested states on to regional sub-committees in accordance with Article 47(4). In that way, the acceptability of the Military Staff Committee would be improved and its capacity to plan and co-ordinate Article 42 activities might in time be brought into action.

ESTABLISH A SIMPLE AND AGREED, UNITED COMMAND AND CONTROL, COMMUNICATIONS AND INTELLIGENCE ORGANIZATION

The greatest possible indictment of the Allied response to the invasion of Kuwait was the fact that two months after the initial deployment little of substance had been achieved in grasping the nettle of command and control. It seemed that the emergence of three distinct alliances was a possibility. Britain and the United States took an independent line from the Europeans, whose co-ordinated response became the aspiration of the Western European Union. Meanwhile, the Arab states insisted that their forces should remain separate entities from non-Arab states. As long as the mixed bag of Muslim, American, Western European, Argentinian, Czech and Polish forces remained on the defensive, the cracks could be papered over. When the force decided to move on to the offensive, against a prepared enemy, enjoying the benefits of operating from interior lines of communication, and commanded through a simple and direct command structure, then the scope for disaster could have been of enormous proportions. That much was evident from the minor incursion at Khafji. For the Allied coalition to work, to maintain its cohesion at times of difficulty, even of reverses, the overwhelming need for one overall commander was apparent to the most elementary of military novices. There were difficulties because there was no prescribed organization and there were divergent opinions. At the eleventh hour, those who had not accepted American leadership fell into line. However, the obvious lack of preparedness and absence of contingency planning is one matter that needs to be resolved within the UN and its Military Staff Committee.

It is a function of that committee to be responsible under the Security Council (47(3)) 'for the strategic direction of any armed forces placed at the disposal of the Security Council'. The circumstances surrounding the random arrival of supporting, polyglot armies, often unsuited to the environment, bringing incompatible equipment to serve under their own specific leadership and speaking as diverse a range of languages as seems possible is undesirable. In two months the number of nationalities comprising the land forces had equalled the fourteen states involved in the Russian Intervention of 1918–20. (In the space of two more months, it had doubled.) Only four of the fourteen states had operated together within the NATO alliance. The UN Charter is precise concerning agreements being reached between the United Nations and the donor states: 'Such agreement or agreements shall govern the numbers and types of forces, their degree of readiness and general location, and the nature of the facilities and assistance to be provided' (43(2)). The circumstances of the 1990s are not those of 1945 but surely today it is possible to negotiate something rather than perpetuate the 'too difficult' syndrome.

In the Gulf, the co-ordination of plans between states took a long time. The major sea body of the French forces, for example, at the time the second largest national contingent after the USA, was already *en route* while their commander, General Michel Roquejeoffre, was desperately searching out a location in which to put them that was 'far enough away from the Americans and from the Arab armies under Saudi command'. In a carbon copy re-enactment of the command discussion between the Japanese General Otani and the American General Graves in Siberia in 1918, the Saudi

General Prince Khaled told General Roquejeoffre that he, the prince, was 'the unique leader'. The French general demurred, restating the official French line that Roquejeoffre's function was limited to co-ordination between the nationally commanded forces in the region. What this meant precisely was put succinctly by M. Chevènement at the French War College: France would retain its 'autonomy of decision and autonomy of action'.

Such imprecise and indecisive hot planning of the role and deployment of international forces invariably means that those who will suffer are the individual members of national contingents. Operations Desert Shield, Granby and Daguet were the separate codenames of the American, British and French operations in Saudi Arabia.

There was a great deal to applaud in America's rapid and professionally executed deployment. No other single nation could have emulated what the Americans had done. The USA was by far the biggest participant with the biggest responsibility and therefore the biggest risks. Power and authority in any alliance can be claimed by the state making the largest contribution. It undeniably made good sense for the overall commander to be an American, as well perhaps as the air, land and sea functional commanders supported by military representatives of the donor states in an Allied military council. Such a proposition could have caused problems for the Arabs and the French but it is a possibility that if the nominated United States commanders reported to the United Nations, then scope would have existed for sensible compromise and early resolution of the problem. The French paper *Libération* indicated that over half of those interviewed would favour French forces serving under a UN commander. It was certainly a condition established by the Soviets before their troops could even be considered for deployment to the Gulf. But President George Bush maintained that US forces would 'be unquestionably under US command'. He pursued a dogged resistance to subordinating his given constitutional right to command US forces to a supranational body. Rarely, if ever today, would the right of full command of one state's forces be passed to another state.

In the Korean War, the United Nations handed the mandate to lead and command the war effort under the UN flag to the United States. The supreme commander, General Douglas MacArthur, reported to President Truman, not to the UN. The war plans, bankrolling of the intervention and the principal decision-making originated in Washington, not in the UN in New York. At the time, this option was realistic and reflected the actual power and position of hegemony enjoyed by the United States.

There is recognition in the Pentagon that the wind has changed. All recent US presidents have been identified by their own doctrine. George Bush's first attempt at a doctrine has been to embrace the inevitability of multilateralism through the New World Order but with America taking first place.

As the principal underwriter of the United States presence in the Middle

East and supplier of the exposed main base, the Saudi leadership insisted on having a say in decisions affecting offensive and defensive operations. The general appointed in charge of Arab and Islamic forces, Prince Khaled bin Sultan, emphasized that any military operation originating from Saudi territory would need to be 'consulted' between King Fahd and President Bush. The US Defence Secretary, Richard Cheney, did say that the chain of command established with Saudi Arabia in November 1990 'adequately safeguards our concerns and their concerns'. While on the defensive, the forces were under joint US/Saudi control, but when the offensive was launched supreme command was assumed by General Schwarzkopf.

It seemed likely during the defensive phase that the United States reserved the right to respond unilaterally in self-defence where an attack on US forces occurred. The attack on North Vietnam was justified on the basis of what proved to be bogus claims that two North Vietnamese motor torpedo boats fired on two US destroyers in the Gulf of Tonkin. What also emerged in the resultant Gulf of Tonkin Resolution was the support given by Congress to the president to take requisite action to repel armed attacks against US forces. The well-known Article 51 invites states to claim that their attack was in the interest of their defence.

The concern that weighed heaviest on the contrastingly cautious Saudi mind was the fear of being drawn into an irretrievable position as a result of the United States' natural impatience and disdain of protracted conflicts.

First and foremost, the Saudis sought to control those troops whose cost they had largely agreed to underwrite and who had been invited on to sovereign Saudi territory. The invitation had been a calculated gamble and offered a propaganda weapon to Saddam Hussein to link the infidels' close proximity to the holy cities of Mecca and Medina. Certainly, the Saudis needed protection, certainly they supported the restoration of the Emir of Kuwait, but with equal certainty they did not relish an unlimited war into Iraq's territory. Their impression of the previous large-scale American deployment in Vietnam degenerating into a very basic but all-out shooting war was not a *modus operandi* they could support in the Middle East. The Saudis recognized that when such a frightening war in the Middle East had ended, the Americans would return home, for better or for worse, leaving the Saudis the legacy of unrestrained military action within their region. There was nothing in the early gung-ho rhetoric of some senior American generals to calm the fears of the Saudis and convince them that all would be well. It was no part of their strategic goal to see Iraq so seriously weakened that she could no longer serve as a plausible buffer between Saudi Arabia and Iran. Certainly, some months after the warfighting had elapsed, when the United States sought to re-establish a modest force level in Saudi Arabia to exert pressure on Saddam Hussein, the Saudis were found to be unenthusiastic.

Successful command is all to do with confidence, both political and military. International forces require the confidence to know that they are waging war in the interest of international peace rather than as the tool for the extension of one nation's singular foreign policy. It is this fundamental suspicion that complicated an early resolution of the command problem. Were the coalition partners the Allies or the auxiliaries of the Americans?

Confidence in a commander stems from his own leadership qualities, which have been described as 'a combination of the will to dominate and the character to inspire; it is that quality in a man which inspires others to follow him'. But a more encompassing description was given by Correlli Barnett to the Staff College at Camberley in 1965, which fits the military situation at the outset of the 1990 Middle East operation to a tee:

> Leadership is a psychological force that has nothing to do with morals or good character or even intelligence: nothing to do with ideals or idealism. It is a matter of relative will powers, a basic connation between one animal and the rest of the herd. *Leadership is a process by which a single aim and unified action are imparted to the herd.*[134] Not surprisingly it is most in evidence in times of circumstances of danger or challenge. Leadership is not imposed like authority. It is actually welcomed and wanted by the led.

It is evident, however, that in a multilateral operation the supreme commander may well be all of these things to his own nationals, but, through no fault of his own, will not be so convincing to other nationals. It may have nothing at all to do with personal qualities but could be due to the acceptable management of a national system which has problems in being credibly translated internationally. These national differences will always produce situations where leadership styles do not induce confidence in the troops of other nations. In short, 'friction' can be at its worst within Allied coalitions. It can be reduced by integrated training, the existence of common Standard Operating Procedures, interoperability and commonality of equipment. The coalition war put together by the Allies in the Gulf was the worst possible example. They were divided by different doctrine, equipment, procedures, languages and national interests. A great equalizer proved to be General Norman Schwarzkopf, the right man at the right time in the right place.

Britain agreed to place the first-to-deploy, 8,000-strong, reinforced armoured brigade under the tactical control of the Americans. Full command was retained by the resident British general, General de la Billiere, who could, if militarily desirable, move the British forces from formation to formation. The scope for natural friction is reduced in the expanse of the desert more so than on the last occasion, in 1982–4, when British and Americans served together in urban Lebanon. The loose command and control that was evident in Beirut had greatly concerned the British Queen's Dragoon Guards group. On one occasion the sky in their tactical area of responsibility (TAOR) was 'black with aircraft' as US carrier-borne planes hit ground targets close to their base. When complaints over the failure to communicate intentions were transmitted to the US Marines at the airport, they were equally in the dark. 'Probably the 6th Fleet Admiral flexing his muscles' was the reply.

Even though the two nations had been serving in NATO for forty-one years, the cross-fusion of formations across national, inter-corps boundaries in the Central Front was only beginning to take its first tentative steps when NATO's military balloon was deflated. Besides, the Americans and British never enjoyed contiguous corps boundaries, so there has not been a compelling need to harmonize operating procedures. In the close quarters of the jungles of Vietnam, the American approach to solving tactical problems was so fundamentally different to that of the Australians that the latter insisted on maintaining their own tactical area of responsibility.

The American solution of dealing with threats with displays of extreme violence is a reflection of the society from which they have evolved as well as having the wherewithal to bring superior firepower down on a given point. Historically, they have had small regular forces but the size was compensated for by considerable firepower engineered out of a rich source of technology and industry. When the armies were expanded for operations in Europe, Korea and Vietnam, they still retained the high ratio of armed support previously enjoyed by smaller forces. Europeans are necessarily cautious and economic with their firepower, regarding its indiscriminate use as profligate.

No one could be certain that the US national command had resolved its own command and control problems before undertaking the additional burden of commanding troops of other nations. Major-General Norman Schwarzkopf, the deputy on-scene commander in the Grenada intervention, said of that episode that although 'the higher HQ screws it up every way', in the end 'it is the initiative and valour on the part of small unit leadership that will win for you every time'. Of the eighteen declared US fatalities in Grenada, ten (or 60 per cent) had been as a result of so-called 'friendly fire', or what the British describe as 'blue on blue'. While serving as a battalion commander in Vietnam in the 23rd American Infantry Division, General Schwarzkopf lost one of his sergeants to US shellfire. The general was then featured in a 1976 book by C.D.B. Bryan entitled *Friendly Fire*.

A more recent opportunity to ascertain whether US command and control problems had been resolved was available in Panama in 1989. That experience acknowledges the particular effort that was made to improve control but the results again were to be a source of great disappointment. The February 1990 edition of *Armed Forces Journal* carried an article on the invasion of Panama, Operation Just Cause: 'Everyone studied the ROE [rules of engagement], and every commander had to brief his subordinates on the ROE until he was sure that they understood them ...'.

All of the Army helicopter crew chiefs and door gunners involved in Just Cause were thoroughly briefed on the risks of injuring innocent civilians, and relieved commanders repeatedly praised the restraint and fire discipline shown by gunners (as well as soldiers on the ground) who avoided returning small arms fire coming from populated areas near some assault zones.

Nevertheless, an estimated 500 Panamanian civilians were killed and circumstances indicate that the blame for the high civilian death toll cannot entirely be placed on troops loyal to Noriega. A report in the London *Independent* of 19 June 1990 claimed that once again up to 60 per cent of the US soldiers killed or wounded in Panama were hit by their own side.

It is an unfortunate aspect of warfare that 'friendly fire' (which is technically amicide but is more usually described as fratricide) will take a toll of its own people. A low figure would be in the region of 5 per cent of casualties while a high figure would be 25 per cent. Statistics from the British Commando Brigade fighting in the Falklands, much of which was at night and involved close-quarter battle, was under 4 per cent. On the other hand, the French artillery at Verdun killed three Frenchmen for every ten Germans. Sixty per cent is therefore a very high figure, but it is distorted by the relatively low number of casualties arising in Grenada, Panama and the Gulf. Headquarters US Central Command in the Gulf admitted that, of the twelve marines killed in the first two weeks of the ground war on the Kuwait/Saudi border, eight had been victims of 'friendly fire'. By war's end, 35 of the 145 Americans killed in action during Operation Desert Storm and 72 of the 467 wounded were 'friendly fire' victims. Nine out of the twenty-five British war fatalities in the Gulf were killed by United States fire. The circumstances of that tragic accident were fully investigated. The valid lessons which arise are the need, as confidence-building measures in coalition warfare, for improved communications, recognition training and a solution to the Identification Friend-or-Foe (IFF) problem. Command and control difficulties are less evident in purely land operations than when the air and naval dimensions are introduced. Seven M-1A1 tanks and twenty of the twenty-five Bradley fighting vehicles lost in the Gulf battle were lost to US fire.

General Norman Schwarzkopf established the USCENTCOM headquarters in Riyadh. In the adjoining office was Prince Khaled of Saudi Arabia. General Schwarzkopf enjoyed an unusual degree of individual authority. The lessons learned from Vietnam and the Lebanon 1982–4 where, in the first instance, the president had involved himself in target selection and, in the second, where every military move had been carefully micromanaged, had thankfully been applied. General Schwarzkopf's authority spanned the four service branches so that in theory inter-service rivalry did not become an unwelcome feature of the war. Power had been delegated down the chain of command to the field commanders responsible for influencing the battle. 'One of the things that I am most thankful for,' said General Schwarzkopf,

> is that the President of the United States, the Secretary for Defence and General Colin Powell, have allowed the commanders in the field to do what the commanders in the field think is correct. Obviously, we brief them on what we are doing. Obviously, if they thought we were doing something dumb, they'd tell us about it, and we'd change it. But they're allowing the commanders in the field to conduct this war. We're going to be able to run this campaign the way it's militarily smart.

General Schwarzkopf's central problem lay in the need to beef up the light forces whose rapid response had been so instrumental in forestalling any possible hostile move against Saudi Arabia. Phase one had been to assemble the 200,000-strong force structure capable of defending Saudi Arabian and Emirate territory. Phase two, the option of using 500,000 men for offensive action, required a build-up of significantly more assets but, more importantly, the overwhelming need was for armour and artillery rather than airborne and light forces. There were too many of the latter group and there was a prevalence of symbolic gestures threatening to make command and control a nightmare. When Britain announced that she was prepared to assign ground forces to the Gulf, the USA was quite specific about what it needed. It did not need 5 Airborne Brigade or 24 Airmobile Brigade; it needed armour to face the threat posed by Soviet T-72 tanks and that meant a brigade, and later a division, from the 1st British Corps in Germany.

There is no small irony in the realization that the British 1st Armoured Division was now faced with the prospect of doing what it had been trained to do: fight Soviet armour – not in Europe's central region but in the desert where its forebears, the 7th Armoured Division, the Desert Rats, had served in the Second World War with such distinction and *élan*. The machinery and means of exercising high-intensity conflict had therefore been imposed upon what had been assumed to be an environment susceptible to low-intensity conflict. The former high-intensity conflict arena of the Central Front had now been relegated by consideration of options for possible low-intensity conflict. The initial placing of the British 7th Armoured Brigade with its Challenger tanks in support of an American Marine division, light in armour, ensured that Britain's response was seen to be more than symbolic. Once it was decided to deploy an armoured division, agreement was reached that the British division would operate with the VII US Corps.

The preoccupation with the command and control problems on land is indicative of where the major problem lay. This is not to say that there were no problems at sea and in the air. Command and control at sea was potentially the least fraught because eleven of the fifteen donor navies were NATO members and the Australian contingent is NATO-compatible. This did not mean however that the normally NATO-assigned forces initially had the same rules of engagement.

The principal difficulty in coordination lay in the fact that there were so many navies. Since the action lay outside the NATO area, NATO was unable to co-ordinate the naval reaction to the UN embargo. Instead, European interests were being co-ordinated by the Western European Union, as had happened in 1987 during the Iran/Iraq War. They made an effort to harmonize the European rules of engagement and air attack precautions as well as to share intelligence and logistics (something the land forces would benefit from). But the fact that the WEU lacks an effective command and control mechanism became apparent. The French naval force, which had numbered seven warships, indicated that it would act independently. Whereas NATO-assigned naval forces used the standard procedures outlined in the NATO Allied Tactical Procedures (ATPS), it proved impossible to adopt totally common ROE, which remained subject to national interpretations and harmonization.

An example of the disinformation rife at the beginning of the Gulf crisis was a false report that the USS *Saratoga* carrier group operating in the Red Sea was forced to scatter to avoid a head-on collision with two Italian warships. Press speculation suggested that the report was made in all probability to underline the need for a more formal command and control structure in the Gulf. Yet the problem was more fundamental than that, because the navies were not operating from the same sheet of music.

Air warfare is arguably the least difficult of the three elements to control, but that remains a relative statement. Six of the ten airforces involved were NATO-assigned. At the outset it was necessary for the British, Saudis and Americans to harmonize the rules under which Iraqi aircraft could be engaged. The British also had to refit their aircraft with an American IFF kit so that the two airforces could avoid shooting each other down. 'Weapons free' and 'weapons tight' policies are but some of the controls that have to be inculcated into multilateral sea and land forces to prevent the shooting down of friendly or neutral aircraft. This is easier said than done when it is realized that Iraq was equipped with French jets and helicopters. Whether on land, air or sea, there is a decided need to draw up common operating procedures in an environment not overshadowed by the threat of war. It is virtually irrelevant to maintain that the crisis enabled a solution to be evolved in time. In the next crisis, there may not be the time. What proved to be beneficial was the computer control of the airspace into and out of Kuwait and Iraq. So comprehensive is the Tactical Expert Mission Planner (Templar) and its supporting information systems that, for example, it would have proven difficult for Israel to have mounted an unauthorized retaliatory airstrike on Iraq with manned aircraft.

The crisis engendered by Iraq served to underline the celebrated dichotomy in the process of intelligence threat analysis between the assessment of intentions and capabilities. The quality and quantity of information is reported to have been extraordinarily good, although the assessment of that intelligence was complicated by the existence of what were, in effect, a number of competing agencies, principally the Defence Intelligence Agency (DIA) and the CIA. Whereas the capabilities had been accurately determined through a wealth of communications assets, particularly signals intercepts, photo-reconnaissance and radar satellites, there arose a serious misinterpretation of this high-quality information. It is possible that Washington assumed Saddam's posturing was aimed at ultimately securing limited border objectives over which the State Department had apparently expressed its neutral position.

There is then the question of the Soviets. There are those who doubt that it was possible for Saddam Hussein to have kept his intentions secret from the large number of Soviet military and technical advisers in Iraq. It is certain that a number of advisers stayed on in Iraq voluntarily, principally because it made economic sense to them personally. There was some speculation that the conservative Soviet General Albert Mikhailovich Makashov was observed in Baghdad immediately prior to the invasion. That would have been significant were it true, for the Volga-Ural Military District, which he commanded, also supplied the Soviet Union's Strategic Reserve. After the August 1991 coup Makashov was replaced by General Sergeev and plans were put in place for the military districts to conform with republic boundaries. It is probably correct to surmise that some in the Soviet military would have been aware of what was about to happen, but this does not mean that the Kremlin was involved. Soviet politics divides between an official line and a conspiratorial line. There is a similarity here with the situation that arose between Colonel Oliver North and President Reagan.

Early in 1991 Andrei Piontkowsky warned of the misconception implicit in the use of the phrase the 'Soviet view'. It is not a monolithic entity; opinion is as diverse as in America. This goes some way towards explaining the prevarication with the CFE agreements. There were at the time in the Soviet Union strong pockets of support for Saddam Hussein, mostly among the military and the business community. The selfsame General Makashov distinguished himself by criticizing the official Gorbachev line during the 1990 Party Congress. Also, politically it was possible in the early months to identify two distinct political threads woven respectively by the westernizer, Edward Schevardnadze, and the Arabist, Yevgeny Primakov. 'Westernizers' identified themselves with the western line intent on removing Saddam Hussein from Kuwait. The 'Arabists' insisted that although

Saddam Hussein's occupation of Kuwait was regrettable, Moscow should nevertheless retain its links with Iraq, her former ally and oil and arms trading partner. In his formative years, Primakov had served as a *Pravda* Middle East correspondent and became associated with Nasser. Nasser had been the subject of his PhD. During his *Pravda* days, Primakov also became acquainted with Saddam Hussein.

The military had also shown some surprising independence in decision-making. Their high-handedness in converting three motor rifle divisions to come under command of the Soviet Navy (which therefore inherited more armour than existed in the British Army) and the removal of military assets eastward beyond the Urals, threatened the viability of the whole CFE process. Elsewhere, other national intelligence agencies, particularly the Arabs, had failed to read the indicators correctly. But it will invariably be the case that human, as opposed to technological intelligence will be difficult to gather within a dictatorship or closed hierarchy such as Iraq.

It was obvious that the United States would take the lead in co-ordinating intelligence. Britain's regional experience was able to make a positive contribution. The Soviets came forward to provide technical information on the Scud missile systems but US intelligence collators became irritated by the French who, keen to protect their defence sales position, proved to be less forthcoming.

In this confrontation the Allies would be almost entirely dependent on technologically based intelligence, unable to fathom the mind of the unpredictable and constantly on the move Saddam Hussein, who made just one public appearance during the first sixty days of the crisis. Technology helped to pinpoint his whereabouts on a day-to-day basis through comprehensive signals intercepts. A British Sunday newspaper gave an insight into the intelligence network at the West's disposal.[135] Lacrosse radar satellites provided important data on what was happening in and around Iraq but perhaps the most important US spy asset proved to be the KH (Keyhole) 12 advanced crystal photo-reconnaissance satellite capable of producing conventional or infra-red pictures. The definition is good down to six inches, making it possible after each cycle to monitor minute changes taking place in the featureless desert below. As for Saddam Hussein, it had been said that he derived a good proportion of his information from an American twenty-four-hour world television news service; he showed his gratitude to that company by giving them for a time sole broadcasting rights from Baghdad. The company became an unwitting conduit for Iraqi propaganda, being unable to research and analyse its own material to be broadcast without first subjecting it to Iraqi censorship.

The 1990-1 Gulf crisis can truly be described as the first of the television wars. The reality of the 'global village' had been evident during, for example, the Romanian revolution. The strong images generated there prompted the USA to mark the tenth anniversary of the invasion of Afghanistan with a suggestion to the Soviets that they intervene in Romania. In Britain, television viewing leapt in the first week of the armed conflict in the Gulf. BARB, the audience research body, reported that in the first week Britons watched nearly four and a half hours more television than normal.

The media corps that assembled in Saudi Arabia was one thousand strong. There were complaints and resentment, particularly among Americans, but most remained understanding and co-operative. An opinion poll published by the American Times Mirror Centre in week two of the war showed that despite press complaints of 'military censorship', 57 per cent of the public supported even greater restrictions. Editors had given instructions that the boat was not to be rocked. The British newspapers were particularly partisan: all twenty-one of the major papers had come out in favour of armed action. Some 300 reporters came within the military-controlled pool reporting system or media response teams, while those not under military control were under constant threat that breaches of military security would lead to the withdrawal of their Saudi visas. Had the Allied victory been less emphatic, it seems likely that many of the free-range reporters would have put themselves in positions of severe risk and grave danger. Press briefings were given nationally, thereby creating an unconvincing impression of collegiality. It seems impossible to recall one occasion when the principal national military commanders were seen together.

PLAN THE FORCE EXTRACTION CONCURRENTLY WITH THE FORCE INSERTION

Precise, unambiguous aims, and therefore the concept of what constitutes success, contribute towards the validation of the principle that a state should pencil in an outline withdrawal plan or plans concurrently with the formulation of the plans for the force insertion. That is a statement difficult to contradict for it has long been an historical maxim that it is folly to start a war without having some idea of how it will end. Such a truism is of particular relevance to the Middle East, since the continuing presence of Allied troops post-conflict always threatened to pose political difficulties in some areas. It is therefore ideal when planning a coalition war, where national variations in aims and perception of success will be evident, that such an important matter as force extraction has to be agreed multilaterally in outline before the initial deployment of forces into the theatre of operations.

There was an impression at some stages in the Gulf War that the Allied political direction was taking a secondary role to the military action. This impression was most assuredly put in its place once open conflict had broken out. For example, the Scud missiles launched by Iraq into neighbouring countries posed no significant military threat. It was, however, the fact of their political significance which conspired to attract the diversion of a disproportionate amount of military assets. In *Vom Krieg*

138

Clausewitz emphasized the primacy of politics, insisting that war was but an extension of politics. Political ideas and plans as to how the peace would be won were released haphazardly from individual capitals like wayward rockets well after hostilities proper had begun.

It was of interest that Iraq had a different approach to the war, as though Saddam Hussein recognized the inevitability of Iraq's military defeat, yet saw the possibility of winning political victory. His use of public relations and propaganda was masterful. His grasp of strategy was dreadful, yet he did understand the politics of war. At what stage after 15 January 1991 the Allies became aware that the Iraqis were fighting a totally different type of war is not clear. It does not require the twenty-twenty hindsight of the Amstrad strategist to observe elements of the unconventional in the skirmish at Khafji, a Saudi town normally of 10,000 inhabitants, which began at 10.30 p.m. on Tuesday, 29 January 1991.

Credence usually given to elementary military principles would have precluded an Iraqi foray which derived its limited success principally from the failures in command, control, communications and intelligence between the responsible American, Saudi and Qatari forces. More surprising was the failure of the Iraqis to support the night attack with artillery, particularly since their air support had been neutralized. Nevertheless, the Iraqis performed bravely, suffering heavy casualties, but their drive into Khafji in normal circumstances should have been caught in the slips. It had been an Iraqi action centred less on the military art than on its political value of gaining for Saddam increased favour among the Arab masses. The Iraqis hoped that the anticipated heavy American casualties would constitute the opening round in a psychological war aimed against a public assumed to be unable and unwilling to accept high casualties. The Allies declared – whether they believed it or not – that Khafji 'was of no military importance' to them, but to Saddam Hussein a limited military success had much significance.

What the foregoing adds up to is the overwhelming importance of stepping into the opponent's shoes as an essential preliminary towards understanding his mind and, therefore, his likely actions. Sandhurst students tasked with planning the defence of a feature were encouraged by their instructors, as a teaching expedient, to look at their position from the enemy's side. Unless a detailed study is made of the courses open to the enemy and a decision taken as to his most likely course of action, then it is impossible to begin to think in advance of uncoupling at war's end. These conflicts are never fought in a vacuum and, despite possessing a prodigious military machine, Saddam posed greater political than military danger within the region. Unless problems are looked at comprehensively from the enemy's point of view it is not possible to come close to the right conclusion regarding the force extraction.

The night of the Khafji battle on Tuesday, 29 January 1991 had been bright, with a full moon. It was not the night that conservative military prudence would have thought sensible for the dispatch of four armoured columns of relatively dated T-55s against the proven high-tech capability of the ground and air weapons in the Allied armoury. But that would have been a military judgement which ignored the political benefits to be accrued from the Iraqi seizure of an important town six miles inside Saudi Arabia and holding on to it for thirty-six hours. A similar misconception had occurred in Australia at the time of the Cowra breakout on 5 August 1944 (see pp. 164–5). The night then had also been clear, starlit, with just a dusting of ground frost. The Australian guards believed that an escape attempt by their Japanese prisoners of war, which was fully anticipated, would be made in misty or foggy conditions. They were guilty of ascribing to their enemy their own, western way of thinking. The weather on 5 August 1944 was ideal for a group determined to die to atone for the dishonour of capture, through the instrument of a kamikaze-style attack on a nearby recruit training camp.

What this all adds up to is simply that to plan the force extraction, if only in outline, requires a sound understanding of the opposition. The courses open to him have to be identified and, if necessary, subsequently updated and refined before troops begin their deployment. In some circumstances, in other places, intervention may need to be immediate. In such an event there has to be a multilateral contingency plan where the groundwork has already been completed. The political debate must identify what the coalition plans for peace happen to be. Unity is essential from beginning to end. There is nothing quite so conclusive as the probability that a successful war-winning coalition which has no collective plans continuing thereafter will most assuredly lose the peace.

ESTABLISH AN EFFECTIVE *CORDON SANITAIRE* AROUND THE TARGET AREA

The Kuwait crisis illustrates very clearly the distinction between an embargo and the escalatory measure of moving to a blockade which is imposed by one belligerent upon another. There was some early sensitivity in using the word 'blockade' due to its common association with war and its legal definition. When President Bush was questioned on 19 August 1990 about whether he was calling for a naval blockade to enforce the UN trade embargo against Iraq, he replied: 'I'm not prepared to use the word blockade, but we are prepared.'

The function of the sanctions imposed against Iraq was to impress upon Saddam Hussein the error of his ways or, taken to the extreme, to cause such devastating misery among his people that he would be overthrown by those interests desirous of a return to the status quo *ante bellum*. Never before had the UN imposed such a comprehensive sanctions regime but it soon became apparent that the UN had no framework to handle the effects of sanctions. Sanctions should and will hurt. The controls imposed upon the importation of foods and medicines into Iraq caused a great moral outcry among the leaders of the Third World: their interest lay in their own neglected nationals in Kuwait and Iraq. Despite two months of a heavy outflow of refugees through Jordan and Iran there were seventeen Third World states with significant numbers of nationals still in Kuwait and Iraq, most too impecunious to leave. The states principally concerned were Egypt (1.25 million); Palestine (470,000); India (126,000); Sri Lanka (85,000: in Kuwait); Bangladesh (75,000); Pakistan (45,000); Philippines (43,000); Morocco (36,000); and Syria (30,000: in Kuwait).

By the end of September 1990 the total number of predominantly male western 'guests' had fallen below 5,000 and, by the end of January 1991, those desirous of leaving had left. Unlike the Third World nationals, those westerners under Iraqi control were being well cared for. Speaking of the Third World representatives, Saddam Hussein said they would starve before Iraqis. Herein lay a potential schism between the developed and the developing world and a real threat to international unanimity which was capable of being exploited. The USA knew that there were indeed adequate food stocks still in Iraq but needed to be persuaded that the *Gastarbeiters* did not have access to these supplies. Once the USA was persuaded to withdraw its objections and Iraq had agreed to relief supplies being distributed by the Indian Red Cross, an exception was made and an Indian ship carrying food supplies was cleared for passage to Kuwait.

Sanctions as an enforcement mechanism are hard, but they are preferable to war. The humanitarian implications of starving women and children, however, are considerations which have to be afforded realistic weighting. If sanctions are to succeed in accordance with the wishes of an undoubted world consensus they must be ruthlessly and exclusively imposed. Iraq did have some reserve stocks but years of mismanagement and an almost zero credit rating meant that these stocks were not of siege proportions. However, it is a trait of human nature that in adversity people very often tighten their belts, close ranks and become commendably resilient. This was a feature of the civilian populations during the Iran/Iraq War. The embargo of Iraq was never going to produce a quick fix, but it could produce a fix. Few countries could be more effectively subjected to a blockade. The Iraqi people would suffer and so, to a greater or lesser degree, would their 'guests'.

The immediate response of the European Community, the USA, the Soviet Union and Japan was to stop importing Iraq's crude oil, thereby in one stroke depriving Iraq of two-thirds of its market. In addition, Iraq's assets were frozen, as were Kuwait's. This was not a significant measure for Iraq since she was estimated to have only $6 billion in foreign banks and was losing revenues of $500 million for each day the crisis continued. The

141

final act of the representatives of the developed world, the Soviet Union and China was to ban the export of arms. Saddam Hussein's ability to wage war and his forces' sustainability thereby came under immediate pressure. What would have surprised the Iraqi leadership was the strength of the opposition mobilized against them. Also surprising was the division that occurred within the Arab League, the majority agreeing to support Security Council Resolution 661 obliging states to impose sanctions on Iraq. On 6 August 1990 the Security Council set up a sanctions committee to monitor the implementation of Resolution 661. Even Switzerland, not a member of the UN and therefore not bound by Resolution 661, agreed to co-operate. In the past, she had declined to take part in economic sanctions against other states. Klaus Jacobi, the State Secretary explained: 'Iraq is guilty of such a flagrant violation that we simply cannot stand idly by. We must sometimes slay sacred cows.'

The extent to which Iraq could ride out an embargo depended to a large degree upon the strength of her sanction-beating assets. To that end she sacked Kuwait, moving everything of value, including strategic food reserves, northward into Iraq. The theft of an estimated $500–800 million in gold provided negotiable currency for the purchase of limited amounts of black-market goods, which contributed to beating the embargo. Since Iran imports 60 per cent of her produce, the cross-border flow of foodstuffs and material was not significant. Iraq's economic condition had grown to be so parlous that it had become her *casus belli*. She had little by way of funds to buy from an inflated black market.

Within a very short time her oil-dominant export market, other than a trickle of gratuitous oil into Jordan, had dried up. It had been a straightforward task to turn the tap off. Ninety per cent of Iraq's oil is exported through two of three pipelines. Syria had already closed down her Iraqi pipeline in April 1982. This central pipeline took oil for export to the Syrian terminal at Banias and the Lebanese refinery at Tripoli. Saudi Arabia had no hesitation in shutting down the southern pipeline exiting at the Red Sea port of Yanbu. There was some hesitation on NATO-member Turkey's part in deciding to shut down the pipeline which runs from Kirkuk in Iraq to Dortyol. Turkey had a trade surplus with Iraq, exporting $445 million in 1989 and importing in return $165 million. Iraq, however, owed Turkey $800 million. The oil problem resolved itself because with no buyers the storage tanks filled and Iraq was obliged to stop pumping. Iraq does not own a significant national tanker fleet with which to ship oil out of the Gulf – even if she could beat the blockade. Her total merchant fleet of only eighty ships was very soon brought to a halt by the influence of sanctions as well as the absence of hard currency.

Iraq had no significant financial assets and now no income with which to buy food. Iraq imports over 70 per cent of its food. Economists believed that Iraq had two to four months of staple foods in reserve, which would be extended a further two months by rationing introduced at the end of August. Most of the food stockpile, principally rice and wheat, was imported on credit from the USA. The value of the US food imported before the invasion was estimated at $2 billion. There is no evidence, however, that there was any effort to stockpile in advance of a long-drawn-out conflict. It would be normal to have operating stocks of two to four months, which indicates that the world's uncompromising reaction to Saddam Hussein had not been anticipated. There would be some smuggling conducted by sympathizers and profiteers but the quantity would not have been significant, principally due to a cash shortage.

Another weapon which could have tightened the screw on Iraq lay in the hands of Turkey. The Euphrates flows from Turkey through Syria into Iraq. Turkey has built the enormous $20-billion Attaturk dam as part of a regional development project. Turkey could *in extremis* have turned off the water, but that would also have affected Syria, a state which, since the crisis, had taken a firm line against Iraq, even supplying troops for the Arab defence force in Saudi Arabia. Water will certainly be a growing source of tension in the Middle East this decade.

The points at which pressure would need to be applied in order to maintain the effectiveness of the embargo are the Straits of Hormuz, Yanbu and Aqaba in the Red Sea, Dortyol in the Mediterranean and Baghdad city. The pipeline terminals at Yanbu and Dortyol proved to be self-regulating. Eighty warships from Europe, the USA, Australia and Argentina among others, vied to police the Gulf. There was an embarrassment of naval assets. In the Gulf context, naval forces proved to be a providential national means of earning 'brownie points' with the minimum of risk and effort. Ships could be positioned well out of harm's way and conduct themselves entirely to their own and their political master's satisfaction.

The imposition of an insurers' war risk premium, UN sanctions and the blockade had combined to ensure that sea traffic through the Jordanian port of Aqaba had all but dried up: Iraqi-bound trade normally accounted for 50 per cent of the cargo handled at the port. Jordan was the only state bordering Iraq to have shown the slightest vacillation in complying with the mandatory UN trade sanctions. The port of Aqaba is her only outlet to the sea and, with no cargoes arriving, the normally busy main supply route from Aqaba to Baghdad had no supplies to carry. Twenty-two thousand truck drivers had gradually become redundant. There is no doubt that some supplies were reaching Baghdad from Amman; indeed Iraqi propaganda films emphasized the leakage in the blockade. There were also reports of food being exported by Iran across her 620-mile-long border with Iraq. The corks, with one exception, had all been placed in their bottles, albeit some fitting tighter than others. The exception was the capital, Baghdad, which was receiving supplies by air in contravention of the trade embargo.

Iraq owns three Boeing 747s and since the invasion of Kuwait acquired a dozen Kuwaiti aircraft. When, to that total, are added the occasional Libyan, Tunisian, Jordanian or Yemeni plane which might be breaking the mandatory UN embargo, embargo-busting by air could have but a minuscule impact upon the importation of goods into Iraq. A diplomat in Baghdad said: 'Jordan's and Iran's compliance with existing sanctions imposed against Iraq will be of far greater importance to the success of the blockade than the new measures taken against air cargo.' It was more likely that these aircraft were carrying strategic goods. It was speculated that Libya was supplying Iraq with chemical weapons, critical spare parts, food and medicine. The importance of the imposition of an effective air embargo relates to its psychological impact as yet a further measure of fostering the impression of siege and isolation. The fact remains that it is almost impossible to fly into Iraq without entering another state's airspace.

The real problem in dealing with embargo-breaking aircraft is the question of what to do with them in the air. UN Resolution 670 does specifically exclude the shooting down of civil aircraft. The shooting down of civilian-registered aircraft would be certain to raise an international furore. This was the case after the Soviets shot down the wayward Korean airliner, KAL 007, over Soviet territory on 1 September 1983, with the loss of 269 lives, and again in 1988 when the USA's missile cruiser, USS *Vincennes*; shot down an Iranian airbus, killing the 299 passengers and crew. The International Civil Aviation Organization (ICAO) drew states' attention to their Convention's amended Article 3 drafted after the destruction of the Korean airliner: 'Every state must refrain from resorting to the use of weapons against civil aircraft in flight.' Even the interception of civil aircraft can only be undertaken as a last resort.

The view is generally taken by international and air lawyers that the Chicago Convention, amended on 10 May 1984, is concerned only with civil aircraft, and that as the Convention does not apply to aircraft used in military, customs and police services, it can be argued that interception of civil registered aircraft used for state/military purposes can be lawful. It follows that a respectable argument can be mounted for the interception of sanctions-busting civil registered aircraft if it is certain that they are being used for state/military purposes. Ultimately, this admittedly fine judgement may well depend on the earlier-rehearsed issue of proportionality. The national and international outcry which would arise from the shooting down of a sanctions-busting, civil-registered aircraft would unarguably give rise to an international row. It might, however, be a successfully defended shooting down if it could be proved, beyond reasonable doubt, that the sanctions-busting was for state/military purposes and this particularly if the military purposes were of an aggressive nature.

The United States is one of a number of states that is reluctant to have its options for action restricted by Article 3 and has accordingly failed to ratify the amendment introducing Article 3, which was ratified by the

United Kingdom in 1987. However, when the amendment of the Chicago Convention was drafted in 1984, the Council of the ICAO accepted the opinion that Article 3 was declaratory of existing customary international law and recognized an obligation not to use weapons against civil aircraft. The obligation therefore exists already and is not dependent upon ratification as an amendment to the Chicago Convention for its validity. Washington lawyers were prominent in the drafting of Resolution 670. They were ill at ease with a sentence in the original draft which only permitted interception which 'did not endanger the lives of persons on board or the safety of the aircraft'. The United States was only too well aware that accidents do happen, and had the draft amended.

Resolution 670, approved by fourteen votes to one (Cuba), permitted only aircraft carrying humanitarian aid and cleared by the UN Sanctions Committee to fly into Kuwait and Iraq. Otherwise, states were requested to 'deny permission to any aircraft destined to land in Iraq or Kuwait ... or ... to overfly its territory'. The Resolution was not confined entirely to air considerations. It approved of restrictions imposed on Iraqi diplomats, stated that Iraqi assets overseas should be frozen and that Iraqi-registered ships discovered to be sanction-breaking should be detained and impounded.

Aircraft identified as embargo-running would need to be dealt with retrospectively. Allied forces in the Gulf had the wherewithal to monitor flights in and out of Iraq. Sanctions which could be imposed against individual aircraft and their operators could include future denial of landing rights elsewhere and the removal of insurance cover. Ultimately, if a state airline were to transgress the mandatory embargo, the UN could react by extending sanctions to apply against the relevant rogue state.

The political, economic and geographical circumstances meant that a strong, effective economic embargo could be mounted against Iraq. The support for the embargo had been unprecedented and beyond what Saddam Hussein could have imagined. There were so many ingredients contributing to the situation in the Gulf that it was predictable that there would be some loose ends to be tied up. There is a need to be particularly cautious in taking action which, though technically legal, might give rise to humanitarian objections. The strong support given to the call for the UN embargo does, unintentionally, introduce an element of weakness. The appearance of a dogmatic pursuit of measures aimed at starving Iraq, for example, could possibly have lost Arab, Asian, African and Scandinavian support. When managing an embargo, it is not enough to be ahead. The real prize is awarded for staying ahead. The danger of one state taking the lead is that it is more certain to polarize opposition than if leadership comes from an invigorated United Nations.

The result of an effective *cordon sanitaire* in modern times shows that the price of collective security comes very high and virtually no state remains unaffected. Two factors have exacerbated the economic profile. First has been concern attendant upon the all-pervading whiff of a world recession, and secondly, when the Middle East sneezes, the whole world catches cold. It happened in 1973–74, 1979–80, and it happened again in 1990. The initial reaction to this last crisis seems to have been exaggerated and unnecessary. It is a sick situation for which there is suitable and available treatment.

The BP statistical review of world energy put the 1989 total Middle East oil production at 16.6 million barrels per day. Iraq produced 2.8 million barrels and Kuwait 1.6 million barrels, a combined total of 4.4 million barrels or just over one-quarter of the OPEC-regulated Middle East production. At the same time, the Saudi production was 5.2 million barrels per day. The principal customers in millions of barrels per day were Europe (3.9), Japan (3.0), and the USA (1.9). The military response to the Gulf crisis was therefore in inverse proportion to the dependence on oil. The maintenance of the flow of Middle East oil to the United States was not the trigger which sent her troops and aircraft into Saudi Arabia and ships into the Gulf. It was merely a contributory factor in a wider tapestry of Pax Americana.

Looking at oil production globally, the twenty-one-nation International Energy Agency (IEA) reported that in the second quarter of 1990 there was an excess production of 2.8 million barrels a day. OPEC intervened to reduce that production but it was subsequently restored by Saudi Arabia. World demand was in the region of 64 million barrels per day so that if the excess production was set against the loss of Iraqi and Kuwaiti oil there was a shortfall of only 2.1 million barrels per day. This additional production was taken up by Saudi Arabia.

In fact, a sensible fuel conservation policy, particularly by the United States, could dampen the impact of any further fuel-related crisis in the Middle East. Oil profligacy in the United States is encouraged by low car taxes and fuel taxes set 50 per cent lower than in most other developed states. In 1990 the *Economist*[136] stated that if the USA achieved the level of fuel economy maintained by the Japanese, she would not need to buy 16.6 million barrels a day (over one-quarter of the world's daily consumption) but only 9.2 million barrels. If such an economy were to be achieved, the loss of the total daily production of both Iraqi and Kuwaiti oil could be ignored almost twice over. The *Economist*'s article went on to recommend that the USA raise its excise duties on petrol. One cent on a gallon of petrol would raise $1 billion annually. 'As a reinforcement for military might, a little economic providence would go a long way.' As one measure to hold down the escalating cost of oil, President Bush authorized the release of a token 5 million barrels (eighteen hours' worth of imports) of emergency stocks from the 600-million-barrel reserve. Yet, in the same week, the president intervened to stop congressional legislation which would have placed mandatory obligations on American car manufacturers to improve their products' fuel efficiency by 20 per cent in 1995 and 49 per cent in 2001.

Having said that, it is necessary to return to the central figure of Saddam Hussein and to consider what his future intentions might have been. The joint deployment into the Gulf and Saudi Arabia was to ensure that his appetite for acquisition did not embrace the highly productive and much more significant Saudi oilfields. An initial estimate of Britain's full cost liability for supporting Operation Desert Shield with ships, aircraft and an armoured brigade was £2 million a day. A month after armed conflict had begun and the force level increased to 40,000 the cost had leapt to £30 million a day. The United States' costs were ten times those of Britain, not counting collateral costs such as the waiving of Egypt's $7 billion arms debt in recognition of President Hosni Mubarak's ready support of Operation Desert Shield. The cost of a six-month war to the USA was estimated at $86 billion or £ 45 billion. High-tech force multipliers come at a price. Twelve months of Gulf War 1990–1 would have cost almost as much as the Vietnam War from December 1961 until its humiliating conclusion in 1975.

The United States' economy, reeling from an acute budget deficit, was unable to accommodate these costs as she had done in the Korean War. In the 1990s, the policeman attracts a salary. The answer was to formulate a US-inspired 'economic action plan', a burden-sharing exercise which identified potential donors on one side and recipients on the other. The donors' liability was divided into two columns: the first, a sum to cushion the effects of sanctions in the Third World and the second, a sum to defray the monthly cost of the multinational force. At the top of the list of possible non-Arab donors was Japan, which relies on the Middle East for 70 per cent of its oil. This plan for the funding of collective security and reimbursing states affected by it is a sensible blueprint which the UN would be advised to take over in order to eliminate possible accusations of 'grace and favour'.

The temporary leap in the cost of a barrel of oil from $19 to $40 impacted on all states, yet it impacted most on those states least able to afford it. Many countries' economies were intertwined with Kuwait and Iraq. There is, however, no equality within a sanctions regime. The low-income countries (under $500 per head per year) tend to be twice as severely affected as middle-income countries. The forty-one countries which comprise the group of Least Developed Countries owe their creditors 80 per cent of their national output. The extra cost of oil imports exceeded $500 million in 1990. Brazil, the Third World's biggest debtor, had to face up to a hike in oil prices as well as write off Iraq's debts principally for weapons supplied on credit. The rise in the price of oil was particularly hard on the emergent Eastern European democracies, who thus far had been cushioned by the supply of cheap Soviet oil. Not one to miss an opportunity to divide and rule the international community, Saddam Hussein offered free oil to the Third World. Any attempt on their behalf to take up the offer by collecting the oil would have been a breach of UN sanctions.

147

It has been estimated that Jordan required a minimum of $2 billion a year to compensate for its losses. Turkey estimated a loss of twice that amount for imposing sanctions against Iraq. A combination of increased oil cost, loss of remittances and non-payment of Iraqi debts, cost India an estimated $3 billion. Remittances from Kuwait alone were worth $100 million to the Bangladesh economy – 0.6 per cent of its GNP. The combined cost to Bangladesh of the sanctions imposed on Iraq exceeded $1 billion.

The imposition of a *cordon sanitaire* around Iraq therefore came at considerable cost. The direct cost of the deployment of forces is high, but understandable. Many observers predicted that the outbreak of the war would send the price of a barrel of oil through the roof. The subdued reaction of the oil market was one of the real surprises of the war. The dampening of the market was achieved by the release of 2 million barrels a day from ample government stocks and through demand restraint measures worth a further half-million barrels a day. On top of this there was significant overproduction of oil, leading the head of the Centre for Global Energy Studies, Sheikh Yamani, to suggest that when Iraqi and Kuwaiti oil came back on-stream, there could be overproduction by up to 5 million barrels a day. For the Third World, the clouds of war would therefore have a silver lining, but for Saddam Hussein, if the forecasts proved to be correct, it would underline the whole pointlessness of the war. In such circumstances, the price of oil could drop to $12 a barrel.

In conclusion, there is merit in being quite deliberately drawn away from this section's central topic to make a number of final observations. If oil prices should fall to $12 a barrel, a tension will arise between the producing world's dissatisfaction with such a low price (Saudi Arabia had a $6 billion deficit at the outbreak of the crisis) and the reappearance in the market of Kuwaiti and Iraqi oil. The last of the Gulf crises had as its *raison d'être* the price of oil, and that is an inescapable factor which intertwines Gulf politics and regional security. Gulf politics and the price of oil are highly volatile issues, which states combine at their peril. It is conceded that, ultimately, the 1990–1 Gulf crisis was the only recent regional upheaval not to have influenced the price of oil. That this was the exception rather than the rule needs to be heeded.

MAINTENANCE OF CONSENSUS

Consensus has to be linked to a precise aim. If the ultimate aim has not been agreed between the parties, then what the consensus is based upon must, by definition, remain imprecise. The danger in drawing conclusions from opinion polls lies in the difficulty of translating simple questions put to an unsophisticated public into what are often complicated scenarios. Early polls are frequently the most misleading because in democracies, in the initial phases of national crisis, there is a tendency for doves and hawks to enter into a bipartisan honeymoon period in support of the administration or government. Monitoring the level of domestic consensus within the Allied sending states throughout the crisis revealed, with the exception of Great Britain, just how temperamentally volatile this subject can be.

An opinion poll published in *USA Today* on 9 August 1990 showed over 80 per cent of Americans to be in favour of sending troops to Saudi Arabia. That is a very limited objective and in the early days it proved to be a limited response to Saddam Hussein's aggression. Only later would the commitment grow, in much the same manner as Felix Cole, the consul at Murmansk in 1918, described the American undertaking in the Russian intervention. As the commitment grows, it draws other interests into the vortex, not least a new threshold consideration of the comprehensive deployment of the reserve forces, something which had not occurred in the USA since the Tet offensive, and in Britain since the 1956 Suez intervention.

The military has provided a beneficial meal ticket for students on US campuses as a means of balancing their college financial liabilities. The sudden prospect of war had a dramatic impact upon many eighteen-to-twenty-one-year-olds. They had never dreamed of the possibility of actually having to fight. The anxiety and cynicism that arose was due largely to a widespread belief, confirmed by the *Los Angeles Times*, that the rationale for the US intervention was to preserve US oil supplies. Where, exactly, the balance lies between principles and interests is open to interpretation or indeed, misinterpretation. 'Standing up for our principles and interests,' said George Bush, 'is an American tradition'. The rationale for the immediate deployment into Saudi Arabia did have an initial oil logic, but that receded in favour both of the concept that aggression should not be allowed to succeed and of concern for Middle East regional stability.

The impression that the USA was prepared to fight for profits and cheap oil was most strongly held among black students. That only 40 per cent of blacks in August 1990 supported US involvement in the Gulf was indicative of a significant white/black divide. If that view was also held by the 30 per cent plus of enlisted blacks in the American armed forces deployed in the Gulf, it would impinge on the third of the 'green lights' – the need for interventionist troops to support what they are doing. The London *Times* of 10 September 1990 reported the view of a black student from the Baruch College in Manhattan: 'We ain't going to fight for some Emir's oil. We're not going to die for profits.' Such a widely held misconception of the USA's aim in the Gulf represents an unfortunate failure in communication but, worse, it represents a serious failure in maintaining consensus. It was upon such a slippery slope that Vietnam foundered.

Ronald Reagan once described Vietnam as a noble cause that was undermined by two factors; the lack of military will, and hostile public opinion. The spectre of Vietnam haunted the Gulf preparations, but

America's confrontation with Iraq would not be another Vietnam: first because she ensured she was not politically isolated, and secondly because it was not a conscript army that had been deployed in the desert. The military resolve was initially emphatic but, out in the desert, the troops would, in time, be influenced by attitudes at home. Certainly there is a risk to morale and stability posed by the dispatch of follow-up troops from an environment already transfigured by an antipathetic consensus within the sending state. The shifting sands imprisoned within the confines of an hour-glass marked out the fact once again of the relationship between the passage of time and the risk of increasing American public hostility. The message seems to be, 'if there has to be war, let it be quick'.

Looking beyond the first sixty days, to the first week in December 1990, American national consensus in favour of a Gulf intervention had slumped dramatically. What was now apparent was not only a division along colour lines but now also by gender. The Harris polls recorded a 'gender gap', with 72 per cent of females aligned against offensive action and only 22 per cent in favour. Males were equally divided, at 48 per cent for and against. Mr Louis Harris was reported in the *New York Times* of 7 December 1990 as saying: 'For the first time, women alone have turned American public opinion about a war. They have swayed the polls against President Bush's using military force in the Gulf.' The gender gap was a new phenomenon. The division that arose in Vietnam had been a generation gap.

The white/black divide and the gender gap were not the only schisms. Potentially more serious was the ideological feud brewing among President Bush's Republicans. The conservatives were on a seesaw, balanced at one end by the isolationists and at the other by a group of interventionists seeking to maintain US global interests. The Republicans were originally weaned away from isolationism by war in Europe and the resultant need to combat Communism. Now that Communism posed a negligible threat to US interests, the ideological division that had remained dormant within America's conservative party had again come to prominence. What could happen, therefore, in an extended or phoney war would be the dissociation not only of the majority Democrats but also of a significant proportion of Republicans. It is chinks in the armour such as these that can be exploited. The existence of such a prospect would have been recognized by Saddam Hussein's propaganda strategist, the then deputy prime minister Nizar Hamdoon. Hamdoon learned the nuances of American political power whilst serving as his country's ambassador in Washington.

On the American domestic front, therefore, the consensus light had turned to yellow. It is possible to identify the exact time that congressional and public consensus were lost: it occurred when troop levels were raised from a sufficiency to defend Saudi Arabia to a sufficiency to take the offensive against occupied Kuwait. So intent had the administration been on securing international consensus that it had failed to maintain its grip on consensus on the home front. Woodrow Wilson and his experience at Versailles was an historic example of international and domestic consensus being out of step.

It was this lack of consensus in the United States which encouraged Saddam Hussein to believe that the United States would not take military action against him. The president's difficulty lay in the possibility that the Democrat-controlled Congress might not give him the backing which he believed the Constitution did not require him to seek. Unfortunately, Congress did not concur with that interpretation and it seemed highly improbable that the president would take America to war without congressional approval. In a television interview given prior to his November 1990 Gulf visit, the president conceded that there had been a failure to explain the rationale behind the administration's Gulf policy.

> If I haven't done as clear a job as I might have on explaining this, then I've got to do better, because I know in my heart of hearts that what we are doing is right. I know what the United Nations has done is correct. I know that we've got to stand up to this aggression.

The Democrat Congress convened to decide whether or not to block a future Gulf War less than one week from the 15 January 1991 deadline. During the Vietnam War, Congress had given the president *carte blanche* as a result of the bogus incident which led to the Tonkin Resolution. It was awareness of this apparent abrogation of Congress's 'power to declare war, grant letters of marque and reprisal and make rules concerning captives on land and water' that made a challenge to the president's policy inevitable. Claiborne Pell argued that every possible alternative should be exhausted before Americans were asked to die. The debate threatened to damage both Democrat interests and the president, yet there was no guarantee that a negative vote would have done anything more than disappoint an increasingly determined Mr Bush. In the event it did not matter. Congress assuaged any lingering sensitivity by giving the president the necessary authority to enter into armed conflict. There was really little choice. The debate was held too late. The president's decision to go 'that extra mile for peace' and the complete Iraqi intransigence demonstrated by Tariq Aziz, a man with no apparent mandate to negotiate, served to turn the yellow light of public consensus for armed intervention back to green. A poll in the *Washington Post* showed not only 63 per cent in favour of using force from 15 January, but also that 68 per cent thought Congress should support the president. Thus it was, for the first time since the attack on Pearl Harbor in 1941, that Congress voted the president the power to go to war.

By February 1991 American public support for the conflict in the Gulf had grown to 80 per cent. It proved, if nothing else, the fragility of US public opinion, so susceptible to mobilization. The Brookings Institution's Catherine M. Kelleher said that the question 'why us, why now, and why there' would be a continuing item on the USA's domestic agenda.[137]

Support throughout Europe was so diverse that it emphasized the real difficulties of achieving a pan-European consensus. The first British opinion poll, published in the *Sunday Telegraph* on 12 August 1990, showed 83 per cent of the British public in support of sending troops to the Middle East. That compared with the 78 per cent who supported the sending of the Task Force to the Falklands and only 37 per cent who approved of Britain's 1956 intervention in Suez. Interestingly, the then troubled Thatcher Conservative government did not attract the jingoistic rise in support that had occurred at the time of the Falklands and that had been so instrumental in carrying the party to parliamentary victory in 1983. In the Gulf crisis the high level of national support throughout Britain was sustained by the unanimity that existed between political parties. It was a unanimity that had the prospect of continuing for so long as Britain's actions were legitimized through the offices of the United Nations and enabling Resolutions scrupulously observed. Support was also sustained by the British sense of fair play and, particularly, the concept that aggression should not be allowed to succeed. 'Of all the contributions the British have made to civilization,' declared Jean Monnet, 'two to me seem essential: respect for freedom, and the working of democratic organisations.'

At the end of sixty days, therefore, the situation in the United States had witnessed the beginning of what would prove to be a significant downturn in support; in the United Kingdom, support was maintained at a high level, but in France support for intervention in the Gulf had actually increased. President François Mitterand's 'logic of war' speech was the trigger which took the early figure of 47 per cent to 60 per cent of people who, in the event of hostilities, favoured French participation in a multinational force. That figure could not be sustained and, in the run-in to the 15 January deadline, the majority became a minority, only for this to be reversed at the outbreak of armed conflict. Mitterand's speech announced the putting into temporary preservation of the twenty-year-old Franco-Iraqi mutual benefit club and some believed in, while others hoped for, the end of French prevarication.

Elsewhere in Europe, the level of support for a Gulf initiative was so unenthusiastic that it became the target of intense American cajoling and diplomatic pressure. Spain was cool. First, the relevance of the conscript factor was evident in relation to the dispatch of non-regular naval forces. The second factor was more relevant to those who might seek to form a military intervention force, a force whose members might have to sacrifice their lives for the benefit of another country. An opinion poll in the magazine *Cambio 16* discovered that only 8 per cent of those interviewed were prepared to die *for Spain*. A report on 13 August 1990 in the Italian *Panorama* news magazine revealed little support for Italian participation in military intervention. Almost 70 per cent of Italians were not in favour of the dispatch of ground and naval forces; over 48 per cent favoured the resolution of the problem by diplomatic pressures and the economic boycott of Iraq.

National consensus was found to be significantly unenthusiastic in Bonn and Tokyo. The unwillingness or expressed inability to subscribe military force in support of possible Gulf action will certainly cause some collateral damage to aspirations within both Germany and Japan to be admitted as permanent members of the Security Council. Such an attitude will be rather more offset by Germany's generous financial support and rather less by Japan's initial reluctance to set aside reasonable funding to offset Gulf costs. What the Gulf crisis will have fostered in Japan is the debate about Japan's position in the world and about the need for a global strategy.

The Bundeswehr possesses the best military equipment in Europe and is the largest of the purely European armed forces. Despite frustrations among the military, Germany is, for the time being, standing by the current political interpretation of the *Grundgesetz*, or Basic Law. Hans-Dietrich Genscher, the veteran Liberal foreign minister in Helmut Kohl's coalition conservative Christian Democrat government, has said that he is prepared to support initiatives which would allow the Bundeswehr to take part in Chapter VI peacekeeping operations. Genscher's East German origins proved beneficial in helping to strengthen his position following the December 1990 all-Germany elections. While this promises a united Germany leading Europe along an unrepresentative Liberal path, it also promises remoter prospects of Germany taking a more robust and positive approach to peacekeeping and intervention. The foreign minister, who has held office since 1974, is not out of touch with public opinion. Defence ministry officials in Bonn estimated that as many as 60–70 per cent of the then West German population would have been against German military involvement in the Gulf. A poll in the *Süd Deutsche Zeitung* of 6 January 1991 revealed that 75 per cent of Germans were against taking on international military commitments. The war legacy weighs heavily upon the public souls of Germany and Japan. So long as there was no direct involvement of NATO, Germany's principal military gesture would remain the sending of five minesweepers to support US naval operations in the eastern Mediterranean and fighter aircraft to Turkey. She was also prepared to make available non-offensive materiel for use in the Gulf. Japan, who has forty-six minesweepers – more than Britain and America possess jointly – sent none until months after the ceasefire.

The second green light of consensus relates to the need for the existence of a form of positive support for intervention within the target country. The first point that is obvious is that the proportion of popular support available to help an intervention would be substantially higher in Kuwait than in Iraq. So broad will be that difference as to underline the earlier recommendation that no rule of thumb should be laid down.

Iraq has the largest internal opposition in the Arab world. The overwhelming support that was given to Saddam Hussein by the West and Moscow prior to the invasion of Kuwait meant that it was an opposition which the significant powers had never thought necessary to cultivate. Indeed, regional dangers were foreseen in cultivating the Iraqi Kurdish opposition. Now there are different thoughts, for it gradually became evident that the implementation of the option of neutralizing Saddam Hussein, short of armed conflict from outside, had to be achieved from within. The problem is that the opposition, like the Mujahideen of Afghanistan, is divided. The radical opposition tends to function out of Damascus where it operates under the protective umbrella of President Assad. The religiously orientated Shia groupings are based in Tehran. The more democratic opposition operates from London, where it has less protection from the attention of Saddam Hussein's assassins. Then there are the Kurds, a quarter of Iraq's population, and the group least likely to be impressed by Saddam Hussein's presidency. The co-ordinated working of some or all of these groups, in co-operation with sympathetic elements in the Army, could provide a base from which the demise of Saddam Hussein might have been orchestrated as a prelude to the introduction to Iraq of a multi-party system. It was significant that Saddam Hussein's military chief of staff was dismissed for having come under the influence of retired officers unimpressed by the president's military planning.

The seventeen-party Iraqi opposition issued a joint statement on 27 December 1990, calling for the overthrow of Saddam Hussein. What had brought them together was a fear that their nation's future insurance policy, the Iraqi armed forces, would be destroyed by the Allied coalition (which may account for the large numbers of aircraft which sought refuge in Iran), and fear of the nation being permanently divided. For the latter reason, they had more fear of Turkey's rather than Iran's intentions. The most important, powerful, and the largest Iraqi opposition grouping is the Kurds, with whom the British Foreign Office opened discussions.

Fortunately, by the end of September 1990 the level of consensus existing among the potential interventionist troops had not been put to a real test. Admittedly there were gripes but, just as squeaky wheels get the oil, the complaints of a small minority whose motives for being in the services must be suspect, should not be regarded as truly representative. The foundation was essentially sound although, Stateside, the number of volunteers coming forward to enlist had fallen significantly.

These circumstances are symptomatic of the tendency among some professional forces to recruit by emphasizing the wonderful prospects available in the services, the opportunity to travel and the immense value this experience will be when it comes to the need to find employment in civilian life. (There is an enormous training machine to correct such an impression.) It is by no means a new phenomenon. A number of British naval ratings in 1982 were recorded as saying they had not joined the Navy to go to war. The US official history of the Korean War reported on the, then, professional, Regular Army:

> The basic fact is that the occupation divisions [in Japan] were not trained, equipped or ready for battle. The great majority of enlisted men were young and not really interested in being soldiers. The recruiting posters that had induced most of these men to enter the Army mentioned all conceivable advantages and promised many good things, but never suggested that the principal business of an army is to fight.[138]

Rarely in recent times had a potential military enterprise in the Gulf attracted so much international political support. It had begun with the prospect, if need be, of becoming a veritable *bellum justum*. One of the threats posed to the maintenance of consensus among the Allied troops would revolve around Saddam Hussein's irrationality. Not all the forces lined up against Iraq had been trained in nuclear, bacteriological and chemical defence. NATO troops had, of course, done so but in the Central Region the threat of retaliation had acted as a deterrent upon a rational opponent. The Gulf was an entirely different matter. No one knew how their ruthless opponent would react. It would prove to be a blessing that Iraq had not had the opportunity to develop nuclear weapons.

Not since the First World War have chemical weapons been used by one party against another party also possessing chemical weapons. They were used extensively on the Western and Eastern Fronts. At least thirty different agents were trialled, of which twelve proved to be of military utility. In the Middle East in 1990–1 there did exist a distinct possibility that the restraint which had lasted for over seventy years would lapse. The need for Allies to operate fully protected in the desert heat could have had such a debilitating influence on both energy and morale as to provide its own trigger for early military action. It certainly sapped the courage and energy of Iranian troops lined up against the Iraqis. In addition, the quantity and the nature of casualties who suffered chemical attacks could have made a significant impact upon domestic consensus. The Gulf crisis promised to be the first operation which could bring back quantities of females in the degrading, so-called 'body bags' for burial by husbands, children and parents. States do not all have the same reaction to mounting casualties. Some will press for withdrawal while others will seek angry retribution.

AGREE AND ADHERE TO NATIONAL CONTRIBUTIONS

This is one principle which was not triggered by the crisis. It is dependent upon pre-planning. That never occurred because the script was virtually written on a day-to-day basis. National contributions could be manpower, equipment, combat supplies, materiel or finance. What this crisis showed is that contributions need a definite elasticity to respond to the changing scales of the conflict. Contributions, therefore, cannot be absolute but will have to be based on ratios of the total.

It is appropriate to make the point here that, in any case, principles are not chiselled in stone. The assembly of the largest, sophisticated force levels since the Second World War obviously established the 1990–1 Gulf intervention as an aberration and, in intervention terms, it should be regarded as such. Principles that are adduced in the intervention field will be extended in attempting to embrace the different levels of conflict, as seen in Grenada on the one hand and Kuwait on the other.

OPERATE WITHIN THE LAW

There has not been a conflict post-1945 which has been so blatantly illegal and shown such utter contempt for international law as that conducted by Saddam Hussein's regime. To take the analogy of international law being more grey than black and white, it is the responsibility of the good (white) to maintain that distinct, essential and unadulterated contrast between evil (black) through the impeccable observance of international law. For the white side to muddy the water, by making dubious claims under the spurious authority of imprecise resolutions, is to hand a propaganda coup to the opponent and thereby dilute the contrast of the extremes of original illegal actions. The maintenance of the anti-Iraqi consensus was predicated upon the reaction being modelled both in defence of and in accordance with international law.

The first part of this exercise will be a short examination of delicts perpetrated by Saddam Hussein. It will not draw on those events which arguably have been condoned by inaction, such as the earlier use of chemical weapons against Kurds and Iranians contrary to the 1925 Geneva Protocol forbidding the use of chemical warfare. In the first months prior to actual conflict, therefore, the major Iraqi transgressions of international law were the invasion and subsequent annexation of Kuwait, the ill-treatment of foreign nationals and the violation of diplomatic missions.

The Iraqi invasion of Kuwait was a total violation of Article 2(4) of the Charter which requires: 'All Members [to] refrain in their international relations from the threat or use of force against the territorial integrity or political independence of any state, or in any other manner inconsistent with the Purposes of the United Nations.' No one gave much credence to the bogus claims of Iraq acting in support of a coup (in itself not a legal justification) or in pursuit of the settlement of a border issue which required Kuwait's voluntary agreement. In consequence, the Security Council invoked Articles 39 and 40 to order Iraq to withdraw its forces from Kuwait. There are two issues which emerge here. First Saddam Hussein's assertion to the visiting Austrian President Kurt Waldheim that his action against Kuwait was no different to the USA's action against Panama, and secondly, a question therefore of the validity of unilateral moves to restore the sovereignty of Kuwait. The first issue makes the point that a state endures the burden of its history. There can be no wiping clean of the slate in international affairs. What is done is done, hence the crucial importance of the prior evaluation of possible future consequences. Under international law the United States had no more right to overthrow a *de facto* Panamanian government than Saddam Hussein had to evict the Emir of Kuwait and his representatives. There is, nevertheless, an admitted difference in kind between the conduct of a secular dictatorship invading and overthrowing an absolute monarchy and a state claiming to act in the interest of putting in place a democratically elected representative.

The second issue, prior to the adoption of Resolution 678 authorizing the use of armed force, would be as a consequence of the legitimate deployment of Allied troops at the request of Saudi Arabia on her territory in accordance with Article 51. The Allied troops would be justified in using force to defend Saudi Arabian territory and there were circumstances in which striking at Iraq could be justified as anticipatory self-defence. The subsequent Iraqi redeployment away from the border to a position of defence in depth would not help a legal argument in support of anticipatory self-defence. It is certain, however, that Saudi Arabia would not wish to inherit the opprobrious legacy attendant upon allowing foreign troops the use of her territory as a launch-pad for violence against fellow Arabs. Some would say that Article 51 would not apply to a unilateral or collective action aimed at relieving Kuwait because the onus was on the Security Council to take the measures she took four months later, 'measures necessary to maintain international peace and security'. Dissenters, who include Christopher Greenwood, maintain that the right of self-defence continues until the Security Council adopts the so-called 'measures necessary to maintain international peace and security'. There is support of this interpretation within the body of Resolution 661 (drafted by the USA) 'affirming the inherent right of individual or collective self-defence, in response to the armed attack by Iraq against Kuwait, in accordance with Article 51 of the Charter'. If it was the view of the Security Council that force was necessary to evict Saddam Hussein from Kuwait, they had the authority under Article 42 so to do.

For a time, the US administration deliberately avoided the use of the 'H' word, preferring to describe their 1,200 or so male nationals in Kuwait and Iraq as 'internees'. There are fewer words more emotive in the US political dictionary than the word 'hostage'. On 4 November 1979 a group of student supporters of Ayatollah Khomeini seized the US embassy in Tehran, incarcerating the diplomatic community of 52 for a total of 444 days. The number was significantly lower than the more recent episode. The blatant flouting

157

of diplomatic relations in Tehran became the *cause célèbre* which hardened attitudes against Iran and drove the USA towards a policy of supporting Iraq. Nevertheless, the mishandling of the hostage episode in Tehran ensured that Jimmy Carter was not re-elected.

That point would have been uppermost in the mind of President Bush as he was seeking his second term of office in 1992. But in this crisis United States public opinion initially was not as flustered by the taking of hostages in Iraq and Kuwait as it had been with regard to the Tehran diplomats. In a poll conducted by the *Wall Street Journal* in mid-September 1990, 53 per cent of voters favoured the USA launching a strike against Iraq, despite the risk to the hostages. On this occasion, the reason why it was accepted that hostages might be harmed may be to do with identity. Diplomats are by nature high profile and since there were relatively few, they became known to the public. In the latter case there were too many hostages to have made an initial identity impact. If the hostages had not been released, that situation could have changed due to the fact that the law of averages would apportion to every city in the nation its own hostage waiting to be embraced by a concerned public. This is one area where the green light theory of consensus is particularly relevant.

Military action under Article 51, to force the release of nationals being treated as hostages, would in all probability be condoned as an 'inherent' right by a majority of the international community. That is of course subject to the caveat that the proper test be satisfied that the action be limited to the necessity of the case and proportionality between the threat and the threatened. The fact of the dispersal of these individuals, United States nationals and others, to be used as 'human shields', would have made the rescue of other than selected individuals from selected sites a virtual impossibility.

Historically, the taking of hostages has been a way in which one side can exert influence over an opponent. It was a ploy freely indulged in, even as late as 1945, when it was used selectively by Axis forces. One trial among over 2,000 post-Second World War trials held in Europe and the Far East, indicated a sea change in attitudes towards the taking of hostages. A US military tribunal convened the hearing of a test case against a certain William List to consider, among other things, the illegality of taking hostages with a view to forestalling military attacks. The formal protection of civilians was established shortly after, in the 1949 Geneva Convention IV, 'Relative to the Protection of Civilian Persons in Time of War'. The definitive Roberts and Guelff *Documents on the Laws of War* gives the opinion:

> In view of the large number of states, parties to the 1949 Geneva Conventions and the status which the Conventions have acquired in the international community, it is reasonable to assume that the Conventions are (at least in part) declaratory of customary international law.

Saddam Hussein has observed only those aspects of international law which suit his purposes. There may be two reasons why he was equally reluctant to use the word 'hostage', preferring instead the word 'guest'. First, the taking of hostages runs entirely contrary to the tradition of Arab hospitality, and secondly, it may have formed part of a safety mechanism within a broader climb-down contingency. It is a more face-saving measure to permit guests to go free as opposed to releasing hostages, with all the implications of making concessions to an enemy.

Geneva Convention IV protects those who 'at a given moment and in any manner whatsoever, find themselves, in case of a conflict or occupation, in the hands of a Party to the conflict or Occupying Power of which they are not nationals'. Iraq is a signatory to the four Geneva Conventions and is therefore bound by them. Article 34 states precisely that: 'The taking of hostages is prohibited.' There is, then, a realistic provision in Article 28 that 'the presence of a protected person may not be used to render certain points or areas immune from military operations'. In general terms, protected persons 'who may desire to leave the territory (Article 35) ... shall be entitled to do so'. Security Council Resolution 663 demanded that Iraq assist all foreigners to leave Iraq and Kuwait immediately. In addition, the individual or 'mass forcible transfers ... from occupied territory to the territory of the Occupying Power ... are prohibited, regardless of their motive' (Article 49).

The line taken by the principal opposing powers in relation to their hostages proved to be unequivocal. While some have negotiated in the past with terrorist groups holding their own nationals captive, there existed a definite consensus on what Mrs Thatcher described as 'a decision of anguish'. She said:

> If you allow the taking of hostages, terrible as it is, to determine your own action against a dictator, he has won, and all he will ever do, or anyone else with similar ambitions will ever do, is to take hostages knowing that other people will never take the requisite action to stop such a dictator.

She then went on to say, to the subsequent howl of protest from relatives of hostages in Kuwait and Iraq: 'So I am afraid we would have to take the necessary action which we feel vital to stop a dictator even though he still held hostages.' At this level therefore it has to be said that the holding of hostages, rather than having a deterrent effect, is likely to be an incentive towards taking military action, if only through indignation.

The Geneva Convention obliges Iraq to treat people in occupied territory humanely. The refusal to provide ration cards to the thousands of Asians trapped in Kuwait and Iraq was a direct contravention of the 1949 Geneva Convention.

Saddam Hussein's order that all missions in Kuwait were to be closed was illegal because such authority is only vested in the legitimate govern-

159

ment of the host state. Article 45 of the Vienna Convention on Diplomatic Relations renders missions inviolable, which serves to emphasize the breach of international law attendant upon the raid on the French embassy in Kuwait. The raid by US forces on Nicaraguan diplomatic premises in Panama in December 1989 was no less illegal. The United Nations Security Council's Resolution 662 confirmed Kuwait's continuing existence by calling upon all states to 'refrain from any action or dealing that might be interpreted as an indirect recognition of the annexation'. The twelve members of the EC agreed *en bloc* to keep their missions in Kuwait open, as did the USA and USSR. While the latter's mission was 'open', it was not staffed. The Allied and European missions closed progressively as water and supplies became exhausted.

It can be seen how the odious behaviour of Saddam Hussein and his complete disdain for international law had served to isolate him from all but a handful of states. There have been investigations into the feasibility of trying Saddam Hussein and his collaborators in Nuremberg-style trials. Mrs Thatcher said, 'we could do what we did at Nuremberg and prosecute the requisite people for their totally uncivilized and brutal behaviour'. The *Los Angeles Times* drew attention to a novel case of poacher turning gamekeeper by reporting the US administration's activities in compiling a list of Saddam Hussein's breaches of international law. In December 1989 a number of Third World countries had demanded a similar trial of President Bush arising from the invasion of Panama. In the interest of maintaining multilateral consensus and an unassailable position on the moral high ground, all that the Allies required to consolidate their position was to do what the Iraqi president had not – operate within the bounds of international law.

So frequent has been the misuse of Article 51 of the Charter of the United Nations that it has come to be regarded as the spivs' article. It has frequently been used by the unscrupulous as a catch-all ploy to sidestep the authority of the Security Council. So it is surprising that two members of the Security Council should invoke that particular article on the occasion when the Security Council was, for the first time in its history, performing as was intended. Such an action might have been more understandable had the Security Council failed to take action but, by its US-drafted Resolution 661, it imposed on member states an obligatory embargo on trade with Iraq and Kuwait. In such circumstances where the UN has taken protective measures, the right to use force in self-defence is generally thought to lapse. Article 51 only permits the inherent right to self-defence 'until the Security Council has taken measures necessary to maintain international peace and security'.

The Emir of Kuwait approached the USA, not the UN, to effect the military enforcement of the UN's embargo against Iraq and Kuwait. Secretary Baker responded very quickly to announce that the 'interdiction [embargo] would begin almost immediately'. After a day in London marked by uncertainty and wobbly diplomacy, Britain followed suit, immediately causing division where there had been unity.

The authority for the USA's and Britain's unilateral move was based on a provision in Resolution 661 affirming the right of individual and collective self-defence for Kuwait against Iraq. This interpretation was regarded by the Soviet Union, China and the non-permanent Third World members of the Security Council as a precursor of premature military moves against Iraq. France declared the proposed embargo to be illegal. In a letter to *The Times* on 16 August 1990, the late eminent authority on United Nations matters, Evan Luard, wrote:

> The effect of the Security Council resolution [661] is to place an obligation to cease trade (except in specified categories) on *individual* member-states. This does not in itself give the right to any particular state or group of states to interfere with shipping on the high seas or in coastal waters to ensure that the embargo is observed. If it appears necessary for further steps to be taken to make the embargo effective it will be for the United Nations, through a Security Council resolution, to call for these measures, and to specify how they should be implemented: as it did in calling on Britain to enforce the oil embargo against Rhodesia 12 years ago.

Resolution 661 contained no authorization to use force, not even the authorization to use minimum force given by President Bush to the US Navy when intercepting ships in the Gulf, Red Sea and the Gulf of Oman. The majority of the fifteen-nation Security Council insisted that a legal embargo of Iraq required a new Resolution. The USA recognized that it did not have the strength or possibly the resolve to implement a unilateral embargo with Britain. The USS *Reid* proved that point when she fired shots across the bows of an Iraqi tanker to force her to stop for inspection. The Iraqi ship ignored the warning shots and made her way through the Gulf of Oman. A Reuters report from Lima, Peru quoted Javier Pérez de Cuéllar as having said that military force by any country to enforce sanctions would be a breach of the UN Charter as long as the Security Council did not approve the use of force. 'Any intervention,' he said, 'whatever the country, would not be in accordance with either the letter or the spirit of the United Nations Charter.' The USA and Britain concurred that a Resolution clarifying the issue was required.

Unanimity was regained in the adoption of a loosely worded Resolution 665, so framed as to satisfy China, the Soviet Union and France. This Resolution authorized naval forces operating in the Gulf to enforce collectively UN sanctions against Iraq in accordance with Resolution 661. So satisfied was Kuwait that she acknowledged that the United Nations had taken the necessary measures in accordance with Article 51 'for the maintenance of peace and security'. Kuwait's isolated comment was neither intended nor taken to suggest the shelving of the option of pursuing military action in support of Kuwait. In normal circumstances it would not be possible to argue a case for collective self-defence in support of a state that has expressed itself satisfied with the UN's diplomatic measures. As ever, there is a difference between the theory and practice, facilitated no doubt by the clever drafting of ambiguous Resolutions. The former Soviet Foreign Minister, Edward Shevardnadze, surprisingly, expressed a view in New York that the forces deployed in the Middle East could take unilateral military action without prejudice to the measures already agreed by the Security Council.

Ethiopia, a member of the Security Council and a state all too familiar with starvation, argued persuasively during the drafting period of Article 661 for food to be supplied to Iraq and Kuwait in 'humanitarian circumstances'. The amendment was agreed but it would be the source of some future problems owing to the stringent controls imposed on food distribution. Article 54 (1) of the 1977 Geneva Protocol 1, concerned with the protection of objects indispensable to the survival of the civilian population, states that: 'starvation of civilians as a method of warfare is prohibited'.

The fact is that the 1977 Geneva Protocol 1 contains so many controversial innovations that it does not enjoy wide support and is, therefore, not entirely declaratory of customary international law. The USA has described it as a 'charter for terrorists'. Of the permanent members of the Security Council, only China has ratified Protocol 1 but, more significantly, it has not been ratified by Iraq. Whereas hostage-taking is no longer a bona fide war option, the denial of food to an enemy remains a legitimate act of war for those states who have not ratified Geneva Protocol 1. Nevertheless, the progress made in international law since 1945 is strong in the emphasis on humanitarian consideration. It is for that reason that the 'Dugan Factor' had an unnerving impact upon the United States' Allies.

General Michael Dugan, former Chief of the United States Air Staff and fighter pilot, revealed the existence of a proposal to bomb Saddam Hussein and therefore, *inter alia*, the inhabitants of 'downtown Baghdad'. Although the general was sacked, the strategy was never disowned. The concept of US strategic bombing had been developed during the Second World War by the bomber commander, General Spaatz. Strategic bombing is designed to break down a nation's ability to wage war as a whole. The 1962 Cuban missile crisis revealed that it was still alive:

> The members of the Joint Chiefs of Staff were unanimous in calling for immediate military action. They forcefully presented that view that the blockade would not be effective. General Curtis Le May, Air Force Chief of Staff, argued strongly with the President that a military

attack was essential ... One of the Joint Chiefs of Staff once said to me he believed in a preventive attack against the Soviet Union. When it was discovered that the Russians were withdrawing their missiles one high military adviser suggested 'that we attack Monday in any case'.[139]

B-52 bombers were used to carpet-bomb North Vietnam and, again, to bomb the Republican Guard on the Iraq/Kuwait border. The latter was not strategic bombing but battlefield air interdiction.

The Dugan affair revealed that some proponents of a strategy of strategic bombing still existed in the Pentagon. The argument related to easing the burden of ground attackers is persuasive, but is the collateral damage inflicted on civilian Iraqis to be achieved without the severest of ramifications? Are they also, the inhabitants of 'downtown Baghdad', no less the victims of Saddam Hussein? In the event, every effort was made to avoid the collateral damage of civilian casualties. Some were inevitable, given the fact that many production units and strategic installations were situated in urban environments, but civilian deaths and injuries were minimized through the wide use of smart weapons and laser designators. In addition, commanders had specific orders to minimize civilian casualties. This influenced attack profiles to the degree that some targets were passed over rather than risk civilian casualties.

It is an unfortunate fact that along the path towards the destruction of Saddam Hussein and his forces lay the destruction of the Iraqi infrastructure. There was no blanket bombing of civilian areas but even pinpoint, high-tech, laser-guided bombs on occasions went astray, resulting in civilian casualties. There were mercifully few mistakes. The bombing of the Baghdad air-raid shelter, killing 400 civilians, received the attention of an in-place media which transmitted the images of the aftermath around the world. Although the Dugan factor never did manifest itself, the political damage was done, particularly among the ultra-sensitive Muslim communities. One single accident such as this, when related to an intended war crimes tribunal, can completely balance out the ghastly happenings among the hapless Kuwaiti residents. Michael Howard suggested that Allied attempts to bring Saddam to trial would be met in many quarters 'with an embarrassing *tu quoque*'.

What seems obvious, that civilians should be spared aerial attack, has only recently been incorporated into treaty law. But this desirable protection has been proven illusory since the percentage of civilians among war casualty totals has climbed steadily since the First World War. At that time, 5 per cent of victims were civilians. In the Second World War the figure had risen to 48 per cent. In Korea it rose again, to 84 per cent and in the Vietnam War it was 90 per cent.[140]

The irony of the situation is that during the Iran/Iraq War the Iraqi airforce carried out a series of indiscriminate bombing attacks against

Iranian civilian domiciliary areas, causing much death, injury and destruction. It was only the intervention of the UN Secretary-General on 9 June 1984 that secured an agreement from both warring states to cease attacks on each other's centres of civilian population. In the 1990-1 Gulf War, Iraq resumed attacking centres of civilian population through the means of Scud attacks on Israel and Saudi Arabia. These were attacks which had no military, but much political, significance as a means of baiting Israel into war and thereby separating the Arabs from the Allied coalition. The missile attack on Israel, not a party in the conflict, was a clear violation of Article 2(4) of the Charter of the United Nations.

History would also repeat itself in relation to the mistreatment of prisoners of war contrary to the prisoners of war convention, the 1949 Geneva Convention III. During the Iran/Iraq War, many prisoners were executed, or tortured during the course of interrogation. Both states were to blame, but UN investigative teams' reports admitted that Iraq was the worst offender. It was not unusual for Iraq to delay the registration of prisoners with the International Committee of the Red Cross for up to six weeks, during which time prisoners were beaten to extract information. Iranian prisoners were forced by the Iraqis to denounce their leaders on radio and television. Prior to this, they would have been processed in special interrogation rooms where the range of tortures included electrical treatment, forceful penetration with sharp objects, beatings, burnings and hanging upside down. There were also psychological assaults through the interminable broadcast of Radio Baghdad political material over loudspeakers installed in every dormitory.

The emotive subject of the mistreatment of prisoners of war revolves around a matter of national standards and a matter of national attitude. It is a two-way street where action and reaction are disproportionately evident. For example, the representatives of a repressive regime are less interested in the fate of those who have become non-combatants than in representatives from a democratic or ordered society. There is plenty of anecdotal evidence to support that fact arising from the Second World War.

In February 1943, in Featherstone Camp, New Zealand, there was a serious confrontation between Japanese prisoners of war and New Zealand guards; forty-eight Japanese were killed and sixty-three wounded in the fracas. More serious was the breakout of Japanese prisoners of war from the Cowra, New South Wales, prisoner-of-war camp on 5 August 1944, in which 321 Japanese soldiers died and 108 were injured. There was much resultant high-level, governmental consultation between the Commonwealth countries and the United States (the New Zealand prisoners were technically the responsibility of the USA who had captured them, as indeed were 118 of the Cowra inmates). Western governments were concerned lest the publicity of these deaths should adversely affect the lot of their own prisoners of war in Japanese hands, 46,000 of whom were being worked on the Burma–Siam railway. It made not one iota of difference.

The Japanese Military Field Code did not recognize the possibility of a soldier becoming a prisoner of war. That part dealing with surrender read:

> He who knows shame is strong and should at all times endeavour to keep before him the honour of his homeland and live up to what is expected of him. Rather than live and bear the shame of imprisonment by the enemy, he should die and avoid leaving a dishonourable name.

To that extent, they were mentally written off: their existence was not admitted. What fate befell people whose existence was not even acknowledged was, therefore, to Tokyo a matter of monumental insignificance. By the same token, the Japanese regarded the Allied prisoners of war in their hands as low life, which accounts for their abominable treatment. The survival rate of Allied prisoners of the Japanese was less than 75 per cent and many, when released, had a severely reduced life expectancy. Allied prisoners in German hands had a much better survival rate, at 96 per cent. The reason why the Nuremberg Tribunal ranked equally with the Tokyo Tribunal was not so much the mistreatment of Allied prisoners of war but the excesses of the Holocaust. It is the 1949 Geneva Convention IV which applies to civilians, particularly to the mistreatment of the Kuwaiti population.

For social reasons, therefore, and for reasons of recent precedent, it appeared highly probable that Allied forces falling into Iraqi hands would not receive the same humane treatment as Iraqi prisoners in Allied hands. The Allies in the Gulf deployed additional medical assets to cope with the anticipated high number of Iraqi casualties. The Prisoners of War Convention is the 1949 Geneva Convention III, to which Iraq is a signatory. According to the Geneva Convention III, it is illegal to parade prisoners, to coerce them to make statements condemning their own governments, and to use them as human shields in high-risk environments. It is not inconceivable that individuals will be arraigned for war crimes. The manner in which those trials would be conducted is not, however, clear. It behoves Allied coalitions to orchestrate their own act to ensure that their conduct towards, and treatment of, their own prisoners in the theatre of conflict and at home is impeccable.

MILITARY INTERVENTION IS THE LAST RESORT OF A COLLECTIVE SECURITY MACHINE

No coalition of states, however strong, would contemplate without real cause taking on, on her own territory, the world's fourth largest military power. The opponent was also an irrational power possessing chemical and possibly biological weapons. Diplomacy was given over five months to run its course, and yet Saddam Hussein remained implacably opposed to returning Kuwait to the Kuwaitis. What he had achieved in that time was to strengthen his defensive positions in Kuwait, muddy the political water by introducing the Palestine dimension, and also polarize opposing groupings in the Middle East. It is, however, true that the Allied coalition needed that time also, to sort out some semblance of order.

There was, at the time when the Allied coalition launched their armed offensive, the residual question of whether or not sanctions should have been given more time to work. There were conflicting reports and opinions. On balance, it did seem that sanctions were having considerable impact upon Iraq, and that the attendant financial haemorrhage through the denial of a daily income of $500 million from oil revenues would, in time, have had serious consequences for a state whose *casus belli* had been its self-inflicted bankruptcy. Logically, the Allies would have preferred sanctions to have been effective within the period of time they were prepared to allow. Not only are sanctions a cheaper option than war, but they also have the compelling theoretical attraction of having no lives penalty. Taking the route to war meant that both the US economy and US lives were put on the line. When political and economic observers looked to see what other contributions other states were making, they perceived, rightly or wrongly, that Japan and much of Europe were not pulling their weight. That perception is certain to have repercussions in future isolation/intervention debates.

There were two distinct forces which, acting together, made military intervention unavoidable. The first was the significant reinforcement of Saudi Arabia by the United States in November 1990 following the mid-term elections. This move from a defensive to offensive posture took account of an important lesson which emerged from Vietnam. Yet it was strategy which, once set in motion and without the acquiescence of the opponent, was difficult to stop. Time imposed itself upon political and military options. The crisis had to be resolved by May 1991, by which time the arrival of both summer and movement of pilgrims to the holy places in Saudi Arabia would signal to the coalition an obligatory cessation of the war on the land and in the air. The second force concerned Saddam Hussein's unassailable position in Iraq, as well as a cult of personality which grew out of control and so ensnared him that he was denied room for manoeuvre. His decision to snub his own generals and assume direct military command is symptomatic of that condition. Militarily, it made good sense to comply with the UN Resolutions and abandon Kuwait in order to save Iraq. Saddam Hussein's future, however, depended upon the retention of Kuwait and, for the currency of his presidency, it remained unnegotiable. The whole fabric and viability of Saddam's regime depended upon his not backing down. Strangely, he regarded his withdrawal from Kuwait as inevitable. 'I am a realist. I know that I will have to withdraw,' he told Gorbachev's special envoy to the Middle East, Mr Yevgeny Primakov. 'If Saddam Hussein stands before the dilemma of either being crushed, as he calls it or fighting,' forecast Primakov, 'he will fight.' That he found himself in a dilemma and did indeed have to fight was a situation of his own making based upon further miscalculation. He misinterpreted the genuine and publicly expressed concerns of the Americans that Kuwait would become another Vietnam. In his first address of the conflict, President Bush was at pains to point out to people that Kuwait was not another Vietnam.

The Iraqi troops dug-in in the featureless desert would have welcomed Vietnam's jungle canopy. It was under that canopy in the early years, along the Ho Chi Minh Trail, that the Viet Cong were resupplied and kept in the battle. Unlike in Vietnam, the Iraqi front line was glaringly obvious. The recent de-ideologizing of international conflict had served to ensure that Saddam would not be resupplied. Every attack on his infrastructure, equipment, logistics and materiel weakened his sustainability. But then, Saddam Hussein was no Ho Chi Minh fighting for the unification of Vietnam, but was seen by a majority for what he was – a murderous tyrant who had illegally annexed a foreign, sovereign state.

The first lesson of conflict analysis is to begin with a blank piece of paper. Saddam Hussein assumed that a combination of Vietnam angst and his own bloody rhetoric would ensure that the United States would not fight. There was an outside chance that he might have made some progress in exacerbating the divide that existed in American public opinion had there been some evidence of flexibility or a display of a willingness to compromise during the course of negotiations. When it became obvious that the talking head of the then foreign minister, Tariq Aziz, had neither the interest nor the authority to negotiate, American attitudes reacted against Iraq. Public opinion hardened when Aziz refused to accept Bush's letter from Secretary Baker. In addition, the provision of a deadline was a statement to the international public that Saddam Hussein could avoid war if he so wished. Psychologically, it was an opportunity lost. When Saddam was faced with the reality of his error, he had been hoist by his own petard. For the United States, it had been an opportunity well taken; the Vietnam syndrome was laid finally to rest. American pride and confidence in herself had at last been restored.

By his conduct, Saddam Hussein had shown to what depths his long-suffering people would be permitted to suffer in order to sustain his own ego and the primacy of the Baath party. The imposition of sanctions against a dictatorship have to be regarded as a long-term expedient unless they encourage a reaction from within which will remove the obstruction by violent force. Naturally, Saddam Hussein took routine precautions. His generals were disarmed before being admitted to his presence and, when he made rare public relations appearances among his troops, all small-arms ammunition had been withdrawn beforehand. Sanctions, therefore, meant that the prospects of the Iraqi people suffering starvation and death could have been a quite realistic outcome. To what degree that would have produced a humanitarian reaction in the West is not clear, but what is clear is the increased importance since Vietnam of humanitarian, legal and environmental considerations. What is likely is that the Allied coalition would have been more sensitive and responsive to the world's ire than Saddam Hussein and the Iraqi Baath party. Starving a state into submission is technically not contrary to international law. As has been stated, Britain, the United States and Iraq are among a significant number of states who have not ratified the 1977 Geneva Protocol I on Armed Conflicts. There have been sufficient detractors for the protocol not to be deemed to be declaratory of customary international law. Yet, realistically, it is unlikely that a policy of starvation could be sustained by democratic states against strong humanitarian objections.

It became abundantly clear in the first weeks of war that peace in the Middle East depended upon the defeat of Saddam Hussein – not the Iraqi people but their leader. This was Saddam's war. Rarely had war been so closely associated with one man. Something emerged from Iraq which created such a powerful image that previously ambivalent German public opinion swung positively in favour of Allied action in the Gulf. The image was not something that had emerged quite so clearly and so obviously from Vietnam, and that was the presence of real evil.

It had been cynical to link the invasion of Kuwait with a solution to the Palestine problem. Saddam Hussein became part of Palestine's problem, for Kuwait had been the region's leading employer of Palestinians. The invasion of Kuwait is estimated to have cost the Palestinians $1.4 billion through lost savings and employment opportunities. In addition, the West Bank Palestinians are estimated to have forgone $1.5 billion in lost remittances. His pan-Arab stance led Yasser Arafat to abandon his painstaking peace initiative to support the Iraqi president. The associated withdrawal of financial support for the PLO from Saudi Arabia and Gulf state clients required an urgent reappraisal of the Organization's commitments. The Scud missile attacks on centres of Israeli civilian population served, as nothing else could, the reconvergence of American and Israeli interests. Whether a deal was struck with Israel for not retaliating is beside the point.

It was the images of captured Allied pilots which really underlined both the regime's depravity and naivety. If Saddam Hussein believed that the appearance of these prisoners of war on television would assist his cause, then he simply had no comprehension of the American psyche. Support for the uncompromising Bush line surged to 80 per cent.

The display of ecoterrorism attendant upon the release of crude oil into the Gulf greatly harmed Saddam's cause. It was not only the haunting images of doomed and dying birds, but the size of Saddam Hussein's miscalculation. The military benefit arising from his action, set against the environmental damage and public relations disaster, had been negligible. It was a sign of the times, and a sign that Saddam had got it wrong again.

Copying the Americans proved not to be beneficial. Between 1962 and 1971 the USA sprayed 11 million gallons of Agent Orange on 7 million acres of Vietnamese jungle. The voices of protest that arose then were distinctly muted. In twenty years, the environment had grown to be an issue which a military commander could neither tamper with nor ignore.

This intervention, then, was justified as the last resort of a collective security machine. Saddam Hussein was either unable or unwilling to make concessions, and the time factor impinged upon Allied options. Sanctions might have worked, but only at great cost and suffering to innocent Arabs and at the expense of the good name of western civilization. Less than a week after the invasion of Kuwait, Saddam Hussein's capacity for evil became readily apparent. Whether the Soviet news agency report of him ordering the execution of his airforce commanders was true or not, what mattered was that it was plausible, underlining the measure of true evil. In the cities of Germany dawned the recognition of a mirror image of Hitler. Whilst not favouring a German commitment to the Gulf, at the end of January 1991 80 per cent of Germans supported Allied actions in the Gulf. They had been the war's fiercest critics. That turn-around compared with 70 per cent support in France, with public opinion beginning to move in much the same way in Italy.

It is generally agreed that the Allied coalition did go 'that extra mile for peace' and, in view of Iraqi intransigence, the resultant military intervention was the justifiable last resort of a collective security regime. What emerged as less clear cut and a source of deep emotion, generating more heat than light, were the events post-3 March 1990, principally affecting the Kurds and, to a lesser extent, the Shiite minorities in Iraq. Military intervention was certainly justified on humanitarian grounds but analysis of the circumstances will reveal that military intervention could not succeed, thereby placing the onus on the Allies to investigate other means of providing assistance. In future, coalition states will need to think through the likely results of their actions in order to be better prepared.

What has unreasonably been described as the trigger to the Kurdish revolt was President Bush's plea that 'the Iraqi military and the Iraqi people [should] take matters into their own hands to force Saddam Hussein the dictator to step aside'. That message was intended for the Iraqi military, not for the disorganized ethnic groups who would have used the opportunity to raise the profile of long outstanding issues even if the Bush statement had never been made. The Kurds have frequently been in major revolt (in 1923, 1932, 1943, 1961–70, 1974–5 and 1986–8) stemming from their dissatisfaction that the 1923 Treaty of Lausanne failed to establish a state of Kurdistan embracing indigenous Kurdish people in Iran, the Soviet Union, Turkey, Syria and Iraq. Today, the Kurdish population is thought to number 18 million, of which Iraqi Kurds total less than a quarter. Foreign ministries throughout the world were only too aware of the implications for regional stability that help and concessions given to the Iraqi group would have on brother Kurds in neighbouring states.

The former prime minister, Mrs Thatcher, said: 'I think we should take very firm steps. It is not a question of legal niceties.' It is, however, a myth to believe that international law in any way inhibited military intervention in support of the Kurds. The 1948 Convention for the Prevention and Punishment of Genocide provides the Security Council with all the necessary authority in international law to initiate military intervention to prevent genocide against the Kurds. The fundamental misconception arises from a misinterpretation of Article 2(7) in the UN Charter, concerned with non-intervention by states within the domestic jurisdiction of other states. The Article contains an important caveat: 'but this principle shall not prejudice the application of enforcement measures under Chapter VII'. We will leave until last the evaluation of the viability of Chapter VII enforcement measures in the case of support for the Kurds and will examine the feasibility of Chapter VI, peacekeeping operations.

The chairman of the Campaign for Nuclear Disarmament (CND) wrote:

> The UN must act now to enforce the terms of the ceasefire. Further slaughter of the Kurdish people must be avoided. Establishing a *genuine* peacekeeping force and strengthening sanctions are immediate steps that should be taken now.

Effective sanctions were still in place, but was the plea to insert a 'genuine peacekeeping force' idealistic or realistic? Traditional peacekeeping operations are predicated upon three basic, recognized requirements. First, the troops are not normally drawn from among the permanent representatives of the Security Council; secondly, blue berets only use force for the purpose of self-defence; and thirdly, the monitoring of interstate borders is conducted with the consent of both states. It would appear, therefore, that the traditional peacekeeping function could not operate because Saddam Hussein would have violently opposed the presence inside Iraq of the traditional, lightly armed blue berets.

The observer force established by mutual consent on the Iraq/Kuwait border at the end of hostilities, the United Nations Iraq–Kuwait Mission (UNIKOM), was both a revolutionary form of peacekeeping and an important precedent. Within the commander's staff and among the body of troops were the representatives of all five permanent members of the Security Council. Backed therefore by the promise of massive retaliation should the need arise, UNIKOM was not a traditional Chapter VI operation but rather a unique Chapter VII operation.

In the post-war phase, *Realpolitik* interposed itself to reshuffle new factors to the degree that the collegiality that had been so essential in evicting Iraq from Kuwait was no longer apparent in relation to the Kurdish problem. It was not just the opposition of China (who feared the impact that intervention in support of minorities might have upon the future of Tibet) or indeed the Soviet Union with her own, considerable, minorities problems; there was also strong antipathy within the Third World for much the same reason. In view of the contemporary circumstances, however, it was illusory to believe that any form of practical military intervention could be achieved without the active support of the United States. President Bush declared that 'our war in terms of the UN Resolutions is finished'. Ambassador Pickering added, 'Iraq is out of Kuwait. We're not going to use military force to intervene internally in Iraq.' Having laid to rest the spectre of Vietnam and restored national pride, the administration was certainly not prepared to risk the political dividend that had been accrued at so little relative cost. Moreover, 75 per cent of the American public were opposed to further military action in the Gulf. It was a public which, since 2 August 1990, had emphatically demonstrated a volatile, collective opinion so susceptible to mobilization.

For all these reasons, therefore, purely military intervention[141] justified on the strongest possible humanitarian grounds was just not deliverable. Other options needed to be examined or, to quote from the principles drawn up earlier, 'the conclusion reached that a satisfactory result could not be achieved'. In the event, the concept of establishing safe havens in northern Iraq from which to assist the Kurds was a unique solution to a unique situation.

UTILIZE THE UN'S LEGAL MECHANISM

Legality is becoming a most important factor in the conduct of international relations. It will be remembered that the United States and Britain reconsidered their position to conform with the Security Council's majority view regarding what action was understood to be possible during the early stages of the blockade. The immense value of the UN's unique legal mechanism as an enabling factor is not universally comprehended.

The *Sunday Telegraph*'s editorial of 10 March 1991 is a case in point. Entitled 'The dangers of the UN Gulf myth', it does make the very valid point that the UN can be both used and abused. The future of the UN's capacity to establish a collective security regime is dependent upon the will of the key players, most notably the one state which, for the time being, has the greatest capacity to facilitate or to spoil – the United States. The *Sunday Telegraph*'s editorial concluded:

> Even without UN backing Britain and the US would have won the war ... and perhaps more decisively. That is the truth, and the west is only forging an almighty stick for its enemies to beat it with for pretending otherwise.

Setting aside the observation that a hundred-hour war is historically one of the most decisive wars ever fought, it has to be said that without the support of international law being exercised through the various UN Resolutions there would not have been a Gulf War. That is the truth.

There is no merit in being dismissive of the Third World's influence in international affairs or in failing to recognize their hidden veto. If the UN had not legalized the coalition efforts to free Kuwait, Saddam Hussein would most surely have orchestrated a highly successful Arab response to frustrate British and American intentions. UN backing also relies upon, amongst others, the agreement of the new Soviet Commonwealth, China and France. All three of these states would have opposed an Anglo-American reaction outside the framework of the United Nations. The UN's legal mechanism is there to be used in the interests of international security.

RESTRUCTURE THE UN'S MILITARY ORGANIZATION

The 1990–1 Gulf crisis reaffirmed how essential it is to plan within the United Nations for peacekeeping or peace enforcement action. The Gulf crisis was yet another in the long list of post-1945 wars which were not predicted. As has so often been the case, the UN was caught flat-footed with no staff, no ideas and no plans to deal with this, the latest major threat to international peace and security. How much longer is this myopia to be perpetuated?

Change must be comprehensive. Those states most likely to be associated with Chapter VII and Chapter VI$\frac{1}{2}$ operations have contributed to this overwhelming impression of *mañana*. Until recently, the USA has used the ambiguous phrase 'low intensity conflict' for interventionist operations. That did fit the bill in relation to Grenada and Panama, but the latest of the Gulf crises required a high-intensity response in what had been regarded as a low-intensity area. The alternative description is the minimalist phrase 'out of area' (OOA) operations. With the exception of the fifteen-month Berlin airlift of 1948–9, the origins of which predated NATO, *all* of the USA's, Britain's and France's post-1945 military operations have been out of the so-called NATO area. A more appropriate term to be used within the power projection spectrum is 'intervention operations'. In order to manage international intervention operations, there has to be a transfer of staff from the Central Region to begin abstract, contingency military planning in the UN headquarters New York, to ensure that crisis management never again has to begin once the crisis is already well under way.

There are of course more ways than one to be unprepared. The UN was simply not organized to implement the enforcement measures as provided within Article 42. In the event, this did not prove to be an insurmountable problem. The mandate came within Security Council Resolution 678, which delegated to member states the authority to use all necessary means to restore international peace and security in the area.

172

The MSC met in August 1990, yet its mechanism was so dilapidated and seized by inactivity that it was unable, and states were unwilling for it, to function positively. What transpired were *ad hoc* meetings of the military members of the permanent representatives. No minutes were taken. The official organs of the MSC were not used, nor did the meetings take place in the UN. Land operations were specifically excluded from discussion. There are indeed more ways than one to be unprepared.

Enthusiasm for the resurrection of the MSC has to be tempered by realism. Political and military values have changed greatly since its inception in 1945. This is reflected in today's moribund committee and its unpreparedness and inability to play a useful role in the Gulf crisis. Moreover the UN member states had failed to implement, or rather to have achieved, contemporary understandings of Article 43. The concept of having a standing military force assigned to the UN is thoroughly unrealistic. Talk should be more logically aimed at the earmarking of troops as a secondary, contingency function. All this of course comes back to the issue of the will of states, particularly the will of the permanent members. It bears repeating that the exclusive membership of the permanent members within the MSC has become anachronistic, yet it is possible to broaden the membership within the Charter rules. Presentationally, such a move would be in the interest of international democracy and is more likely to be supported by those significant states that do not belong to the club of five.

The starting point for the current justification of a role for the MSC lies in its provision and specific mention in the Charter. There is a multiplicity of views as to what its future role might be. Sir Brian Urquhart wrote:

> In case enforcement measures again become necessary, the Military Staff Committee of the Security Council should as soon as possible work out possible agreement both for the provision of forces under Article 43 of the Charter and for their strategic direction and command ... . The Military Staff Committee should now be instructed to embark on an extensive study of how to convert modern military technology, including the various means of deterrence, to the needs of an international system of common security in this highly unstable world.[142]

The continuing pro-Soviet attitude was emphasized by an executive of the Soviet Ministry of Foreign Affairs, Boris Krasulin, who said that the MSC is 'in a position to provide on a permanent basis a comprehensive operational analysis of the politico-military situation in world trouble spots other than the Gulf and to prepare corresponding recommendations for the Security Council'.[143]

There are at least three legitimate paths along which the UN can pursue military intervention. All things being equal, and given the current spirit of collegiality, the MSC could be rejigged to provide a multilateral option to crisis resolution. This could mean a total commitment from planning to command and direction of the enterprise. Current international temperature would suggest that for the moment it is overoptimistic to expect such an eventuality to come to pass. Nevertheless, there is within the literature a general consensus that the MSC should involve itself in contingency planning so that each crisis does not have to be tackled *ab initio*. In addition, the MSC should strengthen its links with the Secretary-General and advise him when requested on Chapter VI and Chapter VII operations. There is no reason why the MSC should not also have a supporting role in the other two intervention options.

The second option can be described as the Korea model, whereby a state is mandated the overall responsibility for operations under the UN flag. The adoption of the Uniting for Peace Resolution accepted that questions of peace and security, for which the Security Council was supposed to have primary responsibility, could be taken out of the Council's hands and placed in those of the Assembly in a situation of crisis if there was deadlock in the Council. UN Resolution 84 authorized the establishment of a unified command, gave the enterprise UN status and approved the flying of the UN flag and the award of UN decorations. The command of UN forces was mandated to one state, the United States. Since the USA funded the majority of the operation, provided half the ground forces and 85–95 per cent of the naval and air forces, her pre-eminent position was incontestable. Fifteen other states provided forces while forty-eight of the sixty members pledged assistance.

The third option, the Kuwait model, is where a state volunteers to lead on behalf of the UN but not under the UN flag. The Kuwait model is of interest because whereas the Korea model skated around Article 42, touching instead upon Article 39 or Article 51 (if a case of collective self-defence can be accepted), the Kuwait model was emphatically dismissive of Article 42. The imposition of the embargo against Iraq should have been couched in the language of Article 42 but no forces had been earmarked, the MSC was non-operational and the Security Council had no experience in overseeing military operations. These problems were circumvented by Resolution 665, which delegated to the American-led *ad hoc* coalition the authority 'to use measures commensurate to the specific circumstances' to halt all shipping and inspect and verify the said cargoes and ships' destinations.

Revolutionary as the adoption of Resolution 665 may have been, it was far less significant than the adoption on 29 November 1991 of Resolution 678. The latter Resolution uses the Chapter VII language that delegated to (coalition) member states the right 'to use all necessary means' to uphold the preceding Resolutions related to Iraq's invasion of Kuwait. What the UN Security Council had done was to recognize its own inability to conduct operations, and had delegated that responsibility into the hands of a willing surrogate, namely the USA. The remit placed upon the USA and her

174

coalition Allies was to keep the Security Council 'informed on the progress of actions undertaken'. Thereafter, the Security Council shut up shop and did not reconvene in public session until three months later. Perhaps the most suitable option for the future is a hybrid model which employs the MSC for planning and advising the Secretary-General while future operations are conducted in line with the more accountable Korea model.

DESIGN A STRATEGY

The absence of a strategy which had considered in advance a short list of participants and the allocation of resources was self-evident. The situation would have been far more serious had the search for a political solution not provided the military with the providential time to put the act together. In future collective security operations, time could well be at a premium, emphasizing the need for international, strategic, contingency planning. The United States is unlikely, or rather should be unlikely, to want to take the lead again in such a formidable, military undertaking including substantial ground forces and the associated political risks. It is also true that other potential contributor states would prefer to see the United States not taking such a prominent lead position.

RESOURCE ALLOCATION

Troops to tasks

Future planning should determine not only the ratio of troops that states might be prepared to set against future tasks, but also their type. This would include the role of the troops and also their designation – i.e. whether regular or conscript.

Equipment

Strategic mobility is achieved at enormous cost. It ought to be possible to spread this cost by states agreeing to undertake and underwrite certain support functions. There would need to be some duplication in order not to put undue emphasis on the achievement of unanimity. There is a worldwide shortage of wide-bodied aircraft and roll-on roll-off shipping. The crisis emphasized the dependence on sea-lift. Seventy-eight per cent of all the Allied land and air arsenal was carried in/on ships. The shortage of these resources would have been indelibly underlined had Iraq provided anything other than token naval and air opposition. Furthermore, strategic mobility was greatly enhanced by the wealth of handling facilities in the Gulf and also by the means of speedy dispersal of incoming equipment, stocks and supplies.

One early and important task for the MSC is to investigate ways in which

175

the level of support required for a force can be reduced through internationalizing the logistic infrastructure. This is easier said than done because of the lack of commonality and interoperability of national arms and equipment. But national bills are enormous.

Only 7,000 of Britain's deployed ground strength of 35,000 in the Gulf were engaged in actual combat.

Finance

If the Gulf crisis is examined in purely monetary terms, it produces an unique conclusion. It was less expensive for the world as a whole to have gone to war than not to have gone to war. If 44 per cent of the world's known reserves had been left in Saddam Hussein's hands, the price of oil would have been manipulated upward to the serious detriment of industrialized states, although those whose suffering would have been most extreme would have been the Third World. The total cost of the war is not yet finalized but it would seem that the speedy and successful outcome of the conflict did provide the Allies with an economic *casus belli*. It also seems that the influence of the resultant reduction in the price of oil by no more than $3 a barrel over a twelve-month period on GNP would adequately cover the total war costs. That benefit is less relevant to an oil-sufficient Britain.

The 1990–1 Gulf crisis is not a crisis which provides good, general guidelines to suggest a way forward for future interventions. In fact, the way in which combatant states touted for financial support while the Third World jostled for pickings was reminiscent of a paraphrasing of Thucydides in his *History of the Peloponnesian War*, whereby the strong take what they will and the weak suffer as they must. Within one month of the invasion of Kuwait, the United States had sent emissaries to the Gulf, Europe and Asia to organize funds with which to pay for the war. That trawl raised promises of cash or donations in kind of $54.5 billion.

The United States has been coy in declaring the actual cost of the war, yet an estimate of her expenditure at war's end was in the region of $42 billion. As is so often the case, states can be quick to promise but slow to pay. If the United States does secure all that was promised, she has agreed to return the surplus.

It is not desirable in future operations for national funding to depend upon the enterprise, guile and bargaining power of individual states. The expenses of the combatants deployed in support of a UN Security Council Resolution and those states who suffer as a result of the imposition of that Resolution should be apportioned centrally, preferably in the UN. Cognizance will need to be taken of a state's wish not to provide financial support for states whose performance in the crisis has been inimical to the donor state's interests.

CONCLUSION

The events of 1990 and 1991 have served to emphasize the plethora of meanings associated with the phrase *military intervention*. The invasion by Iraqi forces of Kuwait was presented to the world as an *intervention* on behalf of the 'democratic forces in Kuwait'. It was a disreputable, bogus cover for a simple territorial aggression.

The Allied military forces operating under the cover of twelve UN Resolutions *intervened* to restore the territorial integrity of Kuwait; in doing so they invaded and temporarily occupied Iraqi territory. That was described at the time as a 'peacekeeping exercise' overwhelmingly sanctioned by the international community.

Then latterly, the forces of the United States, Great Britain and others legitimately *intervened* again on humanitarian grounds to protect the Kurdish population of northern Iraq from the threat of genocide. That intervention was sustained by a force stationed outside the territory of Iraq.

The 'New World Order' outlined by President Bush, 'new ways of working with other nations to deter aggression and to achieve stability, to achieve prosperity and, above all, to achieve peace', has created a great deal of muddled terminology. Until there is some conceptual backup for this vague notion – what we might call New World Thinking – the confusion will continue. What is the underlying reality?

First, international practice is shifting: territorial boundaries are no longer a secure shelter behind which a nation state can mistreat its own population in any way it thinks fit. That is the logic of the *intervention* on behalf of the Kurds.

Secondly, intervention can only exist securely under the cover of international regulation, probably the United Nations. Anything else can be presented as the first kind of *intervention* – a straightforward aggression. The USA does recognize the reality and inevitability of coalition diplomacy. Militarily, this means, *inter alia*, the formulation of representative coalition operations. For its part, the United Nations has a responsibility to ensure that the beneficial convergence of the Realist and Charter paradigms is maintained in the interests of international, collective security.

And thirdly, military organizations will have to accept an extension of their role from the relatively straightforward kind of operation with a clear set of objectives and a definition of 'victory' – as in the case of Desert Storm – to the much more open-ended style of intervention like the protection of the Kurds.

Military intervention is not peacekeeping, as exemplified by the UN operations in South Lebanon or in Cyprus. An intervention force does not just keep two warring parties apart, but seeks to control a situation by the threat of superior force. That was the logic of the Kurdish action.

But intervention in northern Iraq against a potential enemy desperate for peace was a very different matter to the prospect of intervening in a nationalist quarrel between, say, Croats and Serbs in the Balkans; and the Indian experience of intervening in Sri Lanka points to the dangers inherent in this course of action .

So military organizations will have to accept a set of operational doctrines created by the still-developing ideas of intervention. In framing those doctrines they could do worse than look back to the events of 1918–20, for a working roster of elementary principles and 'dos' and 'don'ts'.

ANNEX A: SUMMARY OF UN RESOLUTIONS

660 (2 Aug.): Condemned invasion of Kuwait; demanded immediate and unconditional withdrawal of Iraqi forces; called for immediate negotiations between Iraq and Kuwait.
Vote: 14–1, with Yemen not participating.

661 (6 Aug.): Stringent trade sanctions imposed, excepting medicine and, in humanitarian circumstances, foodstuffs.
Vote: 13–0, Cuba and Yemen abstained.

662 (9 Aug.): Declared Iraq's annexation of Kuwait as null and void.
Vote: Unanimous.

664 (18 Aug.): Demanded that Baghdad allow foreign nationals to leave Iraq and Kuwait and rescind its order to close diplomatic missions in Kuwait.
Vote: Unanimous.

665 (25 Aug.): Allowed member states to use limited naval force to enforce economic sanctions; this included the right to inspect cargoes.
Vote: 13–0, Cuba and Yemen abstained.

666 (13 Sept.): Approved shipments of food to Iraq and Kuwait for humanitarian reasons, but only if distributed by approved international aid agencies.
Vote: 13–2, Cuba and Yemen opposed.

667 (16 Sept.): Condemned raids by Iraqi troops on French and other diplomatic missions in occupied Kuwait.
Vote: Unanimous.

669 (24 Sept.): Adoption of procedural measure entrusting the Security Council's sanctions committee to evaluate requests for help from countries affected by the trade embargo.
Vote: Unanimous

670 (25 Sept.): Prohibited air traffic with Iraq and Kuwait except in humanitarian circumstances.
Vote: 14–1, Cuba opposed.

674 (29 Oct.): Demanded Iraq cease taking hostages and oppressing Kuwait; requested states to document financial losses and human rights violations incurred by the invasion; urged Secretary-General to undertake peace efforts.
Vote: 13–0, Cuba and Yemen abstained.

677 (28 Nov.): Asked UN Secretary-General to safeguard a smuggled copy of Kuwait's population register so as to prevent Iraqi repopulation.
Vote: Unanimous.

678 (29 Nov.): Authorized states to 'use all necessary means' against Iraq unless it withdrew on or before 15 Jan.
Vote: 12–2, China abstained, Cuba and Yemen voted against.

Source: *Strategic Survey 1990–91* (London, 1991), 55.

NOTES

1 Richard Little, *Intervention: External Involvement in Civil Wars* (London, 1975), 2.
2 Philip Towle, *Pundits and Patriots: Lessons from the Gulf War*, Institute for European and Strategic Studies (London, 1991), 32.
3 Little, *Intervention*, 3–4.
4 Cf L. Oppenheim, *International Law*, Vol. I (London, 1905), quoted in Hedley Bull (ed.) *Intervention in World Politics* (Oxford, 1984), 1.
5 Martin Wright, *Power Politics* (New York, 1978), 191.
6 Maurice, *Hostilities without Declaration of War from 1700 to 1870* (1883), quoted in Christopher Greenwood's 'The concept of war in modern international law', *ICLQ* 36 (1987): 285.
7 *Dalmia Cement Ltd* v. *National Bank of Pakistan*, ILR (1967): 611.
8 F.H. Hinsley, *Power and the Pursuit of Peace* (Cambridge, 1963), 318.
9 Bull, *Intervention*, 181.
10 Richard H. Ullman, *Anglo-Soviet Relations 1917–1921*, Vol. II, *Britain and the Russian Civil War* (Princeton, 1968), 353–4.
11 Lawrence Freedman, *Atlas of Global Strategy* (London, 1985), 51.
12 Harvey Starr and Benjamin A. Most, 'Patterns of conflict: quantitative analysis and the comparative lessons of third world wars', in Robert E. Harkavy and Stephanie G. Neumann (eds) *The Lessons of Recent Wars in the Third World*, Vol. I. *Approaches and Case Studies* (Lexington, 1985).
13 William J. Olson 'Low-intensity conflict: the institutional challenge', *Military Review* February 1989: 7.
14 Richard J. Barnet, 'The costs and perils of intervention', in Michael T. Klare and Peter Kornbluh (eds) *Low Intensity Warfare* (London, 1989), 210.
15 Inis L. Claude Jnr, *Swords into Ploughshares* (New York, 1956), 233.
16 Brian Urquhart, *A Life in Peace and War* (London, 1987), 93.
17 *Yearbook of the United Nations* (New York, 1947–8), 494.
18 UN letter S/956 dated 9 August 1948.
19 E.J. Hughes, 'Winston Churchill and the formation of the United Nations organisation', *Journal of Contemporary History* 9(4) (October 1974): 177–94.
20 Hans-Dietrich Genscher, second meeting of the CSCE conference on the human dimension, Copenhagen, 5 June 1990.
21 Hans-Dietrich Genscher, annual meeting of the American Society of News Editors, Washington, 6 April 1990.
22 Before its formation in May 1963, the OAU was preceded by different rival blocs of African groups of which the Casablanca and Monrovia groups were but two. Others included Brazzaville States and the Union of African States (Ghana, Guinea and Mali).

23 Yassin El-Ayouty and William Zartman (eds) *The O.A.U. after Twenty Years* (New York, 1984).
24 E.H. Carr, *The Twenty Years' Crisis* (London, 1939), 8.
25 *The Economist*, 23 September 1989: 16.
26 From the testimony of CIA Director William Webster and quoted in *Time*, 5 June 1989: 18.
27 *Jane's Defence Weekly* of 17 February 1990 reported the Condor-2 project to be in 'complete disarray'.
28 Tai Ming Cheung, 'Build-up backlash', *Far Eastern Economic Review*, 27 July 1989, 18. Reference here and throughout the book is to US $ and US billion.
29 *New York Times*, 9 September 1968.
30 Parliamentary Debates (Hansard), House of Commons, 5th Series, Vol. 292 (13 July 1934): 730–1. Quoted in Kenneth W. Thompson, *Winston Churchill's World View* (Baton Rouge, Louisiana, 1983), 232.
31 *Die Zeit*, 29 December 1989: 24.
32 *The Economist*, 23 September 1982: 16.
33 J.E. Hare and Carey B. Joynt, *Ethics and International Affairs* (London, 1982), 160.
34 *Jane's Defence Weekly*, 26 August 1989: 838.
35 *Jane's Defence Weekly*, 23 December 1989, 1374.
36 Andrew J. Pierre, *The Global Politics of Arms Sales* (Princeton, 1982), 83.
37 *US Army Focus*, November 1989: 7.
38 Ben Lambeth, *Moscow's Lessons from the 1982 Lebanon Air War* (Rand, 1984).
39 Quoted in Jonathan Haslam, 'The UN and the Soviet Union: new thinking', *International Affairs* 65/64 (Autumn 1989): 683.
40 Payment to the UN budget is assessed as a percentage of national income. Brian Urquhart (*A Life in Peace and War*, 354) writes that on that basis the USA should be paying 29 per cent of the budget. He also adds that the UN 'spends more than $800 million [four times the assessed US contribution] in New York city alone'. The conclusion that such matters are relative can be drawn from the fact that the US contribution to the UN Transition Assistance Group (UNTAG) in Namibia amounted to approximately 4 per cent of the annual costs of one US Army Division (quoted in Thomas Weiss (ed.) *The United Nations in Conflict Management: American, Soviet and Third World Views*, New York, 1990, 16).
41 Evan Luard, *The United Nations* (London, 1979), 118.
42 S. Amin, 'Self reliance and the new international economic order', *Monthly Review*, 29 (3) (1977): 1–21.
43 Augustus Richard Norton, 'Drawing the line on opprobrious violence', *Ethics and International Affairs* 4 (1990): 129.
44 Richard Neustadt, *Presidential Power: The Politics of Leadership* (New York, 1964), 42.
45 Sir Nicholas Henderson, Minutes of evidence taken before the Foreign Affairs Committee, 4 April 1984, Question 263, 53.
46 ibid., Question 280, 57.
47 Sir Brian Urquhart, 'Beyond the sheriff's posse', *Survival* 32 (3) (May/June 1990): 204.
48 R.L. Sivard, *World Military and Social Expenditures 1987–88* (Washington DC, 1987), 30.
49 Robert L. Rothstein, 'On the costs of realism', *Science Quarterly* 87(3) (1972): 347–62.
50 Ian Clark, *The Hierarchy of States: Reform and Resistance in the International Order* (Cambridge, 1989), 199.
51 Anthony Nutting, *No End of a Lesson: The Story of Suez* (London, 1967), 95.
52 CAB 128/30 Part 2, 625 (CM. 74 (56)).

53 *Proceedings of the American Society of International Law*, 14 (1963), quoted in L. Henkin, *How Nations Behave* (London, 1968), 266.
54 ibid.
55 Oscar Schachter, 'The right of states to use armed force', *Michigan Law Review* 82 (Apr./May 1984): 1623.
56 Louis Henkin, *How Nations Behave* (London, 1968), 219.
57 Ronald Reagan, *An American Life* (London, 1990).
58 Mark Adkin, *Urgent Fury* (London, 1989), as reported in *The Daily Telegraph*, 26 October 1989.
59 *American Journal of International Law* 78 (1984): 144.
60 David McCollough, *The Path between the Seas: the Creation of the Panama Canal 1820-1914* (New York, 1977), 383.
61 Marko Milivojevic, 'Zone of escalating conflict', *Geographical* 62 (3) (March 1990): 27.
62 *Time Magazine*, 19 February 1990: 35.
63 Carlos Fuentes in *The Guardian*, 31 January 1990.
64 58, 135 killed (including 2,413 missing in action) and 153,303 wounded or injured.
65 General Alexei Lizichev, head of Soviet Army and Navy's Chief Political Directorate, reported in *The Times*, 26 May 1988.
66 A representative of National Public Opinion Research Centre, 146 Lenin Prospect, Moscow, 26 June 1989.
67 Paul Kennedy, *The Rise and Fall of the Great Powers* (London, 1989), 644.
68 Vneshniaia Torgovlia, Statisticheskii Sbornik (1983-1988).
69 *Sotsialisticheskaia industria*, 6 April 1989: 1.
70 Sir Bryan Cartledge, 'The second Russian revolution?', *International Relations* 10 (1) (May 1990): 9.
71 Kennedy, *Rise and Fall of the Great Powers*, 681-2.
72 Richard Connaughton, *The War of the Rising Sun and Tumbling Bear* (London, 1988), 287-9.
73 ibid., 288.
74 Sir Robert Thompson, *Defeating Communist Insurgency* (London, 1967), 50-62.
75 C.E. Callwell, *Small Wars, Their Principles and Practice* (London, 1899), 73.
76 Richard Connaughton, *The Republic of the Ushakovka* (London, 1990).
77 Hare and Joynt, *Ethics and International Affairs*, 160.
78 Mikhail Gorbachev, *Perestroika* (London, 1987), 38.
79 Connaughton, *Republic of the Ushakovka*, 177-80.
80 George Kennan, *The Decision to Intervene* (London, 1958), 414.
81 Virginia Cooper Westall, 'A.E.F. Siberia: the forgotten army', *The Military Review*, 1968: 14.
82 William Sidney Graves, *America's Siberian Adventure 1918-1920* (New York, 1931), 57-8.
83 Michael Harbottle, *The Blue Berets* (London, 1971), 39.
84 Papke, Helmut von Moltke, 316 cf Moltke, *Ausgewählte Werke*, ed. Ferdinand von Schmerfeld (Berlin, 1925).
85 Lieutenant-General Gustav Hägglund, 'Peacekeeping in a modern war zone', *Survival* 32 (3) (May/June 1990): 236.
86 Thomas Cowen, *The Russo-Japanese War, from the Outbreak of Hostilities to the Battle of Liaoyang* (London, 1904), 203.
87 Douglas Story, *The Campaign with Kuropatkin* (London, 1904), 66.
88 Sir David Nicholas, 'The services and the media: thoughts on the future', *Army Quarterly and Defence Journal* 120 (3) (July 1990): 268.
89 *Attitudes in Television in 1990* (ITC research paper).

90 B.H. Liddell Hart, *History of the First World War* (London, 1970), 587–8.
91 Keith Feiling, *A History of England* (London, 1950), 1073.
92 A.C. Bell, *A History of the Blockade of Germany* (London, 1937), 673.
93 In *Asiaweek*, 30 June 1989: 19.
94 Thompson, *Defeating Communist Insurgency*, 52.
95 Cole to Francis, 15 June 1918, F.R.U.S. (1918) Russia, ii, 477–84, quoted in Benjamin D. Rhodes, 'The Anglo-American intervention at Archangel, 1918–1919. The role of the 339th infantry', *International History Review* 8 (3 August 1986): 388.
96 Peyton C. March, *Nation at War* (New York, 1932), 131.
97 Richard N. Gardner, 'The case for practical internationalism', *Foreign Affairs* Spring 1989: 843.
98 D.W. Bowett, *Self-defence in International Law* (Manchester, 1958), 183.
99 Moore, *Digest of International Law* 412 (1906); L. Henkin, R. Pugh, O. Schachter and H. Smit, *International Law* 890–1 (1980).
100 Bowett, *Self-defence in International Law*, 269.
101 Henkin, *How Nations Behave* 2nd edition (New York, 1979), 141.
102 ibid.
103 Schachter, 'The right of states to use armed force', 1635.
104 C.J. Greenwood, 'International law and the United States's air operation against Libya', *West Virginia Law Review* 89 (Summer 1987): 939–40.
105 'Declaration on principles of international law concerning friendly nations and co-operation among states in accordance with the charter of the United Nations', 9 *International Legal Materials* (1970): 1292.
106 Schachter, 'The right of states to use armed force', 1645.
107 Bowett, *Self-defence in International Law* 269–70.
108 James O.C. Jonah, 'Developing a United Nations capacity for humanitarian support operations', paper presented in Niinisalo, Finland, 24–6 October 1989.
109 L. Meeker, State Department memorandum on the legality of US assistance to South Vietnam (1966) 60 AJIL 565.
110 Wang Tieya, 'The Third World and international law', in *Selected Articles from the Chinese Yearbook of International Law* (Beijing, 1983), 19.
111 Barnet, 'The costs and perils of intervention', 41.
112 Valerie Yorke, 'Imagining a Palestinian state: an international security plan', *International Affairs* 66 (1990): 133.
113 Hägglund, 'Peacekeeping in a modern war zone': 240.
114 L.W. Martin, 'The utility of military force', in *Force in Modern Societies: its Place in International Politics*, Adelphi Paper 102 (1973): 14.
115 Claude, *Swords into Ploughshares*, 243.
116 Robert E. Hunter and Stanley R. Sloan (eds) *NATO in the 1990s* (London, 1989), 325–6.
117 ibid, 329.
118 Spoken at a seminar attended by British and French participants in the 1982–4 Lebanon Intervention, held at Wolfenbüttel, West Germany, 20 March 1989.
119 Graves, *America's Siberian Adventure* (London, 1931), 55.
120 Interview in Paris between author and French official, 14 April 1989.
121 Interview in Moscow between author and State Department official, 22 June 1989.
122 Reported in *Armed Forces Journal International* (July 1989): 70.
123 Aleksandr M. Belonogov, 'Soviet peacekeeping proposals', *Survival*, 32 (3) (May/June 1990): 209.
124 Augustus R. Norton and Thomas G. Weiss, 'Superpowers and peacekeepers', *Survival*, 32 (3) (May/June 1990): 212.

125 It has been reported that Arab League emissaries suggested to Saddam soon after the invasion that if he withdrew, they would support his retention of Warba and Bubiyan islands as well as the entire Rumeiliah oilfield. He declined the offer.

126 'Make clear to your rulers, the Emirs of oil, that they serve the foreigner. Tell the traitors there is no place for them on Arab soil after they humiliated Arab honour and dignity' (Saddam Hussein, Baghdad TV, 10 August 1990).

127 In 1989 Jordan exported $200 million of goods to Iraq, representing 23.2 per cent of its commodity exports. The $300 million of imports taken from Iraq consisted principally of oil.

128 A CIA spokesman made the defensive comment that 'We provided policy-makers with very useful and timely information on these events. There were no surprises.' Not everyone agreed that to be the case. In May 1991 CIA director, William Webster, resigned.

129 Stephen C. Palletiere, Douglas V. Johnson II and Leif R. Rosenberger, *Iraqi Power and US Security in the Middle East* (Carlisle, Pennsylvania, 1990), 74.

130 My italics.

131 George Kennan, *The Decision to Intervene*, Vol. II of 2 vols (London, 1958), 165.

132 The war had served to concentrate minds. The 6 March 1991 Damascus Declaration, or 6 + 2 (i.e. 6 GCC states plus Egypt and Syria), drew Syria and Egypt into a Saudi-led GCC in an alliance which had originally confronted Israel in 1970. It had been a marriage of convenience, of richness and of strength. Its success was dependent upon geopolitics and the interrelation of member states. How well it would cohere, therefore, was open to speculation.

133 The presence of national sovereignty in Europe is stronger than some would admit. The thought of a credible common foreign or defence policy embracing the separate will of such states as Britain, France, Germany, Italy, Spain and Ireland is, frankly, difficult to envisage.

134 My italics.

135 Duncan Campbell, 'Under US eyes', *The Independent on Sunday*, 30 September 1990.

136 *The Economist*, 25–31 August 1990, 11.

137 King's College, London, 6 February 1991.

138 R.E. Appleman, *South to the Yaktong North to the Yalu. The US Army in the Korean War* (Washington 1961), 180.

139 Robert F. Kennedy, *13 days: the Cuban Missile Crisis October 1962* (London, 1969), 37-40.

140 Ingrid Detter De Lupis, *The Law of War* (Cambridge, 1987), 241.

141 What did happen in northern Iraq was in a practical sense military interven-tion. There are, however, reservations in describing this action as military intervention. First, it does not fit the adopted definition 'when one or more states intervene militarily within the territory or possessions of one or more other states. The threat or intention of the use of significant force on both sides is implicit.' Secondly, the enabling UN Security Council Resolution 688 does not refer to Chapter VII, the enforcement chapter in the UN Charter. If enforcement action were required, Resolution 688 would have needed Reso-lution 678 as its prop.

142 Brian Urquhart, 'Learning from the Gulf', *The New Book Review of Books*

143 Boris P. Krasulin, 'Current organizational and military requirements for effec-tive action by the Security Council: a Soviet View', in David Cox (ed.) *The Use of Force by the Security Council for Enforcement and Deterrent Purposes: A Confer-ence Report* (Canadian Centre for Arms Control and Disarmament 1990), 51.

BIBLIOGRAPHY

BOOKS

Appleman, R.E., *South to the Naktong North to the Yalu. The US Army in the Korean War*, Washington, 1961

Barnet, Richard J., 'The cost and perils of intervention', in Michael T. Klare and Peter Kornbluh (eds) *Low Intensity Warfare*, London, 1989.

Bowett, D.W., *Self Defence in International Law*, Manchester, 1958.

Bull, Hedley, *Intervention in World Politics*, Oxford, 1984.

Callwell, C.E., *Small Wars, Their Principles and Practice*, London, 1899.

Carr, E.H., *The Twenty Years' Crisis*, London, 1939.

Clarke, Ian, *The Hierarchy of States: Reform and Resistance in the International Order*, Cambridge, 1989.

Claude, Inis L., *Swords into Ploughshares*, New York, 1956.

Connaughton, Richard, *The War of the Rising Sun and Tumbling Bear*, London, 1988.

Connaughton, Richard, *The Republic of the Ushakovka*, London, 1990.

Cowen, Thomas, *The Russo-Japanese War. From the Outbreak of Hostilities to the Battle of Liaoyang*, London, 1904.

El-Ayouty, Yassin and Zartman, William I. (eds) *The OAU after Twenty Years*, New York, 1984.

Freedman, L., *Atlas of Global Strategy*, London, 1985.

Gorbachev, Mikhail, *Perestroika*, London, 1987.

Graves, William S., *America's Siberian Adventure 1918–1920*, London, 1931.

Gurr Ted, Robert, *Handbook of Political Conflict*, New York, 1980.

Harbottle, Michael, *The Blue Berets*, London, 1971.

Hare, J.E. and Joynt, Carey B., *Ethics and International Affairs*, London, 1982.

Henkin, L., *How Nations Behave*, 2nd edn, New York, 1979.

Hinsley, F.H., *Power and the Pursuit of Peace*, Cambridge, 1963.

Hunter, Robert E. and Sloan, Stanley R. (eds) *NATO in the 1990s*, London, 1989.

James, Alan, *The Politics of Peacekeeping*, London, 1969.

Kennan, George, *The Decision to Intervene*, London, 1958.

Kennedy, Paul, *The Rise and Fall of the Great Powers*, London, 1989.

Little, Richard, *Intervention: External Involvement in Civil Wars*, London, 1975.

Luard, Evan, *The United Nations*, London, 1979.

March, Peyton C., *Nation at War*, New York, 1932.

McCollough, David, *The Path between the Seas: The Creation of the Panama Canal 1820–1914*, New York, 1977.

Neustadt, Richard, *Presidential Power: The Politics of Leadership*, New York, 1964.

Nutting, Anthony, *No End of a Lesson: the Story of Suez*, London, 1967.

Oppenheim, L., *International Law*, Vol. I, London, 1905.

Papke, Helmuth von Moltke, 316 cf *Moltke, Ausgewählte Werke*, ed. Ferdinand von Schmerfeld, Berlin, 1925.
Pelletiere, Stephen C., Johnson II, Douglas V., and Rosenberger Leif R., *Iraqi Power and US Security in the Middle East*, Carlisle, Pennsylvania, 1990.
Pierre, Andrew J., *The Global Politics of Arms Sales*, Princeton, 1982.
Reagan, Ronald, *An American Life*, London, 1990.
Roberts, Adam and Guelff, Richard (eds) *Documents on the Laws of War*, Oxford, 1989.
Starr, Harvey and Most, Benjamin A., 'Patterns of conflict: quantitative analysis and the comparative lessons of third world wars', in Robert R. Harkavy and Stephanie G. Neumann (eds) *The Lessons of Recent Wars in the Third World*, Vol.I, *Approaches and Case Studies*, Lexington, 1985.
Story, Douglas, *The Campaign with Kuropatkin*, London, 1904.
Thompson, Sir Robert, *Defeating Communist Insurgency*, London, 1967.
Tieya, Wang, *The Third World and International Law* (selected articles from the Chinese yearbook of international law), Beijing, 1983.
Ullman, Richard H., *Anglo Soviet Relations 1917–1921, Vol. 2, Britain and the Russian Civil War*, Princeton, 1968.
Urquhart, Brian, *A Life in Peace and War*, London, 1987.
Vincent, R.J., *Non Intervention and International Order*, Princeton, 1974.
Walzer, Michael, *Just and Unjust Wars*, London, 1978.
Weiss, Thomas (ed). *The United Nations in Conflict Management: American, Soviet and Third World Views*, New York, 1990.
Wright, Martin, *Power Politics*, New York, 1978.

ARTICLES AND OTHER REFERENCES

Belonogov, Alexandr M., 'Soviet peacekeeping proposals', *Survival* 32 (3), May/June 1990.
Berkhof, G.C., 'The Dutch get their UNIFIL of peacekeeping', *Defence Systems International*, 1989.
Cartledge, Sir Bryan, 'The second Russian revolution?', *International Relations* 10 (1) May 1990.
'Declaration on principles of international law concerning friendly nations and cooperation among states in accordance with the charter of the United Nations', in *International Legal Materials*, New York, 1970.
Gardner, Richard N., 'The case for practical internationalism', *Foreign Affairs*, Spring 1989.
Greenwood, Christopher, 'The concept of war in modern international law', *ICLQ* 36, 1987.
Greenwood, Christopher, 'International law and the United States' air operation against Libya', *West Virginia Law Review* 89, Summer 1987.
Hägglund, Gustav, 'Peacekeeping in a modern war zone', *Survival* 32 (3) May/June 1990.
Haslam, Jonathan, 'The UN and the Soviet Union: new thinking', *International Affairs* 65/64, Autumn 1989.
Henderson, Sir Nicholas, Minutes of evidence taken before the Foreign Affairs Committee, questions 263 & 280, 4 April 1984.
Hughes, E.J., 'Winston Churchill and the formation of the United Nations organization', *Journal of Contemporary History* 9(4), October 1974.
Jonah, James O.C., *Developing a United Nations Capacity for Humanitarian Support Operations*, New York, 1989.
Lambeth, Ben, *Moscow's Lessons from the 1982 Lebanon Air War*, Rand, 1984.

Martin, L.W., 'The utility of military force', in *Force in Modern Societies: Its Place in International Politics*, Adelphi Paper 102, 1973.

Meeker. L., State Department memorandum on the legality of US assistance to South Vietnam, 60 AJIL 565, 1966.

Milivojevic, Marko, 'Zone of escalating conflict', *Geographical* 62(3), March 1990.

Nicholas, Sir David, 'The services and the media: thoughts on the future', *Army Quarterly and Defence Journal* 120(3), July 1990.

Norton, Augustus Richard, 'Drawing the line on opprobrious violence', *Ethics and International Affairs* 4, 1990.

Norton, Augustus Richard and Weiss, Thomas G., 'Superpowers and peacekeepers', *Survival* 32 (3) May/June 1990.

Olson, William J., 'Low-intensity conflict: the institutional challenge', *Military Review*, February 1989.

Parliamentary debates (Hansard), House of Commons, Fifth Series, Vol.292, 13 July 1934. Quoted in Kenneth W. Thompson, *Winston Churchill's World View*, Baton Rouge, 1983.

Rhodes, Benjamin D., 'The Anglo-American intervention at Archangel, 1918–1919. The role of the 339th infantry, *International History Review* 8, 3 August 1986.

Rothstein, Robert L., 'On the costs of realism', *Science Quarterly* 88 (3), 1972.

Schachter, Oscar, 'The right of states to use armed force', *Michigan Law Review*, April/May 1984.

Urquhart, Brian, 'Beyond the sheriff's posse' , *Survival* 32 (3), May/June 1990.

Urquhart, Brian, 'Learning from the Gulf., *The New Book Review of Books*, 7 March 1991.

Westall, Virginia Cooper, 'A.E.F. Siberia: the forgotten army', *The Military Review*, 1968.

Yorke, Valerie, 'Imagining a Palestinian state: an international security plan', *International Affairs* 66, 1990.

INDEX